NEVER-ENDING WATCHMEN

NEVER-ENDING WATCHMEN

Adaptations, Sequels, Prequels and Remixes

WILL BROOKER

BLOOMSBURY ACADEMIC
LONDON • NEW YORK • OXFORD • NEW DELHI • SYDNEY

BLOOMSBURY ACADEMIC
Bloomsbury Publishing Plc
50 Bedford Square, London, WC1B 3DP, UK
1385 Broadway, New York, NY 10018, USA
29 Earlsfort Terrace, Dublin 2, Ireland

BLOOMSBURY, BLOOMSBURY ACADEMIC and the Diana logo are trademarks of
Bloomsbury Publishing Plc

First published in Great Britain 2023

Copyright © Will Brooker, 2023

Will Brooker has asserted his right under the Copyright, Designs and Patents Act, 1988,
to be identified as Author of this work.

Cover design: Ben Anslow
Cover image: Watchmen 3, Second Narrows Graffiti (2012)
(© Colin Knowles / colink. / CC BY-SA 2.0)

All rights reserved. No part of this publication may be reproduced or transmitted in any
form or by any means, electronic or mechanical, including photocopying, recording,
or any information storage or retrieval system, without prior permission in writing
from the publishers.

Bloomsbury Publishing Plc does not have any control over, or responsibility for, any third-
party websites referred to or in this book. All internet addresses given in this book were
correct at the time of going to press. The author and publisher regret any inconvenience
caused if addresses have changed or sites have ceased to exist, but can accept no
responsibility for any such changes.

A catalogue record for this book is available from the British Library.

A catalog record for this book is available from the Library of Congress.

ISBN: HB: 978-1-3501-9874-6
PB: 978-1-3501-9873-9
ePDF: 978-1-3501-9876-0
eBook: 978-1-3501-9875-3

Typeset by Deanta Global Publishing Services, Chennai, India
Printed and bound in Great Britain

To find out more about our authors and books visit www.bloomsbury.com and
sign up for our newsletters.

Dedicated to my students, in my thirtieth year
of teaching

"Oh, god, perhaps a large part of the public, this is what they think
Watchmen was?"

-ALAN MOORE, INTERVIEW IN *GQ* MAGAZINE, OCTOBER 2022

CONTENTS

Introduction: Beginning at the end 1

1   Intertextuality and authorship: Alan Moore and *Watchmen* 7

2   Influence and interpretation: The post-*Watchmen* superhero 55

3   Adaptation and fidelity: Zack Snyder's *Watchmen* 91

4   Influence and interpretation: Grant Morrison and Kieron Gillen 117

5   Prequels, sequels, supplements and remixes: The *Watchmen* multiverse 153

Conclusion: The end of the beginning 197

Notes 203
Selected bibliography 250
Index 253

Introduction
Beginning at the end

In the final chapter of Alan Moore, Dave Gibbons and John Higgins's *Watchmen* (1987),[1] the hero-turned-villain Adrian 'Ozymandias' Veidt, having killed half of New York City with an elaborate stunt intended to prevent nuclear war, is holding what he believes is his final conversation with the *Watchmen* universe's only true metahuman, the blue-skinned, godlike Doctor Manhattan.

'Jon', he says anxiously, using the god's former, human name. 'I did the right thing, didn't I? It all worked out in the end.'

Manhattan cracks a rare smile. '"In the end"?' 'Nothing ends, Adrian. Nothing ever ends.' And he's gone.

His parting line has a further implication for the broader text of *Watchmen*, as the final panel of the last page is seemingly intended to return us to the initial panel of the first. The ketchup-stained smiley face T-shirt that dominates the last image is an obvious visual echo of the smiley badge splashed with blood that opened the narrative, as newspaper assistant Seymour reaches towards the private journal of the vigilante Rorschach, whose narration led us into the opening issue.[2]

'I leave it entirely in your hands', Seymour's editor tells him, and this closing line of dialogue is also loaded with multiple meanings. On one level, it carries a literal message from the author to the reader, as of course we are ourselves holding the book, *Watchmen*, and can physically turn back to the start to read the opening narration from 'Rorschach's journal' again; but it also encourages us to pick a possible option from the open ending. If we choose to believe that Seymour's outstretched fingers closed on the maroon-coloured diary that stands out prominently from the heap of papers in the final panel, then we assume a future where Rorschach's private journal was published and Veidt's ruse came to light soon afterwards; our understanding of the story will therefore be transformed on second reading, because we know that the self-professed genius Veidt's ambitious scheme will eventually come to nothing and that Rorschach, by contrast – doubted as a paranoid outsider and killed for his principles in the final chapter – will ultimately succeed in his mission to expose the truth.[3] Moore and Gibbons leave us with aperture instead of closure: 'nothing ever ends.'

It was already a complex text. And that was *Watchmen* in 1987, when the title referred only to a comic-book maxiseries, and then to a collected edition, often described as a 'graphic novel'. Moore and Gibbons's vague plans for possible prequels, such as a 'Minutemen' miniseries, soon faded.[4] There were discussions of a movie, with complete scripts produced but never filmed, and a broad consensus that the graphic novel resisted adaptation.[5] *Watchmen* embodied the idea that 'nothing ever ends', but as a self-contained, self-referential text that reached its *fin* then began again.

Thirty-two years later, the line 'Nothing Ever Ends' resurfaced as the slogan for the HBO TV series created by Damon Lindelof: not an adaptation of *Watchmen* or even officially a sequel but a 'remix'.[6] By then, 'Watchmen' was already something quite different. A 2008 'motion comic', crudely animating Gibbons's artwork with a single actor providing the voices, served as a modest precursor to the ambitious and controversial Zack Snyder film adaptation of 2009. The film's trailer was soundtracked by a Smashing Pumpkins song, 'The End Is the Beginning Is the End', ironically composed for the 1997 *Batman and Robin* movie whose sculpted costumes, rather than Gibbons's designs, had inspired the superhero outfits in Snyder's film. A video game, *Watchmen: The End Is Nigh*, released in the same year for Xbox and PS3, was a spin-off not from the Moore/Gibbons original but the movie, using its actors and distinct character likenesses.

INTRODUCTION

In 2012, DC Comics, contrary to Alan Moore's clearly stated wishes but with no legal requirement to oblige them, launched *Before Watchmen*, a series of monthly comics that in total consisted of thirty-seven issues, more than triple the twelve chapters of the 1986 story. The slogan at DC's *Los Angeles Times* Festival of Books promotional event promised '*Watchmen*: It's Not the End, It's the Beginning'.[7] This prequel narrative provided extensive backstory for both major and minor characters, including showcase episodes for superheroes who had barely featured in *Watchmen* itself. Five years after the mixed commercial and critical success of *Before Watchmen*, DC announced *Doomsday Clock*, its title referring both to an iconic element of the 1986 narrative and the company's initials. Billed as a direct sequel, it picked up events seven years after Seymour reached for the journal, and immediately closed down the ambiguity of Moore's ending, as author Geoff Johns revealed by the third page that Rorschach's report had been published, exposing Adrian Veidt to charges of mass murder.

Lindelof's HBO series begins thirty-four years after the graphic novel's conclusion and follows its own distinct path. Here, Rorschach's journal is embraced only by a racist organization, dismissed by the police and widely regarded as a crank conspiracy theory: Adrian Veidt's scheme therefore remains intact. The many other differences with *Doomsday Clock* range from major to minor: to pick one small but significant example, Geoff Johns confirms that Seymour was killed shortly after the publication of the journal, while in Damon Lindelof's universe, the former newspaper assistant becomes a successful academic of postmodern theory.

That was the starting point and inspiration for this book: a unique cultural moment, at the end of a decade, when two independent, completely distinct sequels to a 1987 graphic novel – one a comic book, one a TV series, but both produced against the express wishes of the original author – reached their very different conclusions.

'Watchmen' now signifies not a single text but an intertextual network in the poststructuralist sense characterized by Roland Barthes, Jacques Derrida,

Deleuze and Guattari and Julia Kristeva – or a dialogue, in Mikhail Bakhtin's definition. A text, he argues, 'lives and takes shape' through conflict and conversation with other texts, always in process.[8] Any such text

> weaves in and out of complex interrelationships, merges with some, recoils from others, intersects with yet a third group: and all this may crucially shape discourse, may leave a shape in all its semantic layers, may complicate its expression and influence its entire stylistic profile. The living utterance . . . cannot fail to brush up against thousands of living dialogic threads.[9]

'There can be neither a first nor a last meaning', Bakhtin writes elsewhere.[10] Nothing ever ends.

Although *Watchmen* was never a simple text, even at its inception – as Annalisa Di Liddo observes, it was always self-consciously intertextual, and poststructuralism would argue that, in Kristeva's words, 'any text is constructed as a mosaic of quotations; any text is the absorption and transformation of another' – it is now exceptionally complex.[11] 'Watchmen' now refers to a sprawling cross-media matrix of contradictory stories with multiple authors, ranging over thirty-six years at the time of writing.

Even if the franchise had formally wrapped up in December 2019 – *Doomsday Clock* was complete, and Lindelof stated that he had no plans for a sequel to the TV show – the existing texts of *Watchmen* would already have contained infinite chains of meaning. As Deleuze and Guattari put it, 'every sign refers to another sign, and only to another sign, ad infinitum.'[12] Nothing ever ends, in other words. If *Watchmen* had stopped right then and there, we could still trace every existing reference back to its source, and from that source to another source which branched off and led back to further sources, without ever finding a pure point of origin.

And of course, it didn't stop there. The bandwagon rolled on, partly because there was still money to be made. In October 2020, DC Comics launched a gritty twelve-part detective series under its 'mature' Black Label imprint, *Rorschach*, whose relationship to previous stories was left deliberately ambiguous: its references placed it closer to the acclaimed HBO show than to the niche comic-book prequels and sequels. In broader terms, HBO's *Lovecraft County* (premiered August 2020) and Disney+/Marvel's *The Falcon and the Winter Soldier* (March–April 2021) have both been discussed as what we might now call 'post-*Watchmen*' television shows – that is, influenced by the HBO *Watchmen*, with its bold approach to American racial tensions and Black history, rather than the original comic.[13] So the official group of texts continues to expand – as it will, while the storyworld created by Moore and Gibbons continues to yield profitable spin-offs – and around it, in turn, the further echoes and looser connections continue to spread in a wider network, rippling out from the central group. That process currently shows no sign of slowing, let alone stopping.

This book will, inevitably, be out of date by the time of its publication. But we can draw a line, and capture a moment, like a drawing of falling snow in a glass globe, and study a period of time for what it tells us; we can freeze the *Watchmen* network at this stage, examining its crystalline structure not just for its own sake, as an intricate joint creation that has formed over several decades, but also for what it tells us about fundamental concepts such as narrative, adaptation, authorship, ownership, interpretation and our understanding of truth.

1

Intertextuality and authorship
Alan Moore and *Watchmen*

'*Watchmen*', states Annalisa Di Liddo, referring to the graphic novel, 'is an extremely intricate and layered text' as a result of Alan Moore's 'intertextual strategies'.[1] Intertextuality is a theoretical approach which, to put it simply, proposes that every 'text' – which could be a novel, a play, a song, a comic book, a garment or a place – is not a single, isolated entity but part of a vast, in fact endless, broader network of meaning.[2]

Roland Barthes, one of the foremost proponents of this approach, reminds us that it returns to the original meaning of the word 'text', which can be traced back (again, intertextually) through Old French and Medieval Latin variants to a Proto-Indo-European root, all of them carrying the sense 'to weave' and spinning off in turn to 'texture'. 'Etymologically, the text is a tissue, a woven fabric.'[3]

'The Text is plural,' he writes, 'not a co-existence of meanings but a passage, an overcrossing.' He describes it as 'an explosion, a dissemination'; the reader is 'at a loose end', presumably picking up and following a thread through the material.[4] The text is

> woven entirely with citations, references, echoes, cultural languages . . . which cut across it through and through in a vast stereophony. The

intertextual in which every text is held, it itself being the text-between of another text, is not to be confused with some origin of the text: to try to find the 'sources', the 'influences' of a work, is to fall in with the myth of filiation; the citations which go to make up a text are anonymous, untraceable, and yet *already read*: they are quotations without inverted commas.[5]

Barthes warns us against trying to trace a reference back to its 'original'; there is no starting point ('every sign refers to another sign, and only to another sign, ad infinitum'), and the echoes of other texts are invisible, unconscious influences rather than overt citations.

What does this mean, in relation to the original *Watchmen*? (Of course, to Barthes, even the word 'original' here would be misleading.) Inevitably, some of the references will be difficult if not impossible to dig up and identify; Alan Moore's extensive reading will no doubt have shaped *Watchmen*, but many of those influences are so deeply buried and broadly spread that the sources will remain, in Barthes's word, 'untraceable'.

But Barthes is often provocative in his pronouncements and not to be taken strictly literally. Clearly, there are different layers of intertextuality within Moore and Gibbons's *Watchmen*. Some of the references will be lost to everyone but the creators – if they ever realized them, and if they remembered them – while others lie just below the surface, or on the page itself, or are even signalled with inverted commas.

Di Liddo recognizes this in her account of the graphic novel's 'intertextual strategies'. She begins her survey with the title itself, which 'stems from an intertextual reference . . . at the end of the twelfth and last chapter, an epigraph from Juvenal's *Satires* appears: *Quis custodiet ipsos custodes?* Who watches the watchmen?'[6] Already, Barthes's bold statement that 'the citations which go to make up a text are anonymous, untraceable . . . quotations without inverted commas' seems hyperbolic.

The title, connected to a Latin phrase only at the end of the story, follows the pattern of each chapter title, which takes an evocative phrase from a longer

INTERTEXTUALITY AND AUTHORSHIP 9

passage, drawing on a diverse range of sources from 'high' and 'low' culture (The Bible, Elvis Costello, Percy Bysshe Shelley, Albert Einstein, Bob Dylan twice) and offering fuller context in the final panel: thus the bold, initially enigmatic headline 'At Midnight, All The Agents', which interrupts page 6 of chapter 1, is revealed as a lyric from Dylan's 'Desolation Row' ('At midnight, all the agents / And superhuman crew / Go out and round up everyone / Who knows more than they do').[7] Far from untraceable, these intertextual references – showily eclectic in the typical fashion of 1980s postmodernism – are a demonstration of the writer's cultural expertise and the comic's literary aspirations – part of an ambitious and ultimately successful attempt to distinguish it from conventional superhero stories. When the quotations were omitted from early issues – supposedly because of rights issues to the Dylan lyrics – Moore was keen to supply them for fans in person, at a convention.[8]

On the next level down, slightly more obscure and incorporated in the text itself, we could include the references to real-world television shows, films, music and historical events that also feature in the alternate 1985 of *Watchmen*. Despite the existence of costumed adventurers and an actual superhuman, the electric cars and airships and the never-ending Nixon administration, *Watchmen's* New Yorkers can watch Robert Wise's *The Day the Earth Stood Still* (1951)[9] or the 'Architects of Fear' episode of *The Outer Limits*,[10] from September 1963. (This last is itself a knowing reference to the episode that bears similarities to *Watchmen's* alien-invader plot.) This is a world with no mention of Batman but where TV presenters can still make a Bugs Bunny joke ('What's up, doc?' the interviewer asks Manhattan in chapter 3, earning a laugh from the audience) and kids wear Snoopy slippers.[11] The dominant youth subculture is the Knot-Top gang, fuelled on the invented narcotic KT-28s ('Katies') and fans of fictional band Pale Horse, but characters listen to Iggy Pop's 'Neighborhood Threat' (1977)[12] and remember the art-pop band Devo; America triumphed in Vietnam, but Kitty Genovese was still murdered in March 1964, and JFK was assassinated in November 1963, though the Comedian may, in this universe, have had something to do with it. While

Moore creates a whole mini-market of new brands, they also refer back to real-world sources: Gunga Diner (Rudyard Kipling's poem 'Gunga Din'), Sweet Chariot (from an African-American spiritual) and the Gordian Knot Lock Company (from a legend of Alexander the Great, which in turn inspires Adrian Veidt). Mmeltdowns are, Moore explains in the script, an atomic version of M&Ms.[13] (As Julian Darius points out, this alternate universe must have changed course from ours in the nineteenth century, because the beans Rorschach eats are labelled 58 varieties, rather than the 57 named by Henry John Heinz in 1896.[14])

Real-life comics creators (Joe Orlando, Julius Schwartz) are also remembered in the fiction alongside invented ones (writer Max Shea, artist Walt Feinberg), within an alternate industry history that swung from superheroes to pirate stories. In the end-of-chapter supplements, Gibbons adapts his style to draw a racist cartoon for right-wing magazine *New Frontiersman*, a finely detailed illustration for an ornithological journal, the scribbled nightmare of a disturbed child;[15] we are meant to interpret and accept his painted artwork, such as the portrait of young Hollis at Vernon's Auto Repairs in the first *Under the Hood* supplement and the *Nova Express* publicity picture of Ozymandias, as photographs, a simulation disrupted by the inclusion of an actual photograph of Joe Orlando.[16] *Under the Hood's* first chapter offers a particularly interesting example, as a 'news photograph' of a crime scene is contrasted with the 'artist's impression' of Hooded Justice; both of them are drawn by Gibbons.

More subtly, his artwork slips briefly into a cleaner, retro-1940s mode for the (possibly idealized) flashbacks to Hollis Mason's heroic heyday that punctuate the scene of his murder,[17] while the speech balloons, hand-drawn and lettered, alter to signify different periods of (comic book) history: cruder bubbles for the Golden Age 1940s, smooth ovals in the Silver Age 1960s, more angular in the present day.[18] Moore, meanwhile, switches voices with aplomb and evident enjoyment, channelling the earnest blue-collar hero Hollis Mason in three chapters of his autobiography, the frustrated romantic Dan Dreiberg in an essay on ornithology and the *Rolling Stone* flair of Doug

Roth in *Nova Express* magazine. Again, this idea of doing things 'in the style of', without quite parodying or paying tribute, is very much in keeping with 1980s postmodernism.[19]

The most sustained example of this pastiche is the *Black Freighter* comic-book narrative, which runs in the background of the main story from chapters 3 to 11. Initially prompted by the fact that young Bernard is reading this issue at the newsstand, the *Black Freighter* tale returns in glimpses and short sequences that comment obliquely on the action through images and captions: thus the early *Black Freighter* line 'and I knew that life had no worse news to offer me' is followed immediately and ironically by Kovacs's arrival with his 'The End Is Nigh' sign;[20] Detective Steve Fine mishearing Rorschach as 'raw shark' echoes the mariner 'that night, eating shark' from the previous page,[21] while the line 'borne on the naked backs of murdered men'[22] from chapter 5 has its payoff far later, with the reveal of Ozymandias's masterplan and his confession that 'I've struggled across the backs of murdered innocents to save humanity'.[23]

The Black Freighter story is invented by Moore, drawn by Gibbons with a slightly thicker, darker line compared to the main art – emphasized when panels zoom in on detail and acquire an almost woodcut effect[24] – coloured by Higgins in garish primary hues[25] and supposedly authored by Max Shea, a character in the story itself (the article about Shea that closes chapter 5 is published in a fictional *Treasure Island Treasury of Comics*, by an imaginary Flint Editions, located elsewhere in this fictional New York City).

As Di Liddo points out, while the main purpose of *Black Freighter* within *Watchmen* is to provide an ironic chorus and counterpoint to Adrian Veidt's masterplan – 'borne on the naked backs of murdered men' – it also 'echoes literary reminiscences of Coleridge's *Rime of the Ancient Mariner* (1834), Poe's *Manuscript Found in a Bottle* (1833) and *A Descent into the Maelstrom* (1841) and Brecht's *Dreigroschenoper* (1928)'.[26] Here we are moving beyond the top level of quotations, going deeper than visual references and easy puns and descending to a more obscure stratum of 'literary reminiscences' which are open to multiple interpretations: the earlier list is Di Liddo's, rather than

Moore's stated sources, though he (through the anonymous comic-book historian who authors this section) refers to the Brecht/Weill *Threepenny Opera* as a possible influence in the chapter 5 supplement. Moreover, we start to see here the complexity of intertextuality, as *Black Freighter* cannot be mapped to a single referent – in the way that 'At Midnight, All the Agents' is undeniably Dylan and 'Gunga Diner' is clearly Kipling – but evokes a range of possible antecedents, even to a single reader. The matrix becomes more complex if we follow the threads from *Black Freighter* into the future, as well as backwards: Moore evoked Brecht's *Threepenny Opera* more explicitly in his far later *League of Extraordinary Gentlemen,* where it meshes Pirate Jenny with Mack the Knife and Jack the Ripper. Nina Simone's version of Brecht/Weill's song 'Pirate Jenny' was used on the end credits of the 2009 movie spin-off, *Tales of the Black Freighter,* and the character name was borrowed (no doubt deliberately) by Damon Lindelof for a masked cop in the HBO *Watchmen* of 2019 – not so much completing the circle to the original *Watchmen* as linking back to an earlier point in a vast circuit of references.

The same is true of the title itself. The final quotation from Juvenal ties it 'officially' to a maxim that asks who will guard us from our guardians, protect us from our protectors and police our police – echoing Nite Owl's question in chapter 2, 'Protection? Who are we *protecting* them from?'[27] – but prior to that, the word has been floating freely without any confirmed meaning, although it cleverly echoes the musings on watchmaking associated with Jon Osterman and introduced in chapter 4, and other references such as JFK's never-delivered 'watchmen on the walls' speech[28] and Dylan's 'All Along The Watchtower', which gives chapter 11 its title. The linguistic connection between 'Watchmen' and The Minutemen, the 1940s superhero team, the parallel with other established teams such as The X-Men, and the recurring graffito 'Who Watches the Watchmen' give the impression that the word signifies a superhero team within the comic itself, but the group formed briefly by Captain Metropolis in the 1960s was, more prosaically, called The Crimebusters.[29] Zack Snyder's adaptation broke with Moore's original in this respect and used the word in dialogue, presumably to avoid confusion for viewers and to conform to superhero movie convention.[30] 'Watchmen are . . . over', Dan Dreiberg tells Rorschach on their first meeting, referring to their crimefighting prime.

That one word, 'Watchmen' – the very first word of the text – therefore links to multiple concepts including Einstein's quotation about watchmakers at the end of chapter 4 (and its relationship, in turn, to Jon Osterman and his father), the conventions of superhero team names, the final epigram from Juvenal and the fictional team The Minutemen. 'Minutemen' branches off immediately to at least two further meanings: the civilian soldiers of the American Revolution who could be 'ready in a minute' and a slang term about disappointing male sexual performance ('over within a minute'). At a further remove, 'Watchmen' evokes the Doomsday Clock that appears on the back cover of every issue, ticking closer to midnight, the 'real' Doomsday Clock mentioned within the story itself[31] and by implication all the visual echoes of a clock or watch face throughout the artwork, most obviously the blood spatter that intersects Comedian's iconic badge at the approximate 'ten minutes to midnight' position. We could also note that there was a Second World War comic book hero called Minute-Man, initially published during the 1940s as a copy of Captain America – and also named after the American Revolutionary soldiers – who also appeared in DC Comics stories in 1976 and 1996, entirely independently of *Watchmen*. Lance Parkin offers other possible links and precedents, suggesting that the name

> alludes variously to a mobile militia in the War of Independence, a number of right-wing volunteer groups, including a militant anti-Communist group in the sixties, and (after *Watchmen* was published) a vocal group of civilians who patrol the border with Mexico. No doubt Moore was also aware of punk band The Minutemen, and it goes without saying that in a book about the threat of nuclear war, the name is a conscious reference to the ICBMs that had been in service since the sixties (Moore possibly even knew that one of his favourite authors, Thomas Pynchon, worked as a technical writer on the Minuteman project) . . . and so on.[32]

This exhausting but still not exhaustive list gives us a sense of what Deleuze and Guattari mean by 'every sign refers to another sign, and only to another sign, ad infinitum'. We cannot fully explain the meaning of a term like 'Minutemen' without going further down the chain of connections, and then further still. What was the American Revolution? Who was Pynchon? What is a minute? The process is like clicking through pages of Wikipedia, in search of an original source; and theories of intertextuality tell us there is no such thing. Finding the primary reference, from this perspective, is not the point: the pleasure is in enjoying the rich weave of the text as it expands beyond its initial boundaries, leading us down endless threads on unexpected routes.

The main costumed characters themselves – the group once known as the Crimebusters – serve as a prime example. On the most obvious level, they represent traditional superhero archetypes, recalling existing characters in various ways. Comedian could be seen as a hybrid of DC's Captain America with Marvel's The Punisher, instilling the patriotic supersoldier with a grimmer cynicism. Silk Spectre has the generic abilities of a Black Canary, with a skimpy outfit very similar to Phantom Lady's yellow minidress, a dancer's physique and an expertise in martial arts. Nite Owl, Rorschach and Ozymandias each foregrounds a side of Batman: the science hero with geekily branded gadgets, the street detective, the billionaire mastermind with Olympian athleticism. The relationship between Hollis Mason and Dan Dreiberg, and their official titles Nite Owl I and II, reflects the superhero tradition of handing down a title to a former sidekick (see the various dynasties of The Flash, for instance).[33] Dr Manhattan is literally a 'superman' with extraordinary, uncanny powers.[34]

But there is a more specific origin. Moore and Gibbons were adapting a group broadly known as 'the Charlton characters', after their original publisher.[35] DC had bought up the Charlton Comics line and subsequently invited Moore, already celebrated for his work on *Swamp Thing*, to provide their new acquisitions with a story. Moore duly drafted a proposal for 'Who Killed the Peacemaker?', but his editor at DC, Dick Giordano, decided that its bold direction conflicted with the company's longer-term plans for the characters. So Moore and Gibbons went back to the drawing board and created their own analogues based on those originals. Peacemaker became Comedian, and Captain Atom was Dr Manhattan. Peter Cannon, Thunderbolt, became Adrian 'Ozymandias' Veidt. The Question was Rorschach, Blue Beetle was recast as Nite Owl, and Nightshade – a more minor character, described by Gibbons as 'just someone to be Captain Atom's girlfriend' – was renamed Silk.[36] Moore later explained:

> If we had used the Charlton characters in *Watchmen*, after #12, even though the Captain Atom character would've still been alive, DC couldn't really have done a comic book about that character without taking away from what became *Watchmen*. So, at first, I didn't think we could do the book with simply characters that were made-up, because I thought that would lose all of the emotional resonance those characters had for the reader, which I thought was an important part of the book. Eventually, I realized that if I wrote the substitute characters well enough, so that they seemed familiar in certain ways, certain aspects of them brought back a kind of generic super-hero resonance or familiarity to the reader, then it might work.
>
> So, we started to reshape the concept – using the Charlton characters as the jumping-off point, because those were the ones we submitted to Dick – and that's what the plot involved. We started to mutate the characters, and I began to realize the changes allowed me so much more freedom. The idea of Captain Atom as a nuclear super-hero – that had the shadow of the atom bomb hung around him – had been part of the original proposal, but with Dr Manhattan, by making him kind of a quantum super-hero, it took it into a whole new dimension, it wasn't just the shadow of the nuclear threat around him. The things that we could do with Dr Manhattan's consciousness and the way he saw time wouldn't have been appropriate for Captain Atom. So, it was the best decision, though it just took me a while to realise that.[37]

What might initially look like a straight one-to-one adaptation is further complicated by the fact that, as we might now expect, the Charlton heroes were themselves not 'original' but variants on existing characters. Thunderbolt was a copy of Daredevil, created for Charlton when the company couldn't afford the rights to the earlier character.[38] Blue Beetle was based on the Green Hornet, though Andrew Hoberek describes his 1960s incarnation as 'more or less Batman with neither the darkness nor the camp';[39] ironically, once DC bought the character in the 1980s, Blue Beetle was replaced in his regular comic by a copy of a copy, The Scarlet Scorpion.[40] The Question was creator Steve Ditko's mainstream reworking of his own earlier, visually similar but more politically extreme vigilante, Mr A, who was inspired in turn by the philosophical principles of Objectivism associated with Ayn Rand. Captain Atom was cut from the same cloth as contemporary nuclear heroes *Dr Solar, Man of the Atom*, published by Gold Key, and Dell Comics' *Nukla*.[41]

And Moore and Gibbons, given the liberty to invent their own cast, introduced various other influences into the mix, adding them to the basic Charlton templates to create richer, more rounded figures. The first Nite Owl's costume, for instance, was redrawn from young David Gibbons's naïve sketches of a crimefighter called 'Night Owl',[42] while Dr Manhattan's blue skin (described by the artist as 'a cold energy, unlike fire or flame') owed something to Rogue Trooper, the supersoldier Gibbons co-created for *2000AD* in 1981.[43] Facially, Gibbons wanted his superheroes to look like 'individuals, more like the near-caricatures common in European comics, rather than the square-jawed variations on a theme of most American comics',[44] and looked to celebrities for guidance: Ozymandias was, according to his notes, modelled on 'Redford, Kennedy', Michelangelo's *David* and Julio Iglesias.[45] Comedian was facially 'Groucho Marx'[46] and conceptually 'Dirty Harry meets Nick Fury meets Hannibal of *A-Team*' (according to Gibbons), 'using methods similar to those used by the insurrectionist hero of Eric Frank Russell's book *Wasp*' (according to Moore).[47] But the references don't stop there. Moore recalled:

> With our Peacemaker character, Dave and I were saying 'This is a guy who's a comedian', and I believe I took the name from Graham Greene's book, *The*

Comedians. At that point, I'd done quite a bit of research upon various kinds of CIA and intelligence community dirty tricks, so Dave and I saw him as a kind of Gordon Liddy character, only a much bigger, tougher guy.[48]

Another page of Gibbons sketches lists as further inspirations 'Burt Reynolds, Magnum, Clark Gable, circus strongman . . . Esterhaus', the last referring to a character from *Hill Street Blues*.[49] That's twelve sources already, not including Captain America and Punisher: similarly, Rorschach was not just The Question or Mr A but Michael Belker from *Hill Street Blues* (Gibbons)[50] and 'Son of Sam' David Berkowitz (Moore), whose notes to the police directly inspired his journal entries.[51]

Even the female characters based on meagre comic-book source material were rebuilt and redesigned from real-world inspirations: Silk Spectre was Faye Dunaway and Meryl Streep (Gibbons), while Silhouette was 'Marlene Dietrich or Nico' (Moore).[52] 'So yeah,' as Moore put it, 'these characters started out like that, to fill gaps in the story that had been left by the Charlton heroes, but we didn't have to strictly stick to that Charlton formula. In some places, we stuck to it more closely, and in some places, we didn't.'[53]

It's clear that, in di Liddo's phrase, 'every protagonist in *Watchmen* . . . rests on a net of intertextual references'.[54] Indeed, *Watchmen*'s cast is as crowded with cross-references as 'Desolation Row', with its motley parade of wannabe film stars (Cinderella posing like Bette Davis), costumed characters (The Phantom of the Opera), biblical figures (Cain and Abel), scientists and poets (Einstein, Ezra Pound), folk heroes and supervillains (Robin Hood, Dr Filth) fighting, playing penny whistles and chanting protest slogans. One couplet in particular neatly sums up Moore and Gibbons's approach to the Charlton heroes:

All these people that you mention, yes, I know them, they're quite lame
I had to rearrange their faces and give them all another name.

But the influences go back further than the Charlton characters. 'My original idea,' Moore explained, 'for what it's worth, involved the characters of the

MLJ-Archie Comic super-hero line, the Mighty Crusaders.'[55] So instead of Comedian or Peacemaker, the story would have begun with the death of The Shield, perhaps with The Fly and Flygirl in the Nite Owl/Silk Spectre roles, and a version of The Shadow investigating.[56] Some elements of the Golden Age MLJ heroes may have been incorporated into the Minutemen: compare for instance Black Hood with Hooded Justice, Captain Flag with Dollar Bill.

More fundamentally, Moore has admitted a vague debt to the Robert Mayer 1977 novel *Super-Folks*, a spoof of the genre that, he remembers, 'was a big influence on *Marvelman*', his British superhero story for *Warrior* which ran from 1982 to 1984 but which he'd largely forgotten by 1986, 'although I may have had it subconsciously in my mind'.[57] He and Gibbons both agree that *Watchmen*, like *Marvelman* before it,[58] was inspired by *Mad* magazine's comic-book parody 'Superduperman', written by Harvey Kurtzman and drawn by Wally Wood in 1953. 'Superheroes never looked better than when Wally Wood was parodying them', Moore enthused. 'So we decided to sort of take some of those elements from the *Mad* parodies – you know, we were having massive amounts of background detail but it wasn't sight gags: it was sight dramatics, if you like.'[59]

So while Wood's artwork is crowded with satirical advertisements for 'Super Soap', flyers declaring 'Post No Bills' and 'For Rent' signs in place of superhero insignia, Gibbons's is layered with newspaper headlines, slogans, billboards and graffiti that fill in details of the fictional world. 'A lot of the storytelling in *Watchmen* is actually Harvey Kurtzman storytelling', Gibbons added. 'The nine-panel grid comes largely from the EC Comics of the forties and fifties.'[60]

His own technical approach to *Watchmen* – 'remarkably consistent, understated and deceptively simple', enabling that 'high level of visual detail'[61] – was inspired by another artist, Jean Giraud/Moebius.

The kind of line that Moebius uses is a line which detaches the artist from the art. Because you draw in a simple, almost dead-weight outline you de-emphasise the artist's involvement with it – you lose the character of the artist and emphasise the character of what's being drawn. As far as technique's concerned, the way I drew *Watchmen* was I used quite a stiff pen so that there wouldn't be a lot of modulation in the line or much evidence of me being there.[62]

Moore, in turn, has declared that William Burroughs 'is one of my main influences'.

> Not the cut-up stuff, but his thinking about the way that the word and the image are used to control, and their possible more subversive effect. I'm surprised Burroughs didn't do more comic strips himself . . . With *Watchmen* I was trying to put some of his ideas into practice; the idea of repeated symbols that would become laden with meaning. You could almost play them like music. You'd have these things like musical themes that would occur throughout the work.[63]

Already, then, we can see that *Watchmen* sits at the centre of a sprawling intertextual matrix. 'And yet,' as Christian W. Schneider notes, 'this is not the end of it all.'

> Watchmen's complexity does support several readings since 'the meanings of almost every word, image, panel, and page are multiple – *obviously* multiple'. This semiotic polyvalence practically obliges the recipient to reread the text, deciphering new and often coexisting meanings. Nothing is simple in the world of *Watchmen*, not even the seemingly inescapable end of the world.[64]

What Schneider implies here – he quotes from another piece, Thomson's 'Deconstructing The Hero',[65] so even his comment on multiple readings is nested and referential – is that even if we could track down every meaning intended by Moore, Gibbons and Higgins, every reader could nevertheless draw new interpretations from the text on each new visit. His own work provides an example, as it seeks to situate *Watchmen* within the Gothic tradition: not the most obvious candidate, compared to the earlier *Swamp Thing* and later *From Hell*. The critical anthologies *Watchmen and Philosophy* and *Minutes to*

Midnight furnish further instances of interpretations that may never have been considered by the creators. Walter Hudsick lists the 1971 essay 'Man of Steel, Woman of Kleenex' by Larry Niven, with its exploration of supersexuality, as a key influence alongside 'Superduperman' and *Superfolks*,[66] while Chad Nevett ticks off *Watchmen*'s plot against Raymond Chandler's list of elements that make up a perfect mystery.[67]

Watchmen and Philosophy applies Kant, Bergson, Stoicism and – fittingly, as he provides the title to chapter 6 – Nietzsche to the text and uses the closeted gay couple from the Minutemen team, Hooded Justice and Captain Metropolis, as a frankly bizarre case study for examining whether it's OK to be disgusted by homosexuality. 'I have to admit that when I first read about Hooded Justice and Captain Metropolis,' writes Robert Arp with perhaps misguided candour, 'I said, "Oh, no," and closed the book. I have a visceral negative reaction to the thought of another man looking at me with desire or "wanting me", and I'm basically uncomfortable with the gay lifestyle.'[68] The chapter headings include '"Those People" Are Unnatural' and 'They Act Out on Their Screwed-Up Desires', and the author feels the need to reassure us that 'HMs [homosexuals] aren't likely to be child molesters. HMs aren't necessarily cross-dressers or transvestites.'[69]

Inevitably, of course, online commentators come up with their own ideas. Kate Willaert argues that *Watchmen*'s space invader finale could be lifted from a 1959 Jack Kirby comic book, published four years before the broadcast of 'The Architects of Fear' on *The Outer Limits*.[70] James Gifford constructs a convincing theory that Hooded Justice and Captain Metropolis are still alive and enjoying a meal in *Watchmen*'s first chapter.[71] Redditors on r/watchmen continue to debate whether Rorschach is racist.[72] One fan proposes whimsically that Dr Manhattan, after declaring his interest in experimenting with new life at the end of *Watchmen*, went on to create the Smurfs and their universe.[73]

Slash stories about the Rorschach/Nite Owl relationship constitute a subgenre to themselves. One, set during *Watchmen* chapter 10, imagines that Walter Kovacs lost his virginity to Dan Dreiberg while on their flight to confront

Veidt in Antarctica;[74] another has Veidt tricking Laurie into sex during the 1977 police strike.[75] Lavish, lovingly rendered fan art depicts similar moments, alongside Comedian dominating Ozymandias in a violent embrace,[76] while cosplay performers have created gender-swapped incarnations of a female Comedian and Dr Manhattan.[77]

There are manga *Watchmen* fancomics, or *doujinshi*, such as *CatCatch!Rorschach!* (2010), an adults-only depiction of Walter Kovacs as a cute feline, and grimmer volumes such as the *Rorschach Imprisonment Book* (2010);[78] fandom has also produced a filk song by Tom Smith celebrating 'Rorschach Love' (2015)[79] and a *Livejournal* kinkmeme around 'owlbbs', owl babies that were fertilized by Kovacs and laid by Dan Dreiberg.

Moore has acknowledged that readers regularly go against his and Gibbons's intended meanings. In a 1988 interview, his response was mild, tolerating if not embracing alternative explanations:

CHRIS [SHARRETT]: One criticism I've heard of *Watchmen* is that its politics become reversed. The book seems very radical, very progressive, but the bleak ending seems to suggest that the only change in the world is the kind effectuated by charismatic leaders.

ALAN: I could see how people could read that into it, but it certainly wasn't what we intended, and I don't think it's the most obvious sort of message the book conveys. In some ways what we were trying to say was quite the opposite.[80]

Two decades later, his attitude was less forgiving.

I had forgotten that actually to a lot of comic fans that smelling, not having a girlfriend – these are actually kind of heroic. So actually, sort of, Rorschach became the most popular character in *Watchmen*. I meant him to be a bad example, but I have people come up to me in the street saying 'I am Rorschach! That is my story!' And I'll be thinking, 'Yeah, great, can you just keep away from me and never come anywhere near me again for as long as I live?'[81]

And fans, as Moore mentions, sometimes have the opportunity to test their theories in person. Richard Bensam relates a story about comics artist and historian Steve Whittaker, who ran into Dave Gibbons at a convention in 1986. Only four issues of *Watchmen* had been published to date, and Whittaker wanted a clue to the plot. 'Rorschach is the real centre of the story, isn't he? He's the character we should be keeping our eyes on, the one everything else revolves around, right?' Gibbons refused to commit. 'It could be Rorschach or the Comedian or Ozymandias. *You* could be Nite Owl.'[82] I had my own experience of pitching an interpretation to Alan Moore at a 1987 book signing; fired up from A-level language classes, I was convinced that Roy Chess, a minor character in Ozymandias's conspiracy, must be a deliberate pun on the German word for chess, *Schach*. 'Roy Chess', growls Rorschach during an interrogation. 'How's your game?'

'Roy *Schach*', I explained earnestly to the *Watchmen* writer.

'You're too clever for me!' Moore boomed, more generously than I deserved.

'We know now', writes Barthes in 'The Death of the Author',

> that a text is not a line of words releasing a single 'theological' meaning (the 'message' of the Author-God) but a multi-dimensional space in which a variety of writings, none of them original, blend and clash. The text is a tissue of quotations drawn from the innumerable centres of culture . . . the writer can only imitate a gesture that is always anterior, never original. His only power is to mix writings, to counter the ones with the others, in such a way as never to rest on any one of them. Did he wish to *express himself*, he ought at least to know that the inner 'thing' he thinks to 'translate' is itself only a ready-formed dictionary, its words only explainable through other words, and so on indefinitely.[83]

This certainly seems to correspond with a sense of *Watchmen* as, on one level, a dense and detailed architecture of references, a complex structure of ideas and images borrowed from previous work – superhero teams, Hollywood movies,

American politics, German philosophy, European bandes desinées, *Mad* magazine and William Burroughs – mixed together and dressed up in new disguises. We have also seen what Barthes means by 'words only explainable through other words, and so on indefinitely', as the chain of references unspools endlessly from a reference to its source, and then to the source of that reference, without ever reaching an origin.

But how does this square with the broader reputation of Alan Moore as a comic-book *auteur*, a toweringly important creator with a distinctive individual voice and approach? How can Moore be 'one of the finest English-language comics writers'[84] if he is only able to express himself through other people's work? How can *Watchmen* have revolutionized comic-book narratives and shifted perceptions of the superhero genre – *Time* magazine famously listed it as one of the hundred greatest novels, and the 2009 movie trailer described it as 'the most celebrated graphic novel of all time' – if it was just a rehash of unoriginal ideas? Does Moore deserve entire books dedicated to him like Jackson Ayres's *Critical Guide*, which itself opens with a list of plaudits?

> 'Alan Moore is widely regarded as the best and most influential writer in the history of comics.' [. . .] When general reader publications cover Moore, they frequently exclaim his stature: representative headlines include 'How Alan Moore Transformed The Way I Saw Comics' (Berlatsky 2016), 'Legendary Comics Writer' (Wired 2009), and 'Our Greatest Graphic Novelist' (Barber 2006). Comics scholarship also tends to register and accept Moore's high reputation . . . 'Moore is often referred to as the single best writer in the history of the comic book medium.'[85]

There are various answers to this conundrum. First, we should remember that Barthes's essay was a provocation, and that his call for the 'Death of the Author' was a request to shift focus from the traditional creator figure as the only source of truth to the then-neglected figure of the reader. While this was a useful steer and corrective at the time – as he says, 'classic criticism has never paid any attention to the reader; for it, the writer is the only person in literature'[86] – we would equally not want to invest all our faith about the meaning of a work in the vast and diverse community of readers, whose interpretations will inevitably clash and contradict each other and range from the plausible to the preposterous.

Second, while Barthes did help to prompt a significant shift within cultural studies scholarship – which, while it retains an interest in the *auteur*, has also paid increasing attention to readers, viewers and fan interpretations since the 1960s – the lofty authority of the Author-God still dominates broader popular discourse. Journalists still seek out the writer, director or showrunner for the official, intended meaning; fans still tweet the creator for confirmation of their theories; publicity campaigns still foreground the author's name as a brand of authenticity and guarantee of quality.

And Barthes himself proposes a substitute for the traditional author: the 'modern scriptor', who accepts that he bears within himself (Barthes uses the male pronoun throughout) 'this immense dictionary from which he draws a writing that can know no halt'.[87] Moore would perhaps have no dispute with this label – especially fitting because he is literally responsible for the comic -book *script*. He happily admitted in 1983 that he created *V For Vendetta* by making 'a long list of concepts that I wanted to reflect . . . moving from one to another with a rapid free-association that would make any good psychiatrist reach for the emergency cord'.

> Orwell. Huxley. Thomas Disch. *Judge Dredd*. Harlan Ellison's '"Repent, Harlequin!" Said the Ticktockman'. 'Catman' and 'Prowler in the City at the Edge of the World' by the same author. Vincent Price's *Dr Phibes* and *Theatre of Blood*. David Bowie. The Shadow. Nightraven. Batman. *Fahrenheit 451*. The writings of the *New Worlds* school of science fiction. Max Ernst's painting 'Europe After The Rain'. Thomas Pynchon. The atmosphere of British Second World War films. *The Prisoner*. Robin Hood. Dick Turpin.[88]

'There was some element in all of these that I could use', he admits of his early struggle with the material, 'but try as I might, I couldn't come up with a coherent whole from such disjointed parts'.[89] Moore's role in the process, from his own account, involved joining those things together into a structure that made sense.

As such, we can still admire and celebrate him as 'author' (or co-author, or 'scriptor'), not for crafting entirely original material from nothing – which, as the earlier discussion demonstrates, is clearly impossible – but for the skill with which he constructs new edifices from recycled material; for his ability to combine and rearrange familiar ideas and motifs in startling new formations. And we can recognize his distinctive traits and themes through the ideas he returns to and reworks, the favourite items he retrieves from the archive and the recurring patterns he forms from them. As Ayres notes, this perspective fits the notion of intertextuality 'as a virtuosic technique deployed by a knowing artist'.[90]

At this stage, then, I want to spend some time exploring those traits, themes, motifs and patterns, in order to gain a more detailed sense of the elements that combine to make up Moore's style in *Watchmen*. In doing so, we can identify how they developed and evolved from his previous work – not just the obvious superhero examples but also his lesser-known stories – and, in turn, can see how they continue into his later writing. And crucially, by establishing a detailed model of what Moore does in *Watchmen*, we then have a baseline for comparison against tributes, parodies, prequels, adaptations, sequels and other remixes, in the chapters still to come. This is not intended as an exhaustive list but a usefully indicative one.

We have of course extensively covered *Watchmen*'s intertextuality: its plundering of the past and collaging of previous, diverse sources. Far from denying this practice, Moore admits and embraces it. Di Liddo points out that his magical practice embraced the notion of 'Ideaspace, an immaterial dimension acting as repository for both individual fantasies and the collective imagination'; in his words, Ideaspace is 'a kind of medium or field or space or dimension in which thoughts occur . . . I believe that this "space" impinges to some degree on all consciousness and that it is co-accessible'.[91] We can see similar ideas at work in *Supreme*'s alternate reality The Supremacy (with its own alternate titles the Psychoverse or Cognitive Zone)[92] which houses variant heroes; the Underspace or Infraspace where the 'change bodies' of Miracleman and his fellow superhumans are kept between transformations, the Immateria, or plane of existence devoted to the imagination, from *Promethea,* the utopian Blazing World from his *League of Extraordinary Gentlemen* and the *Roger Rabbit*-style cartoon city from the short 1986 strip *In Pictopia.* These all convey similar ideas of a treasure house, archive or warehouse where archetypes, ideas and icons are stored for later retrieval, with obvious echoes of Fredric Jameson and his definition of postmodern pastiche: 'In a world in which stylistic innovation is no longer possible, all that is left is to imitate dead styles, to speak through the masks and with the voices of the styles in the imaginary museum.'[93] While Jameson sees this cultural turn as a dead end – his museum sounds more like a mausoleum – Moore tends to celebrate it as a dressing-up box, a chest of marvels. In *V For Vendetta* we are invited to visualize this space, even visit it: the protagonist's Shadow Gallery is a hidden archive of forbidden music, old film posters, theatrical sets and vaudeville costumes.

But what does Moore do with that treasure house of material? Rather than simply reuse it uncritically and unchanged, he transforms it: he reactivates, revives and revises it.[94] 'Revisionary' is the term comics scholar Geoff Klock uses for Moore's approach. 'It sends a wave of disruption back through superhero history by asking, for example, what would make a person dress up in a costume and fight crime?'[95] As Klock points out, one of Moore's key techniques is to seriously consider the broader implications of superhero tropes that are, in conventional narratives, taken for granted. 'Superheroes only make sense in a world where masked opponents support their fantasy',[96] without them, as Dan Dreiberg realizes, 'it's all crap dressed up with a lot of flash and thunder. I mean, who needs all this hardware to catch hookers and purse-snatchers? I mean really?'[97] That 'really' is significant, standing for the underlying question: what would it *really* be like if superheroes had existed since the late 1930s? What difference would it make to the superhero comic-book genre? What relation would their outfits and accessories have to sexual fetish? How would a genuinely superpowered individual change the community of costumed crimefighters, affect technology and change history?

Perhaps the most obvious precedent can be found in Moore's *Swamp Thing*, 'Book Four' of the first volume, cover-dated May 1984. This is his first engagement with DC Comics' big-hitter superheroes, the Justice League of America – Superman, Wonder Woman, Batman and their close colleagues – and his opening narration immediately achieves the effect of making these familiar commercial icons seem strange, marvellous and miraculous again.

> There is a house above the world, where the over-people gather. There is a man with wings like a bird . . . there is a man who can see across the planet and wring diamonds from its anthracite. There is a man who moves so fast that his life is an endless gallery of statues . . . in the house above the world, the over-people gather.[98]

Compare to – to give a typical example of the conventional approach – the introductory captions from *Justice League of America* 21, twenty years earlier.

> In the secret sanctuary of the Justice League of America, the members meet in an emergency session. Acting as chairman for this meeting is the famous crime-fighter from Gotham City – Batman! Picking up the gauntlet of battle hurled down by the master criminals, the champions of justice set out.[99]

Some of the differences between these introductory texts lie in Moore's distinctive prose style, which I'll discuss further later in this chapter. The repetition of 'house above the world' creates a sense of echoing rhythm, adding portent and gravity, slowing the pace and suggesting an epic, even biblical mode: we are among gods, and Moore provides a suitable chorus. His vocabulary is precise as well as poetic, often seeking less familiar terms – Superman squeezes diamonds from the more scientific and evocative 'anthracite', here, instead of simple 'coal' – and suggesting new ways of seeing. While the classic Silver Age *Flash* comic 'Flash of Two Worlds' conveys his powers through the mundane comparison 'I could outrun a taxicab',[100] Moore places us in the speedster's position, realizing that a man who moves so fast would see the world as a 'gallery of statues'. Notably, of course, he avoids any use of the term 'superheroes', preferring the Nietzschean 'over-people'. The effect is to distance us, to encourage us to see the familiar in a new way – closer to how it might 'really' be than the conventional generic narrative that treats these gods, aliens and titans as if they were friendly scoutmasters and sports mascots.

Swamp Thing consistently follows this rule of restricting itself to real-world logic – or something closer to it – rather than taking the easier way out through superhero convention. As with the 'gallery of statues', his revisions often reverse what was previously assumed. His central character, Alec Holland, did not simply transform into a plant monster, as the previous stories had it; instead, he is revealed to be a plant which thinks it is Alec Holland, building a skeleton of wood and furnishing it with vegetable lungs, a heart and brain.

In *Miracleman*,[101] Moore decides that rather than simply changing into a superhero through a magic-atomic word – as was the case in the optimistic original stories of the 1950s – the body and mind of the civilian alter ego Mike Moran must actually be swapped with that of a superior being, Miracleman, which is otherwise stored in an extra-dimensional limbo. Inevitably, following the grim logical implications of this unequal dynamic, the all-too-human Mike decides he cannot handle sharing his life with a deity – his wife has left him, unable to deal with marriage to a 'higher species' – and commits suicide, leaving Miracleman alone to forge a new Olympus on Earth.[102]

The strategy in each case is to take a familiar and safe icon or idea – often simple and optimistic, perhaps even childish and naive – and to think it through rigorously, asking how it would work in a world like our own. Moore was open about the fact that he planned to apply the same strategy to the Charlton characters that had worked with his previous projects, and DC welcomed it: 'they were interested in other stories from Moore that applied real-world logic to superheroes', Lance Parkin reports.[103] In the process, the original is made 'darker': sometimes literally in visual terms but more often in the sense of mature, challenging, sophisticated 'adult': the cliché of 'grim and gritty' that came to summarize this era of superhero comics.

The concept is neatly captured by a page at the end of *Miracleman*'s first issue, where, across an eight-panel grid, we zoom in slowly on an image of the grinning protagonist, his face rendered in 1950s primary colours, until shadows consume the brightness, the hero seems to glower and the Pop Art portrait becomes vague, abstract shapes. The last frame is dominated only by the blue-white gleam in his eye. The captions that run across this zoom are drawn from Nietzsche: 'I teach you the superman! He is this lightning . . . he is this madness!'[104] *Watchmen* performs a very similar routine at the end of chapter 6, moving steadily closer in on a Rorschach blot until its black blotches fill the panel. 'We are alone', runs the narration. 'There is nothing else.' Cue another quotation from Nietzsche ('If you gaze into the abyss, the abyss gazes also into you').[105]

Even more succinctly, Moore's revisionist approach is symbolized by the Comedian's yellow smiley-face badge, splashed with blood – a simple, bright icon defaced by detailed, realistically painted gore[106] – and articulated by Ozymandias, when he reveals his plan to Dreiberg in the penultimate chapter. 'Dan, I'm not a Republic serial villain. Do you seriously think I'd explain my master-stroke if there remained the slightest chance of you affecting its outcome?'[107]

While Moore's superhero stories of the 1980s are the most obvious examples of this method, it can also be seen, to an extent, in work like *Halo Jones*, especially Book Three, which subverts easy clichés about war narratives by placing a scared and confused everywoman, rather than *2000AD*'s usual battle-hardened soldiers, in the midst of horrific conflict, and *Skizz*, which reinvents the boy-befriends-alien narrative by having the visitor land in working-class Birmingham, where he is discovered by, again, an unassuming teenage girl.

This process of seriously thinking through the implications of familiar tropes – 'wading through cold logic', as a character in *Miracleman* puts it[108] – often leads Moore to an unflinching portrayal of the consequences, which, without implausible last-minute escapes and convenient plot armour to rescue the characters, edge into the horror genre. Characters who crash through high windows plunge in terror among shards of shattered glass – the Comedian's descent in *Watchmen* echoes near-identical panels in *Swamp Thing*, from a year before.[109] A extraterrestrial landing in New York City would, he and Gibbons demonstrate across six garish full-page splash pages at the start of *Watchmen* chapter 12, result in horrific levels of destruction, with buildings pierced by tentacles as thick as tree trunks, and characters we've come to know over several issues bleeding to death in the rubble.[110]

These grim tableaux – which have clear precursors in the glimpses of apocalypse in both *Swamp Thing* (1986) and the even earlier *Captain Britain* (1983)[111] – are an obvious pairing with the double-page spread in *Miracleman* depicting the grotesque cruelties inflicted on London by the sadistic villain Johnny Bates.[112] Artist John Totleben, drawing on sketches by Goya,[113] rivals Hieronymous Bosch's visions of Hell with his tableau of impaled faces, missing limbs and bodies trussed with barbed wire against a backdrop of burning buildings.[114] The lesson here is similar to that in *Watchmen*, too: Miracleman, closely resembling Ozymandias in his Aryan perfection, muses that 'there's never been a heaven; never been a house of gods . . . that was not built on human bones'.[115] As the notes to those pages put it:

> The creators' goal for the story was not to be gruesome or extreme, but to depict the plausible damage inflicted by a battle of superhumans – to show the real horror of violence. [. . .] Action in fantasy-adventure entertainment often has no meaningful impact – everything is back to normal in the end, which can be seen as a glorification. Here the results are hideous and true.[116]

Again, 'real' and 'true' are key words.

'Wading through cold logic' enables Moore to realize that an obsessive street vigilante like Rorschach would be likely to live in squalor, wearing the same musty outfits and restricting himself to a desperately unhealthy diet as he pursues his mission; it also results in the progressive, for the mid-1980s, inclusion of gay and lesbian characters. 'Given the world of *Watchmen*,' he told Christopher Sharrett, 'it seemed likely that there would be roughly the same percentage of gay people as in our world, and that certain professions might attract a higher percentage of gays than other professions.'[117] (As Ayres notes, times have changed, and to contemporary readers, 'his observation that superhero activity might "attract" queer people plays out problematically'.[118])

An unflinching embrace of 'realism' in genre stories led to the joyfully explicit scenes of childbirth in *Miracleman*, the admission that superheroes would need to use the bathroom mid-adventure in *Watchmen* (and that when terrified they might even wet themselves, in *Captain Britain*),[119] the well-meaning allegory of menstruation in *Swamp Thing*'s 'The Curse' issue and the mention of periods in *Halo Jones*, unusual for a boy's comic.[120]

The focus on 'realism' inclines Moore to restrict *Watchmen*'s violence largely to Rorschach moving a man's finger a single agonizing inch and to consider that a middle-aged man like Dan Dreiberg might struggle to perform sexually without his costume. It also leads to horrors of a different kind, in the sexual violence that pervades Moore's work. Comedian's brutal attempted rape of Sally Jupiter in *Watchmen* is just one in a series of similar traumatic scenes, such as the sexual assault of Barbara Gordon in *The Killing Joke*, the violation and torture of Evey in *V For Vendetta*, the rape of Johnny Bates and Avril Lear in *Miracleman*, of The Invisible Man in *League of Extraordinary Gentlemen Volume Two*, of Janni in *League of Extraordinary Gentlemen: Century 1910* and of Agent Brears in *Neonomicon*. Some of the 'grim and gritty' graphic novels that followed *Watchmen* regrettably attempted to emulate this aspect of *Watchmen* as a sign of 'maturity', as we'll see; but it must also be noted that Moore himself continued to experiment with variations on this disturbing theme, for several decades. As Ayres observes, 'depictions of rape and sexual violence . . . are rampant across Moore's comics.'[121]

As we saw earlier, Moore's prose style plays an important part in his making strange process, encouraging us to see the familiar from new perspective. It tends – again, as we've seen – towards portentous repetition and strikingly poetic imagery: overdone and overripe in places, perhaps, but undeniably imaginative. A line from *Swamp Thing*, 'clouds like plugs of cotton wool dab ineffectually at the slashed wrists of the sky', is frequently quoted as an example of Moore's excesses.[122] This style remains remarkably consistent throughout the 1980s.

In 1983, the alien interpreter Skizz arrived in Birmingham. 'Lights spin and blur into a neon nightmare. As his lungs absorb more and more of the stupefying oxygen into his blood, incomprehensible images pulse into his shock-dilated eyes. He changes direction again and again, losing himself amidst the dark geometries.'[123] In a short story, also from *2000AD* in 1983, Moore opens the scene at dawn: 'The rains had ceased, and amber sunlight burnished the steaming jungles of the Rhine Valley to a deep bronze. Somewhere, a mammoth screamed . . . He lay and watched the ochre clouds scudding across a brazen sky.'[124]

These are the first lines of Moore's *Swamp Thing*, from February 1984: 'It's raining in Washington tonight. Plump, warm summer rain that covers the sidewalks with leopard spots. Downtown, elderly ladies carry their houseplants out to set them on the fire-escapes, as if they were infirm relatives or boy kings.'[125] The issue ends with an echo: 'It's dark. It's late. I have a lot to do tomorrow. No matter. For the moment I am content simply to think, and to plan . . . and to listen. It's raining in Washington tonight.'[126]

Moore's Superman story 'For the Man Who Has Everything', drawn by Gibbons, was published in 1985: the Man of Steel battles his nemesis Mongul.

Eyes spit out suns. Muscles shift like continental plates, rolling under a hide of jaundiced leather. . . in the Chamber of Archives, a machine with a brain made of light is counting the distant pulsars. Within ten feet of its algebraic reverie, alien engines of fury grind together unnoticed.[127]

INTERTEXTUALITY AND AUTHORSHIP

In 1986, Moore wrote 'Tygers', a tale of the Green Lantern Corps, for DC:

> Years later, he died. Colliding with the radiation girdle of the turquoise planet, his ship suffered a critical malfunction. His ring of power was similarly useless. There was nothing he could do. He watched helplessly as the melanoma drive began to devour itself, and he knew then that he had been deceived . . . he fell . . . and all the way down, in his mind, he could hear them laughing.[128]

The story ends at its beginning, with slight variation: 'He fell. The yellow radiation girdle around the turquoise planet rendered both starship and ring of power useless within instants. He fell . . . he fell . . . and all the way down, in his mind, he could hear them laughing.'

This is a fight scene from *Miracleman*, May 1987:

> The brute crouched upon my chest, grinding sparks from its jaws. They showered hot upon my cheek, upon the petrol of my desperate rage . . . fracturing two of my own fingers I punched through its abdomen, immediately drenched in its scalding fluids, steaming and phosphorescent. Shuddering in the way that pigs do upon realising their throats are cut, it pronounced five dreadful syllables. Briefly, I embraced an infant sun that scribbled bright, autistic crayon lines across each retina. It became something like a giant, severed hand, a sticky mouth glistening in its palm. I pulverised one of its knuckles. The black lips writhed, incontinent, about a profanity coined beneath other constellations. I could not stay the recital of its bare, incendiary rhythm. I could not slam the covers shut upon its hideous vocabulary. It spoke . . . God clapped his hands.[129]

Although the passage about rain in Washington is the first-person account of plant-based supervillain The Floronic Man, and the final fight scene is described after the fact by the triumphant, godlike Miracleman – while the others are simply anonymous storytellers – we can identify the same voice across all of them and recognize it also in the line about cotton wool clouds, and

34   NEVER-ENDING WATCHMEN

the introduction to the house of the over-beings, discussed earlier. Whoever officially narrates, the ventriloquist is usually Moore himself in what we might call a mode of epic grandeur, occasionally overegged. (When he speaks as Swamp Thing, the narration is slower, spaced out with ellipsis, but otherwise unchanged: 'He stares . . . static crackling . . . in eyes . . . that have travelled . . . beyond reason . . . a boulder shifts its hue . . . from gray . . . to red . . . to white . . . and finally shatters. He howls . . . and a hurricane . . . spills from his lips . . . I . . . dare not . . . look. I . . . dare not . . . look away'.)[130]

If anything, this tendency is toned down in *Watchmen*, as there is no omniscient narrator; instead, Moore's descriptive prose is channelled into the baroque conspiracy theories and revenge fantasies of Rorschach's journal and the more fragmented, abstract observations of Dr Manhattan. While they are perhaps more similar than they should be, and both still clearly bear the imprint of their author – Rorschach's is meant to be a street-level brutal poetry, but he, like Manhattan and indeed Moore, enjoys looking down on the world like a god – they operate within their own specific ranges, with their own recognizable tones and distinct vocabularies, and are clearly not interchangeable.

> Soon it will be dark. Beneath me, this awful city, it screams like an abattoir full of retarded children. New York. On Friday night, a comedian died in New York. Somebody knows why. Down there . . . somebody knows. The dusk reeks of fornication and bad consciences. I believe I shall take my exercise.[131]

> Come . . . dry your eyes, for you are life, rarer than a quark and unpredictable beyond the dreams of Heisenberg; the clay in which the forces that shape all things leave their fingerprints most clearly. Dry your eyes . . . and let's go home.[132]

As Dr Manhattan tells Laurie on Mars, 'we gaze continually at the world and it grows dull in our perceptions. Yet seen from another's vantage point, as if new, it may still take the breath away'. The line embodies Moore's 'revisionist' agenda – not revision for the sake of it, or for shock, but in order to make

INTERTEXTUALITY AND AUTHORSHIP

strange and make new – but in *Watchmen*, significantly, he gives this role to two key characters, allowing us to see 'from another's vantage point'. Rather than dominating with his own heavy, heady style – which, it could be argued, has become familiar through his previous work – Moore's approach in *Watchmen* tends towards exercises in pastiche and experiments in diverse voices, especially in the prose sections at the end of each chapter.

Moore's restless love of language leads him not only into the epic, apocalyptic mode but also towards lighter dimensions. Though *Watchmen* is associated with a 'dark' trend in superhero comics, it – like much of Moore's work – is also full of puns and wordplay. Indeed, the slogan 'At play amid the Strangeness and Charm', which Dr Manhattan finds handwritten on a Gila Flats pinboard, could summarize this aspect of his approach; it also serves as a clever, throwaway pun about the qualities of quarks, hidden in darkness at the back of a panel. We might not go so far as Lance Parkin, who provocatively claims that the entirety of *Watchmen* is a giant gag – '*Alan Moore was joking*'[133] – but we shouldn't forget to see the funny side of the story, either.

The more obvious comedy, perhaps, falls flat. Comedian's schtick is to claim that everything in life is a big joke, but there's little laughter to be found in his scenes. Dan's story about Captain Carnage, who was pushed down an elevator shaft when he tried his 'punish me' kink on Rorschach, prompts Laurie to helpless guffaws, but as Ayres points out, it's 'gallows humour' about someone being 'killed over his non-normative sexuality'.[134] Rorschach's routine about the clown Pagliacci is memorable more because of his utterly humourless delivery and his clumsy attempt at the social conventions of comedy rather than for the anecdote itself. 'Heard joke once . . . Good joke. Everybody laugh.'[135] His apparently off-the-cuff pun about 'human bean juice' is better.

In fact, Rorschach accidentally provides some of the story's moments of humour. 'That's what they're saying about me now?' he growls to Dan. 'That I'm paranoid?'[136] As Parkin observes, it's 'straightforwardly set up and paid-off',[137] neat as a music-hall punchline. 'Why are so few of us left active, healthy, and without personality disorders?' Rorschach asks himself later in the first chapter, not long after he's told us he'd like to see New York's drains scabbing over, the streets filling with blood, the vermin drowning in filth and all the 'whores and politicians' begging him for salvation, so he can look down and whisper 'no'.[138] His condemnation of his fellow crimefighters for retiring comfortably – Veidt is 'pampered', Dan is 'flabby' and 'the first Nite Owl runs an auto-repair shop' – is richly ironic from a filthy, unhinged loner.[139] His effort, later in the story, to comfort Dan about the death of Hollis Mason by pointing out that it fits his conspiracy theory – 'by finding mask killer, can have revenge for Mason's death'[140] – is almost touchingly clueless.

Rorschach is also the butt of a straightforward visual joke in chapter 1, when his hard-boiled private-eye spiel meets the cosmic power of Dr Manhattan: 'Not leaving before I've' he declares, vanishing into a blue mist, and finishes 'had my say' alone outside the government base.[141] In the adjacent scene, he rages to Veidt that if Comedian was a Nazi, 'you might as well call me a Nazi, too'. We are treated to Veidt's amused response as he strokes his chin, his back turned to the oblivious Rorschach. With an exclamation mark in the corner of the bottom frame, this could be the wry ending of an Alan Moore *Future Shock*.[142]

Part of Rorschach's complexity, in fact, is that while he initiates and leads the plot, and is for most of the book the only character to correctly believe that a conspiracy lay behind all the deaths and disappearances, his 'mask-killer' theory remains ridiculously naive and narrow: in chapter 5 he accuses the decrepit old man Moloch of organizing Comedian's assassination and Manhattan's exile, and later wonders aloud whether the mastermind is 'Jimmy the Gimmick or The King of Skin', two-bit costumed criminals so irrelevant to the story that they are never mentioned elsewhere.[143] His persistent belief that a small-time former foe might be behind the grand plan is one of *Watchmen*'s subtlest running gags.[144]

As already noted, the text is closely woven with double meanings: a curry chain called Gunga Diner, a band called Krystalnacht, a singer called Red D'Eath (from the Edgar Allan Poe story), an autobiography from a superhero-turned car mechanic called *Under the Hood*. Detective Fine mishears Rorschach as 'Raw Shark'; Ozymandias makes laboured puns about the vigilante 'blotting out reality' and hardly being 'without stain'.[145] This linguistic experiment echoes Moore's earlier work, such as *Skizz* from 1983 – the name itself is Roxy's attempt at pronouncing 'Zhcchz' – in which the alien eats 'moo-zee' for 'beck-fuss' in 'Burmy-gam' and exclaims 'flippi-neck' when things go wrong.[146]

Swamp Thing's tribute to the comic strip *Pogo*, as Di Liddo notes, 'offers the opportunity to experiment with new linguistic formulas' ('I whish I could explicate, but I don't squeak your linguish').[147] It also includes extensive ventures into poetry, through the rhyming demon Etrigan with his iambic pentameter, and more subtly, in a sequence where Moore's captions ('The night can make a man more brave / But not more sober') end with an image of a roadside billboard reading simply 'BURMA SHAVE'.[148]

V For Vendetta's vigilante adopts not only the rhythms of a Renaissance theatrical hero – "Midst insurrection's clamour, we may easily forget just what it is for which we strive . . . isn't it dancing? Scented shoulders? Pupils widened by desire or wine?'[149] – but also quotes with postmodern eclecticism from Enid Blyton,[150] Yeats[151] and Lou Reed,[152] like a living embodiment of the impulse behind *Watchmen*'s chapter titles. There are Christmas-cracker puns here, too – a dour government agent is described waggishly as 'bitter Almond' – and ambitious tricks with sound and language. The vigilante takes his name from the Roman numeral for five, but when he uses Beethoven's Fifth as a musical cue, the meaning is more complex. 'Da da da *DUM* . . . it's Morse Code for the letter "V".'[153]

Halo Jones Volume 1, set in a cramped futuristic conurbation called The Hoop, is crowded with wordplay, both in the dialogue – 'Oubliay the Clara Pandy! The Rumble-Jacks'll be here for a hoop-scoop any minute now . . . I could have crumped that shmoo without any inbutt from you, Fido!' – and in the cultural environment itself. The delinquent youth group, equivalent to *Watchmen*'s Knot Tops, is called the Different Drummers, after a quotation from Henry David Thoreau. A washroom sign shows silhouettes of girls, boys and aliens, a beggar's sign reads 'Be Glad You Have a Tail – I Haven't' in two languages, and consoles in the background are labelled MAM, indicating the maternal welfare system 'Municipal Aid and Maintenance'. These details are reminiscent of the *Mad Magazine* style and Wally Wood's *Superduperman*, though here they serve the broader purpose of worldbuilding rather than just providing bonus jokes. *Watchmen* employs the same technique with its 'sight dramatics' like the repeating graffiti, posters and smiley faces.[154]

Even closer to *Watchmen* in visual terms is the short strip 'Chronocops', drawn by Dave Gibbons as a *2000AD* Future Shock in 1983. The story of time-travelling detectives Joe Saturday and Ed Thursday – themselves a parody of Joe Friday from *Dragnet* – returns regularly to the same busy lobby scene, where, as the intrigue develops back and forth across various past and future dates, we learn to identify doubles of the main characters in the background, hiding behind a potted plant and disguised as nuns. A similar 'sight dramatic' occurs in *Watchmen*, where Rorschach appears distantly in the background of a street scene, dressed in his civilian disguise, and walks around the block unremarked while the *Black Freighter* captions comment obliquely on his presence: 'His eyes, his nose, his cheeks seemed individually familiar, but mercifully I could not piece them together. Not into a face I knew.' As Rorschach passes in the foreground and disappears around the corner, the newsvendor remarks, 'I bet there's all kinda stuff we never notice.'[155]

Puns pervade Moore's science-fiction stories for *2000AD* from the early 1980s. 'Grawks Bearing Gifts' (1981) ends with a joke about the humans having 'reservations', meaning caged resettlement areas;[156] 'Salad Days' (1982) revolves around 'humanitarian' being interpreted along the lines of 'vegetarian', as a dietary preference.[157] 'Sunburn' (1982) not only revels in solar wordplay – 'I shouldn't have flared up like that', 'we call it the Ra-Ra skirt, after the Egyptian sun-god', 'C'mon everybody! Magma's up!' – but also introduces a character called Rorschach.[158] The punchline to 'An American Werewolf in Space', from February 1982, involves a vampire giving his name as 'Count Alucard';[159] Moore's 'Reversible Man', discussed later, is called Lamron Namron.[160]

In fact, several of Moore's *Watchmen* concepts were first explored in these twist-in-the-tale fast fictions: 'The Regrettable Ruse of Rocket Redglare' (1981) is about a retired superhero squeezing back into his costume for a final fling, and 'The Reversible Man' (1983) tracks its protagonist's life backwards, with an effect not unlike Dr Manhattan's overview of his personal history, and a black frame at the end. 'Eureka' revolves around a contagious idea: 'If all time is simultaneous and all events happen in a single instant, then time is but a figment of mind.'[161] Many of Moore's tales from this period, like 'Chronocops', share a fascination with time's direction, duration and speed and the changes to perspective that result: 'Brief Lives', written for DC Comics in 1985, even features two naked, bald blue men sitting on a red planet's rock under the stars, watching civilizations rise and fall in an image strikingly similar to Manhattan on Mars.[162]

At the end of his chapter, Parkin relents a little on his claim that *Watchmen* is a funny book. 'Is *Watchmen* cheerful and life-affirming, then? No, not for the most part, but neither is it written in a monotone, endlessly dark and dreary.' To fully understand it, he convincingly proposes, we have to also understand that it is 'by the writer of *D.R. & Quinch*'.[163] And if we look back at Moore's *D.R. & Quinch* stories for *2000AD* – the two characters were themselves based on O.C. and Stiggs from *National Lampoon*, just as Rorschach was The Question and Nite Owl was Blue Beetle – we find an actually amusing version of the Comedian in Pulger, the grizzled, lantern-jawed veteran of a science-fantasy Vietnam. 'Boys! I thought you were dead . . . I thought you'd become victims of this war . . . this damned, dirty little war.'[164]

Another key form of wordplay and linguistic double meaning is what we might call the use of counterpoint: the occasions, so frequent in *Watchmen* that they become a trademark of its storytelling, when a narrative caption or dialogue balloon seems to comment on an otherwise unrelated image. A very simple example occurs on the opening pages of chapter 1, when the detectives' guesses at what happened to Edward Blake ('which means that the occupant was home when it happened . . . he would have put up some kinda fight I'm certain') become, in cinematic terms, 'voiceover' to the red-tinted flashbacks of an intruder kicking open Blake's door and punching him in the face. By page 3, this technique has started to stray away from the literal and into the playfully ironic: the dialogue 'Ground floor comin' up' is not about Blake at all but an elevator, yet to us as readers, it seems to comment mordantly on his plunge through the window.[165] On page 4, 'What say we let this one drop out of sight' continues Fine's suggestion that they 'follow it up discreetly', but combined with the image of Blake tumbling towards the sidewalk, it acquires a double meaning.

Sarah Van Ness's analysis of *Watchmen* usefully discusses similar moments as a departure to an 'elsewhere' and 'elsewhen'. The earlier example is, strictly speaking, only an 'elsewhen', as the detectives are exploring the crime scene where Blake was killed the previous day, but as Van Ness points out, when Veidt discusses Blake at the end of the story, occasioning another series of puns, he refers to another place as well as another time.

> Again, the colour scheme alternates between cool and warm colours; Karnak is predominantly coloured in blues and greens, and the murder in shades of red. Veidt explains, 'Upon learning the creature's intended purpose, Blake's practiced cynicism cracked.' These words are shown in a dialogue box with an image of Blake thrown against a window, which has cracked and shattered from the impact . . . the silent location (Blake's murder) is elsewhere and elsewhen in Veidt's mind.[166]

Another example, highlighted by Klock, parallels two events that occur at the same moment but 'elsewhere': Dan and Laurie fight off Knot Tops, while Dr Manhattan's TV interview seems to comment on the action. 'Wally Weaver . . . died of cancer in 1971', declares journalist Doug Roth, in the green-tinted studio audience. We cut to a panel of Dan crushing a thug's nose, the palette a sickly combination of bile yellow, blaze orange and blood red. 'I believe it was quite sudden and quite painful.'[167] 'In this context of intertextuality,' writes Klock, '*Watchmen's* scene juxtaposition is crucial. Again and again two seemingly unrelated scenes are juxtaposed, and the dialogue from one is a running commentary on the other.'[168]

We can see Moore developing this narrative device in his earlier work. 'The Vortex' chapter from *V For Vendetta*, originally published in July 1983, uses a dead woman's journal as narration in a manner reminiscent of Rorschach's diary, except that in *V* the accompanying images merely illustrate the text in a conventional manner. 'The ones at the front ran straight into the gas' echoes what David Lloyd shows us – silhouetted figures clutching their faces and staggering through clouds of smoke[169] – rather than providing an oblique, accidental or ironic commentary.

In November of that year (the 'Video' episode), however, Moore confidently mixes multiple soundtracks from television channels against visuals of V's infiltration of a media hub so that a sitcom's crass innuendos – 'If I show him I'm willing to get stuck in, I think he might try me in a more advanced position!' – supply the captions for V performing acrobatic judo moves on a group of guards, and 'what if somebody comes in?' accompanies a shot of him kicking his way through a fire exit.[170] The technique here is almost identical to the juxtapositions from the Dan and Laurie fist fight that Klock praises earlier: the key difference is that the captions are taken not from another ongoing major plotline – as is the case in *Watchmen* chapter 3 – but from an isolated soundtrack that serves only to provide ironic counterpoints and is therefore easier to manipulate than a full-blown narrative scene.[171]

Moore's two-part *Vigilante* story, dated May 1985, employs what in film would be parallel editing, introduced in the early days of cinema as a technique for building drama by cutting between two simultaneous scenes. In the opening pages we watch a predator break into a woman's home – busting the lock, pushing against the security chain, booting the door down – alternated with panels showing the eponymous vigilante rushing in vain to stop him.[172] While this instance is comparatively simple, lacking the extra level of overlapping commentary, we can see Moore experimenting further with the double meanings and visual overlaps that would become his trademark. *Watchmen* chapter 5 plays extensively with puns around an image of Buddha and the words 'enlightenment' and 'inspiration'.[173] In *Vigilante*, as the protagonist investigates the woman's murder, a dialogue caption at the bottom of the page declares, as if calling from the next scene, 'Hey, let's have a little illumination in here.' Turning the page, we realize that the voice belonged to sex worker Fever, who switches on the lights of her apartment to reveal a prominent Buddhist shrine.[174] In cinema, we would call this a 'sound bridge'.

Moore's *Superman* tale 'For The Man Who Has Everything' (1985), again with Gibbons as artist, uses the technique extensively for the same transition-smoothing purpose but with greater ambition. Faced with the mystery of Superman's apparent paralysis, Batman comments, 'Really, it's just a case of putting the pieces together', meaning that they need to assemble clues into an explanation, but his words appear over an image of Superman's father on Krypton – not just elsewhere but within Superman's delirious fantasy – standing over a shattered glass sculpture.[175] Further examples can be found in *Swamp Thing* issues from late 1986: the banal saying 'the world keeps on turning', conveying simply 'life goes on', is lent a more literal meaning when it appears over a wide shot of the Earth.[176]

'Similar panel compositions', Van Ness goes on, 'thematically unite one location (elsewhere) or time (elsewhen) to another through a repeated visual pattern or motif. In similar panel compositions, one or more compositional elements (shapes, colours, character positions and body language) join two different locations or times through their recurrence in two consecutive panels.'[177] An instance can be found in *Watchmen* chapter 2, when a slow zoom into Adrian Veidt's face at Blake's funeral in 1985 transitions to a close-up of the adventurer as a younger man, in costume, at the first meeting of the Crimebusters two decades before. The priest's sermon – 'O Lord, who for our sins art justly displeased' – segues into the off-screen voice of Captain Metropolis announcing that 'I'm pleased to see so many of you here'.[178]

This example closely parallels a memorial service from *Swamp Thing*, cover-dated December 1986: here a close-up of the grieving Abigail Cable's

INTERTEXTUALITY AND AUTHORSHIP   43

heels (facing right) cut to a similarly framed image of her bare feet (facing left) in a happier time and place, with her voice-over bridging the transition: 'I want to keep you sharp in my memory, even though it hurts. Sharp enough to cut me.'[179] However, as Van Ness points out, *Watchmen*'s scene changes become increasingly sophisticated, and by its mid-point are transcending anything in his previous work, to the point of becoming almost unconscious echoes of abstract patterns. In chapter 5, a splash of blood across the pyramidal poster of a Buddha, spreading right to left, cuts to a splash of mud across the triangular logo of a Pyramid Deliveries truck, vaguely mirroring the previous image with a left-to-right trajectory.[180]

Visual transitions dominate *The Killing Joke*, released in March 1988 but, according to Parkin, written in 1985.[181] In this case, perhaps because artist Brian Bolland has a heavier touch than Gibbons, perhaps because Moore overuses his device, or perhaps simply because he was still finding his way with it, the scene changes sometimes feel forced and inelegant. A frame of the younger Joker reaching out to touch his wife's hand transitions to the adult villain extending his fingers to a reflection in the glass of a 'Laughing Clown' machine;[182] an image of the adult Joker raising a shot glass as he unbuttons Barbara Gordon's blouse cuts to the younger man lifting a tumbler, fingering a basket of prawns.[183] As this last example suggests, the effect can be crass, and as we'll see, Moore became disillusioned with it himself.[184]

Watchmen follows a tight formal structure in its panel layouts – most precisely in chapter 6, which forms a symmetrical pattern around Adrian Veidt's action sequence on the central pages – and returns consistently to a nine-panel grid, with all major scene changes taking place at the start of a new page – a clean storytelling technique that Moore perfected in 'For the Man Who Has Everything'.[185] 'The grid of nine uniform panels on each page,' writes Paul Gravett, 'allows you to follow the fine-tuned passage of multiple stories moment by moment. Panels tick by like a metronome or a timebomb, counting down to midnight.'[186] While there are frequent variations on this pattern for effect, as Elizabeth Sandifer notes, 'momentary lapses aside, the nine-panel grid really is the beating, or perhaps more accurately ticking heart of *Watchmen*'.[187]

We can sense the effect of this grid by looking at the exceptions to the rule. In chapter 1, Rorschach leaves Adrian Veidt with the words 'Be seeing you', his departure depicted in three panels that take up a third of the page's height. Their size restricts their detail – they show simple figures, their meaning quickly understood – so we stick with them only for as long as we need to read the dialogue, as Alan Moore knew we would. 'A panel containing the standard 35 words of dialogue', he explained in his *Guide to Writing Comics*, 'will take maybe seven or eight seconds to read, depending on the complexity of the image accompanying it.'[188] Then, filling two-thirds of the page, is an image of Veidt, hands clasped contemplatively behind his back, staring out of his skyscraper at the rainy city. Time has passed, for the window open in the previous frame is closed. Veidt has clearly been in this position for at least a few moments, which cues us instantly, perhaps unconsciously, into a more leisurely pace.

The foreground of the picture contains the latest paraphernalia of his superhero brand – articulated action figures, some of which, we now realize, Rorschach has twisted into painful shapes as a comment on Veidt's moral bankruptcy – an upside-down newspaper which requires that we study it in order to read the latest headline about the Doomsday Clock, and fancy purple-and-gold executive desk furniture. ('Look upon my works, ye Mighty, and despair!') We linger on this panel not just because its details invite inspection but also because of its size, affording it the extra time and thought that this moment needs; in film, it would be a shot of long duration, in contrast to the quick cuts that carry Rorschach and Veidt's earlier conversation. Perhaps without knowing why, we stay with it, almost hearing the rainfall.

The scene echoes another from just a few pages earlier, where Rorschach walks away from Dan in four quick, small panels snarling 'You quit', and we are left with a large tableau of Dan, slouched in a baggy suit in a corner of his tatty warehouse, while his Nite Owl costume stands behind him in silent rebuke and reminder of his glory days. Note that after Rorschach's parting barb, Moore and Gibbons include a single silent panel showing Dan's head slightly lowered as Rorschach walks away into the darkness – a beat of reaction before he slumps, reflecting on his life.[189] The Veidt scene also slows its pace before the shift to a larger image. The first two panels on the page contain thirty-five and thirty-six words of dialogue, respectively, as Veidt earnestly defends himself from charges of hypocrisy and Rorschach snipes back. The third has only four: 'Sure', Veidt murmurs almost to himself, gazing down from his balcony – Rorschach is already descending the building by grappling rope, off-frame. 'Have a nice day.'

This confident manipulation of pace and rhythm across smaller and larger panels leads us to the shock of the six full-page splashes, packed with gruesome detail, in the final chapter: but it also allows Moore to employ other 'cinematic' techniques that convey pace and movement. While he cautioned at the time about making comics into inferior movies – you will be left with a film that has neither movement nor a soundtrack'[190] – he also freely admitted that he used filmic terms like pan, zoom, long shot and close-up in his scripts.

> If you understand cinematic techniques then you'll be able to write better, more gripping comics than someone who doesn't, but if cinematic technique is seen as the be all and end all of what comics can aspire to, then at the very best comics are always going to be a poor relation to the cinema.[191]

This form of cinematic storytelling is most obvious in Watchmen's silent scenes, such as Rorschach's initial investigation of Comedian's apartment: there are only three dialogue balloons across the four pages of this sequence, and they consist of puzzled grunts and growls. The nine-panel grid encourages a sense of consistently timed, rhythmic cuts as we follow Rorschach's progress through the window down a corridor, into a bedroom, to the drawers and then the wardrobe; almost entirely visual, these panels give the impression that they could be adapted directly to cinema, like a storyboard. Unsurprisingly, they closely resemble Moore's earlier scenes of a silent vigilante in *V For Vendetta*.[192]

Some sequences in *Watchmen* go beyond the storyboard, though, and resemble short strips of celluloid, a series of images in order. As we read them, we have a strong sense of movement flowing across frames. When Rorschach breaks the man's finger in chapter 1, for instance, the digit changes position from *here* to *there* as abruptly and cleanly as the tick of a clock's second hand.[193] The effect is heightened by the fact that the 'camera' is fixed in place, with the two images that cover the movement adjacent and almost identical. The overwhelming similarity between them enables us to immediately spot the difference at the centre of the frame – finger where it should be, finger bent backwards – while other slight changes such as the toppling beer glass, the wide-eyed grimace of the unfortunate perp and his other hand rising slightly, clutching at the air, sell his agonized reaction.

As we saw with the slight zoom on Ozymandias's face in the funeral scene, sometimes the camera is mobile, accentuating the moment: when Ozymandias opens his fingers to reveal that he caught Laurie's bullet in chapter 11, we also dolly in closer for effect.[194] A far more dramatic movement bookends chapter 1, with its slow crane shot out from a close-up of the badge in the gutter – an extreme close-up if we include the cover of this issue and indeed the detail from the graphic novel's cover as part of the sequence – to just above human height, then up and back to the third floor, and higher yet until we are looking down with Detective Joe Bourquin at the vertiginous plunge from Blake's apartment. 'Hmm. That's quite a drop.'[195]

While this simulated camerawork is particularly striking in *Watchmen* because of Gibbons's self-effacing art and the consistency of the grid, we can find examples of these techniques throughout Moore's 1980s writing. The spectacular pull back from Mars into deep space that occupies three full pages at the end of *Watchmen* chapter 9 is, for instance, outdone in its ambition by a four-page sequence in *Swamp Thing* 55 (published months earlier) which starts at ground level in Gotham City, rises to skyscraper height, then travels back and back, revealing cities, countries, the globe itself . . . and then, incredibly, reverses through space, past planets and stars, out of our very galaxy, until it comes to rest on an alien world where Swamp Thing reforms his body out of strange blue weeds.[196]

One of Moore's *Green Lantern* stories from 1985 experiments with a similar perspective – though it is treated as a swiftly executed sight gag – as a mercenary searches a distant planet for a hero called Mogo, only to realize as he blasts off and sees the planet from a distance that the entire globe was Mogo.[197] The first issue of *Halo Jones*, from July 1984, opens with a slow zoom in from above Manhattan, through traffic jams of aerial vehicles towards Halo's apartment, and then through her window until we frame Halo herself in close-up: perhaps a deliberate tribute to Hitchcock's *Psycho*, as Moore praises the director in his guide to writing comics.[198]

Despite the far more organic, fluid, even psychedelic storytelling of *Swamp Thing*, the fixed-camera technique is employed to show the plant creature growing 'live', as we watch: in a playful scene from October 1986, it happens literally on camera, while a cynical TV presenter speaks into the lens and out to us, as his viewing audience. 'Does he exist? Many people insist that the swamp man is a creation of the media.' Meanwhile, shoots are forming at his waist – 'spluk! flek! kwelk!' and combining into the form of a green mossy elemental.[199]

The device is used effectively in *Miracleman* from February 1986 to convey the slow descent of a blood droplet from a blade of grass,[200] in Moore's 'Night Olympics' story from *Detective Comics* (May 1985) to capture Green Arrow's preternatural speed with a bow[201] and in *Vigilante* to show the protagonist closing a victim's staring eyes.[202] We can see it again in 'D.R. and Quinch Go Straight' from 1984, watching the teenage anti-heroes in the dock over four near-identical frames while Quinch silently intimidates a clerk and D.R. notes down the name of the prosecuting judge for future revenge,[203] and in a March 1983 issue of Captain Britain, holding attention on the protagonist and his sister, again for four frames, as they meet after many years and catch each other's eye in a crowded café.[204] It recurs several times in *V For Vendetta*, though usually in a minimal two-frame unit, to convey a light on, then off,[205] a door open then closed,[206] or a gun barrel clicking through a single revolution[207] and as such can be traced back at least to 1982 in Moore's work alone.

As was the case with the nine-panel grid, this 'fixed camera' was not a device invented by Alan Moore by any means.[208] We'll later see it employed by Steve Ditko in the mid-1960s, and it was a staple of the mainstream Marvel storytelling style by 1970;[209] ironic in a way, as Gibbons states that he deliberately went in the opposite direction to the classic *How to Draw Comics the 'Marvel' Way* approach.[210] What distinguishes *Watchmen* is, in accordance with the concept of a 'scriptor', not its creation of a new language but the level of ambition and complexity with which it wields and combines existing techniques.

It was only with chapter 3, it seems, that Moore realized the full potential of the story he was writing. Chapters 1 and 2, in isolation, are relatively straightforward introductions of the main characters – motivated by Rorschach's investigation, which visits them all in turn – and flashbacks from a funeral to the shared past. While elegant, these issues are no more complex than *Swamp Thing* of the same period, which, as we saw, included very similar crane shots and visual transitions around the main character's memorial ceremony. Chapter 3, however, introduces the *Black Freighter* story-within-a-story, which enables Moore to refer to 'black sails' against Gibbons's tight close-up of a fallout shelter sign.

> So I dropped in a caption in the comic that the child was reading about a hellbound ship's black sails against a yellow Indies sky. And I have a word balloon coming from off-panel, which is actually the balloon of the news vendor, which is talking about war. The narrative of the pirate comic is talking about a different sort of war. As we pull back, we realize that we're looking at a radiation symbol that's being tacked to the wall of a newly created fallout shelter. And finally, when we pull back into the beginning, into the foreground, we realize that these pirate captions that we've been reading are those in the comic that is being read by the small boy. This was exciting. There was something going on here. There was an interplay

INTERTEXTUALITY AND AUTHORSHIP 49

between the imagery, between the strands of narrative, the pirate narrative, the dialogue going on in the street. They were striking sparks off of each other, and they were doing something which I hadn't actually seen a comic do before. I think it was around those first three pages of *Watchmen* #3 that I started to realize that we'd got something different on our hands here.[211]

Watchmen, then, drew on an armoury of techniques, motifs and themes that Moore had been exploring for years. It refined them, evolved them and expanded them. It was brand new in some ways, familiar in others. As it grew, its complex structure becoming clear, Moore and Gibbons grew with it, raising their game and rising to its challenges. They filled this cathedral of a text with ever more intricate details, thrilled by the synchronicities and coincidences that emerged within their intended designs.

What did Moore do next? What could he do next, after pushing his approach so far? He retained some aspects of his distinctive style but ditched others. By 2003 he was brutally dismissive about some of *Watchmen*'s trademark devices:

If you can even detect or notice a particular trick then this almost certainly means that you have done it more than once, and that it is thus in danger of becoming 'part of your style', to put it charitably, or, more accurately, of becoming a cliché. All that stuff I said . . . about changing scenes with clever panel-to-panel linkages? Forget it. It was becoming a cliché even as I was writing those words, a technique that I pretty much abandoned straight after *Watchmen*. The captions filled with thoughtful, image-laden prose that initially drew so much attention to my work and which for a while I assumed to be the commercial backbone of my writing abilities? Dead in the water after those last issues of *Swamp Thing* and *Miracleman*; extravagant verbal showing-off that was fine for its time but in danger of becoming a joke if incessantly repeated.[212]

Directly after *Watchmen*, he claimed he was moving away from superheroes, too,[213] but that wasn't the case, or not for long – after the collapse of his hugely ambitious real-world drama *Big Numbers* in 1990, he returned to the genre with the retro Marvel Comics pastiche *1963* in 1993. *Supreme* (1996–2012), *Tom Strong* (1999–2006), *Promethea* (1999–2005), *Top Ten* (1999–2001), *The Forty-Niners* (2005) and *League of Extraordinary Gentlemen* (1999–2019) all explore costumed adventurers from various angles and create extensive histories for those characters and their generational predecessors – based on archetypes and cultural icons in thin disguise – much like the Minutemen and Crimebusters. The sadistic secret agent 'Jimmy' from *League of Extraordinary Gentlemen: Black Dossier* (2007) is, essentially, to James Bond what Rorschach is to The Question: an existing anti-hero with the serial number filed off, reimagined for the 'real' world, or something like it.[214]

Horror remained a key theme, too: the demons of *Swamp Thing* – and their science-fiction variants in *The Green Lantern* 'Blackest Night' story – return, their debt to H. P. Lovecraft made explicit, in *Black Dossier* ('What Ho, Gods of the Abyss') *The Courtyard* (2003), *Neonomicon* (2010) and *Providence* (2017). The vast, eldritch monstrosities from this later work have smaller, milder predecessors in the tentacled 'Black Mercy' plant that clings to and consumes Superman in 'For the Man Who Has Everything' and indeed in the 'squid' that Ozymandias inflicts on New York City.

Less obvious, and perhaps more interesting, is the evolution of Moore's narrative techniques. Although he declared that he'd ditched his more recognizable trademark devices, many aspects of his approach to *Watchmen* – which, as we saw, can in turn be traced back to the early 1980s – persist in his later work. 'For the Man Who Has Everything', for instance, plotted its fight scene around an actual schematic of the Fortress of Solitude, provided by Dave Gibbons.[215] Gibbons, a meticulous draftsman, also ensured that the New York streets of *Watchmen* were consistent throughout its twelve issues.[216] This insistence on a plausible, mappable environment clearly informs Moore's masterpiece *From Hell* (1989–99), an interrogation of the Ripper crimes with Eddie Campbell, set in a convincing and connected Victorian London. The scene in which we are confined with Dr William Gull in the tiny room of

Mary Jane Kelly as he mutilates her is unbearable partly because of Moore's commitment to the details of time and space: the action takes place solely within 9 Miller's Court on the night of 9 November 1888.

The 'sight dramatics' and crowded backgrounds, inspired by *Mad Magazine* and developed in *Halo Jones* and 'Chronocops' before they helped to build *Watchmen*'s bustling, busy alternate 1985, persist in *Top 10* and *Promethea*, each with a host of invented brands (Nukola, Elastagel, Weeping Gorilla) and in-jokes (a band called the Blues Beetles, with Blue Beetle and Beetle Bailey in the Lennon/McCartney roles). They reach their peak in *League of Extraordinary Gentlemen* (1999–2019), whose frames are rammed with cameos and cross-references that need several volumes of annotations to fully decipher. In one 1969 scene alone, set in Soho, we find a sex show starring Vril aliens from 1871 science-fiction novel *The Coming Race*, a club named after Andy Pandy's doll-friend Looby Loo, a nod towards the British TV series *Lovejoy*, a poster for the Treen School of English and a bus promoting a fictional magazine from the obscure early 1960s soap opera *Compact*.[217]

League of Extraordinary Gentlemen also took *Watchmen*'s endpapers to an extreme: in *The Black Dossier*, the comic-book story becomes a supplement to all the back matter, which includes pastiches of Shakespeare, *Fanny Hill*, Kerouac and Woodhouse-meets-Lovecraft. There's even a Tijuana Bible – the sex comic starring Silk Spectre in *Watchmen* – though this grim leaflet is a product of Orwell's Airstrip One. *Providence* (2017) ends every chapter with a 'Commonplace Book' of handwritten material, including a sketch in issue 4 that evokes Walter Kovacs's scribble of a childhood nightmare.

These more recent stories employ the same techniques of fixed camera and crane shots that Moore perfected in the mid-1980s: the final chapter of *Providence*, for instance, watches an FBI car approach and round a corner across three tall panels, our viewpoint static and steady as CCTV;[218] *Neonomicon*, in its first issue, pulls back from inside an agent's car to just above its roof, then rises over the streets until we look down at the entire city.[219] While the grids are less rigid and the overlapping captions have been phased out,[220] the parallel narratives are still in place: *Black Dossier*, for all its experiment with diverse forms, is based around a straightforward chase that cuts between Allan Quatermain and Mina Murray, on the run with the dossier, and their MI5 pursuers.

The Courtyard even features a narrow-minded detective – a 'smug little Nazi' – his face cast in different colours by the lights outside his derelict apartment, narrating the world in bitter Rorschachian poetry:

Clinton Street, down in Red Hook, is striped cobalt as ten thousand fireworks explode over Brooklyn.

I can hear . . . slabs of bass shuddering out down the river. They mix with distant ambulance sirens in shimmering, science-fiction voluntaries.

Is it just me who finds sirens beautiful? Miserable Wagnerian divas, threatening fire, plague or murder. [. . .]

Club Zothique: a strange neon cancer grown out from the crumbling stone of a waterfront church, a cheap dance-hall and immigrant dive since the late 1920s. A toxic and lurid agaric of light bulbs, enduring the centuries.[221]

In *League of Extraordinary Gentlemen*, a more fragmentary urban patter is given to Andrew Norton, the fictional avatar of author Iain Sinclair – '7-7, concussed bus driver shambles from here to Acton, King's Cross fire memorial storage site . . . explosion a momentary light-show glitch at Joe Boyd's UFO club'.[222] In this context, perhaps Rorschach's journal can be reread as a kind of New York psychogeography.[223] Norton is, we are told, 'the Prisoner of London, but in time he's completely free. His perspective is different'.[224] We see him standing placidly in one place while the city changes around him, not unlike Dr Manhattan.

In *Neonomicon*, Agent Brears also gains a transcendent vision of time that 'doesn't distinguish between past, present and future', explaining how the Lovecraftian gods 'were, are and shall be'. *Providence*'s penultimate chapter ends with its red-headed investigator slipping his journal into an envelope

INTERTEXTUALITY AND AUTHORSHIP

and mailing it to a detective (on the final page of the last issue it is ripped in half in front of our eyes, its revelations lost). For someone who claims, understandably, to left *Watchmen* far behind – 'hey, *Watchmen* was 1986, that was almost fifteen years ago, and today's a completely different time', he declared in 2000[225] – Moore seems sometimes to have circled back to it.

He still finds wordplay impossible to resist, just as he did in his *Future Shocks*. One plotline in *League of Extraordinary Gentlemen* hinges on Bob Cherry, from the Billy Bunter stories, being the same character as Harry Lime from *The Third Man*, based on their fruity surnames. The traumatic ordeal of *Neonomicon* is lightened slightly by a central play on words: 'your annunciation, Mary' is misheard as 'you're a nun, see, Asian Merry' – while the Lovecraftian horrors of *Nemo: Heart of Ice* conclude with a similar linguistic puzzle: the expedition's sole survivor can only mutter 'Tiger Lily', an approximation of the nightmarish chant 'Te-ke-li-li' that echoed across the occult Antarctic.

We could, in fact, trace a line directly from the opening scene of Moore's 'For the Man Who Has Everything', through *Watchmen* chapter 12 to *Nemo: Heart of Ice*.[226] All three are set in the frozen wastes of Antarctica, where a small team of adventurers trudges through the snow towards a legendary destination (The Fortress of Solitude, Ozymandias's Karnak, the Mountains of Madness). Hot breath trails in the icy air. There are remarks about the cold and the suitability of costumes. So far, perhaps, the similarities are superficial. But the panel from page 2 of the 1985 Superman story, where Wonder Woman raises her left hand, stepping forward on her right leg, to point towards the entrance to the Fortress,[227] almost precisely matches the panel in *Watchmen* – also by Gibbons, of course – where Dr Manhattan raises his left hand, his right leg forward, advancing towards Karnak. And in that panel, Jon is speaking both to Laurie at his side and to Rorschach, ninety seconds later, in a different scene (but in the same pose), one page on.[228] 'I – I'm sorry. It's these tachyons. They're muddling things up.'

In *Heart of Ice*, Janni Nemo gasps 'What did she mean?', and her crewmate explains, 'It's my proposed warp, affecting our brains so that we . . .'. The panel seems entirely out of context, unconnected to its surrounding frames, and it recurs five pages later, with identical composition, but suddenly making sense in relation to the images and words that surround it. There are twenty-six years between *Nemo* and the end of *Watchmen*, but the same experimental intelligence is clearly at work, with the same fascinations. Alan Moore is still interested in the possibilities of reanimating pulp tropes and making them fresh, of conveying time through the unique form and structures of comic-book medium, of asking 'what if' and, at his most simple and straightforward, of telling a rip-roaring adventure that will grip readers for half an hour or so, just as he wanted to in the mid-1980s.[229]

He said he'd give up superheroes. He didn't. He said he'd given his last interview.[230] He hadn't. He said he'd given up comics.[231] He might have.

He said, after some brief musing about a *Minutemen* prequel or a *Black Freighter* series, that he wasn't going to write any more *Watchmen*.[232] He didn't. But other people did.

2

Influence and interpretation
The post-*Watchmen* superhero

Watchmen ends by returning to its own beginning – the smiley face, the journal – and inviting us to read the book again from the start with a changed perspective. As such, it was a self-contained text, despite all its intertextuality – a complete story about a new set of characters, many of whom have died, departed or disguised themselves for new undercover lives by the conclusion. But inevitably, because of its popularity and prominence, *Watchmen* had an impact on comics in general and the superhero genre more specifically, both in the years immediately following its publication and in the decades after. Perhaps surprisingly, that influence is often seen as negative. As Ayres reports, some commentators view it as 'Moore's obituary for the concept of heroes in general and superheroes in particular' and the 'genre's epitaph';[1] according to film critic David Hughes, it was supposedly 'intended to be the last word on comic book superheroes'.[2]

But *Watchmen* – despite its critical engagement with clichés – was never meant to end the superhero, any more than Barthes's 'The Death of The Author' was intended as a memorial notice. If anything, Moore hoped that others would follow his example and build on it further. 'I'd have liked to have seen more people trying to do something that was as technically complex as *Watchmen*, or as ambitious, but which wasn't strumming the same chords as *Watchmen* had strummed so repetitively'.[3]

He expressed similar views in a 2001 interview with Jonathan Ross: 'When I did *Watchmen*, I thought, great, people are going to feel compelled to look at the clever storytelling involved and they'll feel compelled to match me or better me in coming up with ways for telling stories. But instead, it seems what most people saw was the violence, the grimness . . . that's what got regurgitated and recycled.'[4]

So, contrary to popular belief, Moore wanted to revive the genre and inspire other creators. Instead – so he tells us, and this version of events has become official comics history – the industry was swamped with a glut of inferior cover versions or, as Van Ness puts it, 'a proliferation of copy-cat works with similar themes'.[5] 'After *Watchmen*,' writes Millidge, 'the grim'n'gritty, deconstructive, postmodern superhero comic became a genre, the prevalent mode for writing contemporary superhero comics.'[6] Moore, again:

I think that what a lot of people saw when they read *Watchmen* was a high degree of violence, a bleaker and more pessimistic political perspective, perhaps a bit of sex, more swearing. And to some degree there has been, in the years since *Watchmen*, an awful lot of the comics field devoted to these very grim, pessimistic, nasty, violent stories which kind of use *Watchmen* to validate what are, in effect, often just some very nasty stories that don't have a lot to recommend them.

It seemed that the existence of *Watchmen* had pretty much doomed the mainstream comic industry to about twenty years of very grim and often pretentious stories . . . although that had never been my intention with the work.[7]

Gibbons expressed similar misgivings. 'In *Watchmen*'s wake there were some, frankly, tedious grim'n'gritty comics done, but these completely missed the point. It was affection and truth that the fans bought into, not disdain and distortion.'[8] Looking back in 2009, he reflected:

what we slightly deplored was that following *Watchmen* and *Dark Knight* everything in comics became dark and dirty, and grim and gritty, and often really depressing and somewhat tedious. I would hate to think that from now on the only possible flavour of superhero movies would be, you know, dark and down. I think that the superhero genre has many, many flavours. It's a shame if any one of them pushes out the others, because I think it's the diversity that is probably the saving grace of superhero books.[9]

Gerard Jones and Will Jacobs's history of late 1980s superhero comics offers a telling snapshot of the dominant mood. *The Shadow* (1987) was a showcase for 'twisted sensibility . . . a surreal burlesque'.[10] *Martian Manhunter* (1988) was 'deep into mournful character exploration'.[11] *Doom Patrol* and *The Spectre* (both 1987) were characterized by 'darkness and angst'.[12] *Marshal Law* (1987) was 'violence-heavy . . . it made some fierce satirical comments on the genre' but 'also wallowed in its own violence and sexual titillation'.[13] *Deadman* (1989) was 'bloody . . . with the powerful horror art of Kelly Jones'; *Nexus,* which had begun in 1981, now turned 'grimmer and darker',[14] while *Green Arrow: The Longbow Hunters* (1987) was 'one of the bloodiest and cruellest comics yet published'.[15] *A Death in the Family,* which killed off Batman's sidekick Robin after a phone-in vote, had 'a special cruelty'[16] and 'a love of sneering violence'.[17] *Batman: The Cult* was 'even more mean-spirited',[18] and *The Killing Joke,* whose 'greatest gift to the Bat-line of comics . . . was an injury gruesomely inflicted on Batgirl by the Joker', was 'a complex story but a cold one'.[19]

Though they acknowledge the existence of lighter, brighter titles at the same time, like Keith Giffen and J. M. DeMatteis's *Justice League International* (1987), Jones and Jacobs present these as 'a salve for the wounds of *Watchmen*';[20] the main trends, according to their report, were either attempts to emulate Moore and Gibbons's work or reactions against it. 'DC was learning the calculated pain and rage game', the authors sum up at one point;[21] comics were now characterized by 'sadistic villains and snarling, unthinking vigilantes' and even decent industry veterans 'had lost sight of how sickening it all was'.[22]

'The lesson that most people took from *Watchmen*,' suggests Elizabeth Sandifer, 'would be taken to perverse extremes, as comics entered a morbid race to the bottom to see who could tell the most violent and sexualised stories.'[23]

> The core of the problem was that from DC's perspective, the lesson of *Watchmen* could only be one thing: things like this sold. And within the post-*Crisis* reality of the direct market, what DC specifically cared about was what fans said. The simple reality is that what the vocal fans who showed up and bought *Watchmen* in their specialist comic stores liked most about the book wasn't the moving explorations of sexuality in 'A Brother To Dragons'; it was Rorschach being a moody badass in 'The Abyss Gazes Also'. And so this is what DC imitated.[24]

Joe Queenan's 1989 article 'Drawing on the Dark Side', published in the *New York Times Magazine*, picked on *Watchmen* as the epitome, if not the root cause, of the trend towards depravity and gives a sense of what 'darkness' came to mean in comic books:

> The vindictive, sadistic tone of comics of the 1980s is best exemplified by the work of Alan Moore, author of *Watchmen*, which appeared in 1986. This is a well-written and elegantly drawn series that opens with a retired superhero named The Comedian being tossed out of his high-rise apartment building. The Comedian doesn't elicit much sympathy, however, for we learn in flashbacks that he had previously gunned down his pregnant Vietnamese girlfriend and attempted to rape a superheroine. *Watchmen* also features a boy who laughs when he finds out that his mother committed suicide by drinking Drano, a heroine forced into early retirement because of lesbianism, and a child hacked to pieces and fed to German shepherds. This is all in the service of a sophisticated literary technique called 'foreshadowing' that prepares the reader for the riveting climax, in which half of New York City's population gets annihilated.[25]

We could argue that Queenan missed the point of *Watchmen*. But according to Moore and Gibbons – and their view is confirmed by multiple commentators –

INFLUENCE AND INTERPRETATION

other creators also misread what *Watchmen* was aiming for. Sandifer, in turn, suggests that 'vocal fans' – though the evidence in her account seems anecdotal – shared this misreading. In trying to reproduce its impact, these critics agree, the industry focused largely on *Watchmen*'s relatively explicit sexual content and its scenes of violent horror, dressing this 'mature' content up in cod psychology and bad poetry and ignoring much of its complex potential.

Jackson Ayres's overview, 'When Were Superheroes Grim and Gritty?' from the *LA Review of Books* in 2016, adopts this discourse from its title onwards but adds a further sense of historic periodization.

> The genre's formative years, 1938–1945, are grandly referred to as the Golden Age. Then – after a decade-long interregnum when superheroes were overshadowed by other genres such as horror, crime, and romance — DC Comics' October 1956 relaunch of the Flash in *Showcase* #4 inaugurates the Silver Age. This period, which features the revitalization of DC's Golden Age superheroes and the ascendency of Marvel Comics, lasts until 1970, when it gives way to a Bronze Age. This narrative of decline has recently been taken even further by a newly christened phase: the Dark Age of Comics.[26]

Though he challenges the discourse in several ways, Ayres agrees that the shift was prompted by 'groundbreaking', 'milestone' titles, including *Watchmen* and Frank Miller's epic story of Batman's last battle, *The Dark Knight Returns*. While he praises Moore and Miller's work as 'serious, self-reflexive', Ayres characterizes this period in terms of

> a shift toward darker themes, graphic violence, sexual explicitness, and a generally cynical tone, an approach commonly summed up by professionals and fans with two words: grim and gritty. This metonymical expression has inspired portmanteau neologisms like 'grimdark' as well as related phrases like 'darker and edgier' or its counterpart in superhero film, 'grounded and realistic'. If Moore and Miller are the creators most responsible for this grim and gritty turn, both are ambivalent about its legacy. Moore has frequently

insisted that publishers misunderstood *Watchmen*, claiming they and culpable creators used it as validation for nihilistic, nasty, and insubstantial stories presented as sophisticated fare for 'mature readers'.[27]

Geoff Klock, drawing on the literary criticism of Harold Bloom, would call this process a 'misprision'[28] – 'a complex act of strong misreading',[29] part of the network of influence and interpretation that surrounds any text. 'Influence', writes Bloom, 'as I conceive it',

> means that there are *no* texts, but only relationships *between* texts. These relationships depend on a critical act, a misreading or misprision, that one poet performs upon another, and that does not differ in kind from the necessary critical acts performed by every strong reader upon every text he encounters.[30]

So, as we saw, readers and critics draw their own interpretations from stories like *Watchmen*, and fans sometimes put their reading into creative practice; but Bloom reminds us that professional writers (and artists) do too, expressing that interpretation in their own work. Klock extends this theory beyond poetry – Bloom's field of study – to comics. 'Superhero comic books are an especially good place to witness the structure of misprision,' he asserts, 'because as a serial narrative that has been running for more than sixty years, reinterpretation becomes part of its survival code.'[31]

This chapter critically examines the relationship between *Watchmen* and the DC superhero comics that surrounded and immediately followed it, taking as its focus the years between 1986 and 1989. As such, it necessarily narrows down a broader and more sprawling matrix. Most obviously, it does not consider *Watchmen*'s influence on contemporary Marvel titles, though it touches on *Watchmen*'s relationship to Vertigo, the 'mature', dark fantasy imprint launched by DC in January 1993. The trend for *Comedian*-style cynical, militaristic anti-heroes within the Image Comics of the mid-to-late 1990s is also significant but lies outside this particular survey.

INFLUENCE AND INTERPRETATION

61

I further neglect, for reasons of space, *Watchmen*'s broader cultural influence such as its connection with the late 1980s rave scene, which started with the use of the smiley face – its blood squiggle over the right eye – on the 1987 Bomb the Bass single 'Beat Dis'. As Parkin observes, 'by 1988, the badge was cropping up in all sorts of places: as set dressing in a Lenny Henry sitcom, on a *Doctor Who* companion's bomber jacket.'[32] There were rapidly produced spin-offs and spoofs like the 1987 'funny animal' comic *Watchcats* and Neil Gaiman's 1986 sketch of *Watchdogs*,[33] and *Watchmen* even crept into the contemporary culture of home computer games, with bloodstained smiley badges and the words *ego ipse custodes custudio* (roughly, 'I watch the watchmen') in the graphics of *Agent X II*, released for the ZX Spectrum, Commodore 64 and Amstrad in 1987. Part of *Watchmen*'s achievement – part of what established its reputation as a phenomenon, rather than just a superior story within a specific genre – was its transcendence of the comic-book sphere and its impact on popular culture more broadly. I have chosen to focus more narrowly and investigate more deeply through close textual analysis, rather than undertake a broad trawl.

Before we begin, there are a few other points to consider. *Watchmen*'s influence is usually discussed, as we saw in the commentaries earlier, in relation to the tone, style, form and mood of its successors, but we should also remember that the physical aspects of the *Watchmen* trade paperback as a glossy, substantial volume that could be sold in conventional bookstores shaped the production of subsequent graphic novels. Indeed, while that term had existed since at least the late 1970s,[34] it was only in the late 1980s that 'graphic novel' firmly entered broader public discourse[35] – and led not just to significant changes in marketing, promotion and distribution but also improvements in paper quality and printing.[36]

It is also important to recognize that *Watchmen* was, as a graphic novel, commonly discussed alongside *Maus* and *The Dark Knight Returns*, which were grouped into an unlikely 'big three' based on their publication format and popular impact.[37] Art Spiegelman's holocaust memoir is an uneasy fit here,[38] but the 'post-*Watchmen*' superhero was undoubtedly also the post-*Dark Knight Returns* superhero. Indeed, many of the 'darker' Batman titles of the late 1980s, such as *A Death in the Family* and *The Cult*, owe more to Miller's four-issue Batman epic from 1986 and its follow-up *Batman: Year One* (1987) than they do to Moore, as does Mindy Newell's *Catwoman* (1989), which Queenan uses as the opening hook of his article: 'The prostitute squats in the shadows, her leather-clad haunches poised atop black leather boots. Her cruel face is encased in a leather mask; in her left hand she clutches a leather whip.'[39] Newell's depiction of Selina Kyle is a self-conscious, even cynical, continuation of Miller's characterization in *Batman: Year One*, with scratchy art aping the more confident lines of David Mazzuchelli. To fully account for Miller's role in shaping the superhero narratives of the period, we would have to go back through his *Ronin* (1983–4) to his early 1980s work on *Daredevil,* and that could fill another book in itself.

Furthermore, the post-*Watchmen* tendency to reinvent, reimagine, retcon and reboot existing properties has a number of complex origins. On one level, DC was attempting to reproduce the success of Moore's work on *Swamp Thing*, which had rescued a hokey, forgotten character by considering how he might rationally and logically function, if such a plant creature could actually exist. *Miracleman* and *Captain Britain* confirmed Moore's talent for this revitalizing and updating of old tropes, and of course *Watchmen*, while it still involved the Charlton characters, was originally an opportunity to let a comic-book auteur perform his magic on another stale set of superheroes. In Moore's own words,

> they could see that I was capable of moving them to a new area that comics had not ventured into before. So, they offered us *Watchmen* and it worked out very, very well for them. They were able to suddenly claim that all of their comics were 'graphic novels' now – that they were seriously committed to a progressive comics medium that could produce works of art and literature.[40]

But the late 1980s trend for fresh takes on familiar titles must also be considered in context of the DC 'event' series, *Crisis on Infinite Earths* (April 1985–March 1986) which aimed to simplify the company's fictional universe by wiping out numerous alternate worlds from continuity,[41] relegating redundant characters to a narrative 'limbo' and starting others again from scratch.[42] Moore's 'Whatever Happened to the Man of Tomorrow?' was part of this process as the last Superman story from before the Crisis, a farewell to some of the sillier, Silver Age elements before John Byrne revamped the title with *Man of Steel*. On a formal level, it is worth noting in passing that *Crisis* issue 4 ends with a sequence strikingly similar to the final page of *Watchmen* chapter 11, though it was published two years earlier – six tall panels bleaching out to pure white and then a nine-panel grid during which black smoke fills the whiteness, until the final frame is entirely dark. While it lacks *Watchmen*'s elegant symbolism, it reminds us that many of Moore and Gibbons's techniques were refinements of and elaborations on existing comic-book devices, rather than inventions.

There are a number of ironies and ambiguities about the *Crisis* project. Some titles rebooted wholeheartedly, wiping characters' memories, while others continued as if the Crisis hadn't happened or underwent a partial, half-hearted restart. It was far from the advertised clean break and reset. Superman, for instance, began again, with even the destruction of his home planet Krypton rewritten, while Batman's pre-Crisis history with Robin, by contrast, remained only lightly altered. Superman had no knowledge of any Crisis, but Kid Flash clearly remembered its traumas and the death of his mentor, Barry Allen. Other daft discrepancies, like the existence of two different Hawkmen with similar names but entirely different backstories – Carter Hall the archaeologist, Katar Hol the alien policeman – were unreconciled.

There is a further fundamental paradox in the idea that what was meant to be a clean-up of DC's overly complicated mythos resulted not only in accidental loose ends and inconsistencies but also a deliberate move towards more complex, challenging characters and narratives. A company-wide reset could have led to a simpler mode, a single, streamlined universe with accessible stories and bright icons. Instead, it aimed for maturity and adult sophistication in both theme and content; and in this, the success of *Watchmen* and to a lesser extent *The Dark Knight Returns* were no doubt a major influence. If the bestselling graphic novel of 1986 had been Scott McCloud's lighter, more playful teen superhero title *Zot!*, DC might have chosen a different route.

We should note, though, that even within the same publishing company and in the same year, there were oddities that didn't fit the trend. In the month that Adrian Veidt was explaining his master plan to destroy half of New York, DC published a special issue of *'Mazing Man*, its quirky, cartoony series about a deluded little man from Queens who thinks he's a superhero and his talking dog sidekick. It was advertised with the slogan 'DC. We've made comics fun again'.[43] By contrast, DC's *Angel Love*, drawn in the whimsical style of an innocent newspaper strip like *Cathy* or *Love Is . . .*, highlighted the risks of cocaine addiction in its first issue, a month before *Watchmen*'s debut. While the consensus that this period was overwhelmed by dark, gritty superhero reboots accurately captures a cultural shift, it was not without its exceptions.[44]

Finally, it would be misguided to imagine that the dominant mood in superhero comics before 1986 was light, simplistic and benevolent, and that *Watchmen* flipped a switch. Moore's *Swamp Thing* dates back to 1984 and *Miracleman* and *Captain Britain* to 1982, while Miller's *Daredevil* started in 1981 – its gritty violence was parodied by Moore in his own 'Dourdevil' of 1983[45] – but neither author single-handedly transformed the genre to a 'mature' approach. The comic book industry's Bronze Age, usually dated as 1970–85, was itself characterized by a dramatic break from the relative silliness and science fantasy of the previous Silver Age (1956–69). Denny O'Neil and Neal Adams's *Batman*, debuting in 1970, had brought the character back to street-level vigilantism. By comparison to the comics that had inspired the 1966 TV series, this Batman was decidedly 'grim'n'gritty' – as were the 'socially relevant' Green Arrow and Green Lantern stories of the 1970s that dealt with racism, politics and drug addiction.[46] As Moore pointed out, 'dark treatments of the super-heroes . . . had been done before. I mean, you could even say that

INFLUENCE AND INTERPRETATION

Stan Lee and Jack Kirby were going for a gritty, darker treatment of the super-heroes back in 1961 with the Fantastic Four.'[47]

'Darkness' in the superhero genre, then, is not a binary on-off; it is more like a gradual dimmer, transforming the mood from bright midday to dusk or twilight. 'Darkness' can only be defined in terms of what has come before: it constitutes a relative shift in tone that affects different titles in different ways at different times. *Watchmen* certainly dialled up certain aspects of the superhero genre and dialled others down, but, like *The Dark Knight*, it did so by working with and amplifying existing material. Rather than a complete reset and rejection of the Bronze Age, *Watchmen* was, in both theme and aesthetic, a creative picking and choosing from previous trends, an adjustment, a push and a twist; it represented a steer in a distinct direction but not a dramatic change of course for the genre.

We have looked at the key traits and techniques that Alan Moore developed throughout his 1980s career and refined, perhaps perfected, in *Watchmen*. Which of these aspects do the 'post-*Watchmen*' comics adapt from it, and how are these tropes combined with other sources and styles in different ways across different texts?

An obvious place to start is the Charlton characters themselves, some of whom (Blue Beetle, Peacemaker and Captain Atom) were reintroduced into the DC Universe after being withdrawn at an early stage from the *Watchmen* project. Moore and Gibbons, interviewed in March 1988, could already see a direct influence.

> DAVE GIBBONS: To my way of thinking, once they've been integrated into DC they're just another bunch of superheroes, who more or less duplicate a whole line of existing ones.
> STEVE WHITAKER: . . . almost uniformly they smell – I mean, doing that to Captain Atom, doing that to Peacemaker. I mean writing Blue Beetle as Spider-Man meets Tony Stark.
> ALAN MOORE: The irony of it is, when they said we don't want you to do the Charlton characters it was because they could see what a radical

interpretation we were going to put on them – which would spoil them. I think that the problem that we have post-*Watchmen* is that we now have a Peacemaker with a lot of facial hair, who's a really nasty sort of gung-ho character. We've got The Question who is leading a fairly seedy existence in the world of real crime and horror. We've got Dr . . . uh . . . Captain Atom, sorry, who is sort of all blue – I don't want this to come over as saying to all the writers of those series 'You've ripped us off', but it's ironic. I don't think those characters would have been quite the same if it hadn't been for *Watchmen*.

STEVE WHITAKER: I must say, I remember seeing that cover of Blue Beetle where there's presidential posters all over saying 'Heroes get stuffed!', there's Blue Beetle walking away, and it's very 'Spider-Man No More', hunched shoulders, all that, and you think 'What have you been reading?' I know what they've been reading! And ironically, these are the characters they were based on.[48]

The traits Moore identifies here as borrowed from his own work amount to superficial appearance ('sort of all blue', 'a lot of facial hair') and general tone or milieu ('really nasty . . . gung-ho', 'fairly seedy . . . real crime and horror'). This fits the theory that late 1980s superhero comics lifted surface elements from Moore and Gibbons in order to cash in on a popular trend, and that they misread *Watchmen* as cynical, violent and pessimistic, reproducing those themes without attending to its other elements.

Whether this would constitute a misreading of *Watchmen*'s central mood is itself open to discussion. Parkin, as we saw, presents *Watchmen* as a gigantic joke, but Andrew Hoberek describes the series as 'melancholy', typified by 'sadness and ambivalence',[49] and Klock makes a similar point, distinguishing it from the world of Miller's noirish, 'operatic' heroes. 'Gibbons' characters . . . all have a distinct sadness, and his frumpy characters stand in stark contrast to Miller's very "cool" Batman. Moore's realism does not empower, as Miller's does, but empties out the power of previous superhero narratives.'[50]

But to see *Watchmen* as unrelentingly grim would be a narrow view. It certainly includes moments of violence and cynicism but also of beauty, love and forgiveness; there are examples of bleak nihilism – like Dr Malcolm Long's recognition that Rorschach blots, like life itself, only offer meaningless dark patterns – and also of wonder, when Dr Manhattan realizes that every human birth is a rare and precious miracle. As Moore put it, 'Yeah, you've got Rorschach, you've got the Comedian. I don't think that Dr Manhattan is dark; I don't think that Nite Owl is dark.'[51]

Is Moore correct that the four Charlton characters who were introduced into DC's continuity in the mid-to-late 1980s – *Peacemaker, Captain Atom, Blue Beetle* and *The Question*[52] – follow this superficial form of influence, borrowing only the miserable and pessimistic aspects of its mood, along with a couple of its characters' visual traits? We can best assess this by looking at the comics themselves, in turn.

The post-*Watchmen* Peacemaker from January 1988 is dressed identically – and just as absurdly, with his red fitted T-shirt, white leggings and science-fiction silver helmet – to the Peacemaker who made his first appearance in *Fightin' Five* issue 40 (November 1966), where he was introduced as 'a man who loves peace . . . so much so, that he is willing to fight for it!'[53] Moore is correct that by issue 3, having gone without sleep for days while battling his inner demons and external enemies, Peacemaker has become a stubbled, tormented figure who, at one point, grins with gritted teeth: 'That's funny . . . really . . . very . . . funny . . . HA HA HA.'[54] A climactic shot from the same issue shows Peacemaker, silhouetted by the lights of a military aircraft, hoisting his rifle and warning a crowd that 'If you surrender now, we'll let you live'[55] – strongly recalling *Watchmen*'s chapter 2 splash of the heavily armed Comedian hanging onto the illuminated front windows of the Owlship, yelling at a protesting mob, 'Lissen, you little punks, you better get back in ya rat holes!'[56] Writer Paul Kupperberg later confirmed that he was told to amp up the brutality, presumably to keep up with a prevailing 'post-*Watchmen*' mood: 'my editor's marching orders to me had been to push the envelope on crazy and violent.'[57]

However, *Watchmen*'s influence on the 1988 *Peacemaker* goes a little further than cartoonish reproductions of a few key Comedian scenes. Kupperberg concludes each of its four issues with a dossier on the main character, complete with field reports, psych profiles, logos, handwritten dates and signatures. While the effort and immersion falls far short of *Watchmen*'s back pages, the intention is clearly to provide backstory and insight into character: we learn for instance that the military needs to keep Christopher Smith's traumas unresolved in order to fuel his hostility 'on a level conducive to his continued operation as Peacemaker',[58] which lends a further, albeit thin dimension to his noisy adventures.

Captain Atom follows a similar pattern of partial borrowing, combining *Watchmen* with a grab bag of other loose ideas and contemporary trends. Its issue 1 was dated March 1987, three months after Moore's readers first learned Dr Manhattan's origin, and its cover sets the tone for a Saturday morning cartoon version of that traumatic episode.[59] 'After they blow him to bits', the caption announces over an image of Atom, half-naked, radiating energy – one key difference from Gibbons's visuals is that Captain Atom's genital area is conveniently covered up. – 'The adventure begins!'

Moore is correct that this Atom is 'sort of blue', in contrast to the brightly costumed 1960s incarnation, though the comic describes it as 'silver skin'.[60] Government agents discuss using a 'laser dye process' to decorate him with an insignia, to eliminate 'the need for the requisite mask and costume'[61] – similar to Manhattan's decision to ditch his uniform and draw a hydrogen atom on his forehead. Nathaniel Adam's transformation into his new form also resembles *Watchmen* stylistically, with a nine-panel grid depicting his body melding with an alien metal. A glowing humanoid form then appears on the military airbase ('—Errrghhh—'),[62] while in *Watchmen*, a floating brain and nervous system appears in the Gila Flats men's room ('Eeeeiiighh!').[63] Atom's powers are explained in terms of a 'quantum field . . . everyone and everything is a part of its never-ending flow'. He has 'the power to "tune-in" on the quantum flow',[64] but he is also a man out of time, undergoing an experiment in 1968 and waking up to find himself in 1986.

INFLUENCE AND INTERPRETATION   69

These are clearly variations on the Dr Manhattan tune, but the performance style is very different. While Cary Bates and Pat Broderick occasionally adopt a disciplined approach similar to that used by Moore and Gibbons – a nine-panel grid for the transformation and a tight set of three frames tracking a fighter plane's unsteady descent to a landing field[65] – *Captain Atom* is, for the most part, content to be crudely unsubtle. Mouths gape open, eyes bulge, fingers jab out of the panel, speed lines emphasize movement and characters deliver lines like 'The thing speaks!'[66] When Captain Atom snaps his bonds, the word 'SNAP' appears helpfully behind them.[67] If *Watchmen* is a symphony, this is a jingle.

As with *Peacemaker*, though, *Captain Atom* goes slightly further than simply adapting key character beats from *Watchmen* for a less demanding readership. It is suffused with the ongoing media discourse about its new hero – the covers of fake magazines like *Timely, Omna, Newsworld* and *Todays' Life* interrupt issue 2, like a public chorus – and its third issue deals with the inconsistent history of the character through a TV interview that explains the previous Captain Atoms as a government cover-up. While the interview itself matches Dr Manhattan's TV appearance in *Watchmen* chapter 3, and the rationalization of naive older stories into a new modern continuity recalls *Miracleman*, the storytelling style, using TV screens as panels, is straight out of Frank Miller's *Dark Knight Returns*. The primary opponent in these early issues, meanwhile, is not a conventional supervillain but Plastique, head of a separatist group 'who have long lobbied for Quebec's right to secede from Canada'[68] and who shoots explosives from her fingers at Ronald Reagan during a White House press conference. *Captain Atom*'s overreaching exuberance and messy compilation of ideas from various sources make it more than just a copy of *Watchmen*.

'It looks like the darker tone *Blue Beetle* has been taking lately is about to get even darker', writes C. P. Cagle of Tennessee, in the May 1988 issue of that comic.[69] Darkness, of course, is relative, but note that Steve Whitaker's complaint about *Blue Beetle* in the roundtable with Moore is not about its gritty grimness but that they have made the character into 'Spider-Man meets Tony Stark'. One of Spider-Man's trademarks is his playful commentary on action, and in contrast to the *Watchmen* sequences where a solo character moves silently through a mission – such as Rorschach's investigation of Comedian's apartment in chapter 1 – this Blue Beetle chats constantly to himself, very much in the style of the Marvel Comics webslinger.

> Wouldn't want the bashful Bug to just sit around getting rusty! Systems check reads clear green – so it's time to exit straight down – irising open the Bug's landing platform – so I can drop through the specially-reinforced tunnel beneath Kord, Inc – shoot out through the secret hatch-lock hidden in the bed of Lake Michigan – and it's – up, up, and away! Or has somebody already trademarked that line?[70]

Although Dan Dreiberg offers similar explanations as he takes the Owlship for a tour – 'I ran a scan on Archie earlier: not a feather out of place . . . better wash these windows down before we hit the exit tunnel . . . it's a forgotten section of subway I converted after buying the building above. Let's pick up a little speed here'[71] – he is an overgrown boy playing with his toys for the first time in years, and his narration is meant to impress Laurie; he is enjoying her anxiety and his own confidence, which help to compensate for their earlier unsuccessful sexual encounter. Blue Beetle's patter is for nobody but the reader.[72]

Compare, in turn, a vintage issue of *Spider-Man* from 1967. Peter Parker, in civilian clothes, hears a cry of distress and starts talking to himself or, rather, to us:

> Something's wrong – atop that warehouse roof! And no one else around . . . except me! It's the watchman . . . he's outnumbered . . . if I don't get there fast . . .! They're too dangerously close to the edge of the roof!! Have to move fast . . . so fast that they won't recognize me! The watchman hasn't seen me yet . . .! And these two hoods won't get a chance to see anything![73]

There is nothing in *Watchmen* to resemble this narration, but it strongly echoes that *Blue Beetle* monologue from twenty years later.[74]

INFLUENCE AND INTERPRETATION 71

Similarly, Blue Beetle's fist-fight banter from 1986 is far more reminiscent of the 1960s *Spider-Man* than of the almost silent combat in *Watchmen*, right down to its staccato phrasing and abrupt punctuation. The climactic superhero conflict between Ozymandias and Nite Owl in chapter 11 has six words of dialogue: 'Manners'. 'Adrian . . . don't . . . make . . . me . . . kgguh'.[75] Here are Blue Beetle and then Spider-Man:

For all I know, you could be Dr Ruth Westheimer under that mask! In fact, that's an excellent point! What say we take a little peek under all that asbestos!? I've heard of people being shy, Firefist . . . but isn't this a trifle extreme?!? I'm afraid we'll have to – Eh –? Someone in trouble –!?[76]

I hate to shatter your pipe-dream, guys, but – us Spider-Men don't demolish that easily! Now I don't want you to think I'm getting bored or anything – 'cause you're a real swingin' fun group – but I'll have to wrap this tea party up now! Don't think it hasn't been a real pleasure waltzing around with you – although, just between us kids – it hasn't been![77]

This example is drawn from the very issue of *Spider-Man* that Steve Whitaker cites in his complaint that *Blue Beetle* is copying *Watchmen*:

I remember seeing that cover of Blue Beetle where there's presidential posters all over saying 'Heroes get stuffed!', there's Blue Beetle walking away, and it's very 'Spider-Man No More', hunched shoulders, all that, and you think 'What have you been reading?' I know what they've been reading![78]

Len Wein, author of the new *Blue Beetle*, had indeed been reading *Watchmen* – he edited it – and the cover Whitaker refers to, from *Blue Beetle* 9 (February 1987, drawn by Paris Cullens), does have the gritty, gutter-level detail of Gibbons's work, complete with empty cans, graffiti and an abandoned newspaper. But the more pertinent question is, perhaps, 'what had Alan Moore and Dave Gibbons been reading?' The hunched-shouldered pose, overflowing trashcan, shadowy fire escape and hard rain of the 'Spider-Man

No More!' splash page from July 1967 were clearly one of the influences on the sequences of Rorschach (rather than Nite Owl) wandering grimy New York backstreets. The final panel of *Watchmen* chapter 1, page 24, for instance, reproduces several elements from this iconic *Spider-Man* image, while the cover and opening panels of chapter 5 have a similar focus on abandoned trash and puddled, reflective sidewalks.[79] What Whitaker identifies here is more accurately a two-step tribute: *Blue Beetle* referring to *Spider-Man* through *Watchmen*.

So far, we have seen little sign of *Watchmen*'s formal influence on the new Charlton titles. *Peacemaker* may have lifted a vague sense of its cynical violence and psychological torment, *Captain Atom* its political and media backdrop and *Blue Beetle* the occasional visual reference to its crowded, detailed mise en scène, but we have found no echoes yet of the major storytelling devices that structure Moore's work of this period: no counterpoint captions, no scene transitions based on similar imagery, no crane shots, no recurring symbolism.

There is another tantalizing moment of similarity in *Blue Beetle* issue 2, which again turns out to be more complex than it first appears. Page 3 presents a twelve-panel grid which cuts for suspense between the hero, trapped beneath a collapsed building, and the flaming roof that gradually threatens to fall on him. On the next page, two rows of four panels hold the same steady angle and position, giving a 'fixed camera' effect as we focus on Blue Beetle's efforts to lever himself free. Appearing too early (in July 1986) to be directly shaped by *Watchmen*, this could nevertheless be taken as a sign of Alan Moore's broader influence on comic-book form; as we saw, the technique recurs throughout his earlier 1980s work. Yet once more, the core reference is to an old issue of Spider-Man.

Amazing-Spider-Man 33 (February 1966) famously – Len Wein would have known it well – features its hero trapped under tons of wreckage, straining in agony and narrating every moment in a melodramatic monologue. 'The weight – is unbearable! Every muscle – aches –!' protests Spidey,[80] while Blue Beetle tells us, 'Feels like my spine is gonna snap . . . but I can't quit.'[81] Even the page layout of the 1986 comic, with two rows of tight panels then a larger one beneath for intensity and emphasis, echoes the 1966 *Spider-Man* scene as much as it does *Watchmen*, which uses the pattern for moments of explosive drama such as Rorschach bursting from the fridge and Comedian crashing through the window.[82] Fittingly, in a further addition to this complex web of references, the Spidey sequence was planned and drawn by Steve Ditko, who of course also created the original Charlton character.

Yet Blue Beetle is not just a Spidey tribute, either. While, as Whitaker accurately observed, the wisecracking most obviously recalls Spider-Man with Iron Man's gadgets, Len Wein's monologues for this 1986 incarnation are in fact not far removed from the Charlton version of *Blue Beetle*. In 1967, he declared to himself, 'Gotta bring the Bug down fast . . . 'fore I splatter the sidewalk! I guess it's too late to worry about what'll happen if I miss the hand-hold! Not bad . . . considering that I don't practice this stunt too often!'[83] In 1986, he announced, 'With a little help from the Bug . . . and my handy-dandy sky-wire – I may be able to find another way in! If I'm wrong about this, I'm about to become a charcoal-broiled blue smear . . . boy – talk about your dramatic entrances!!'[84]

This apparently simple comic is, then, surprisingly complex in its influences. Issue 1's opening narrative captions perhaps take a stab at Moore's prose of the *Swamp Thing* era:

> Chicago: They call it the Windy City . . . but the chill spring wind that blows this day blows ill indeed – carrying only the plaintive wail of congregating fire engines and the acrid smell of smoke and fugitive sparks.[85]

But elsewhere, the editorial voice is straight out of Stan Lee's mighty melodramas. Issue 3 bears the quasi-Shakespearian title 'If This Be Madness . . .!', technically a near-quotation like 'At Midnight, All the Agents' but far more reminiscent of the grand Marvel tradition: compare for instance 'If I Kill You . . . I Die!' from *Hulk* 130 (August 1970) or indeed 'If This Be Doomsday!' from *Fantastic Four* of April 1966.

Far from a direct copy of Nite Owl, this is a hybrid, multifaceted Beetle. What the series has most in common with *Watchmen* is its approach to raiding the archive, poaching from history and giving the classics a twist; what Nite Owl and Blue Beetle fundamentally share is the fact that both are archetypal heroes dressed up for the 1980s but with their roots in the nostalgic past.[86] And both, crucially, are coming out of retirement for these adventures. Like Batman in *The Dark Knight Returns*, christening himself anew in Gotham's rain; like Captain Atom, restored to a new decade; and like Dr Manhattan, reassembling himself into a new form, this Blue Beetle is making a comeback, re-entering what, even in this relatively lightweight title, is presented as a more complex world. ('The people of a simpler time and place knew him only as . . . Blue Beetle', proclaims the first page.[87]) Dan Dreiberg's return involves brushing the dust off his old equipment and squeezing into his costume, but it makes him feel as if he's on fire.[88]

This concept of rebirth, whether literal or symbolic – and again, the reboots and retcons of the *Crisis* played a significant role, as did the commercial remarketing of the superhero genre for 'mature audiences' – is a key trope, perhaps the key trope, of the period and, as such, it may constitute Moore's most significant influence on the genre. The idea underpinned all his major superhero stories from the early 1980s onwards: issue 1 of *Miracleman* brings the hero back to life and out of retirement, punching the air triumphantly ('I'm back!!');[89] his first episode of *Swamp Thing* has the protagonist return from the dead, and Moore's *Captain Britain* starts by killing the character off, only to rebuild him in the next chapter. What plot device could be more fitting for a superhero renaissance? No wonder a mid-1980s industry keen to both reboot its tangled mythology and reposition itself for adults seized on the concept.

The fourth Charlton character to enter DC, *The Question*, opens with a similar twist in his first issue of 1987, as the protagonist has only '25 hours and 15 minutes to live'.[90] Dennis O'Neil, the writer-turned-editor who had brought Batman down-to-earth in the 1970s, was offered this title or *Captain Atom*

INFLUENCE AND INTERPRETATION   75

and chose the more street-level story. He was told by DC boss Paul Levitz that he didn't have to make it commercial and could just write what he wanted. He took the job, with conditions.

> If I accepted the assignment, I was going to change the character. That's why in the first issue, he dies, symbolically, to be resurrected in the second issue. I thought that was a strong story point, and it was also our way of saying that the old Question is dead, and this was something new.[91]

The Question had first appeared in *Blue Beetle* 1, back in June 1967, so it was fitting that his 1980s debut was in Len Wein's revamped *Blue Beetle* title.[92] The buddy-movie rivalry between the two characters, needling each other affectionately as they share the Bug, offers an intriguing alternate perspective on Rorschach and Nite Owl's team up, and there are moments so reminiscent of *Watchmen* that the reader would be forgiven for thinking Wein had cribbed from Alan Moore's scripts as he edited them. The Question describes 'Using this garbage can – to take out the trash!'[93] while Rorschach muses that he's 'never disposed of sewage with toilet before. Obvious, really.'[94] Blue Beetle makes a gag about the phrase 'under the hood', the punning title of Hollis Mason's book, and a cop strolls into a gang lair, breaking a thug's finger in vivid close-up. At the end of this storyline is a twelve-frame grid which pulls slowly back from a dead body as the rival warriors surrounding it start to clap in respect. 'The play at last is ended', Wein announces. A black panel: 'The curtain falls.'[95] *Watchmen* issue 2, published two months before, had closed with an entirely red panel and the word 'Curtains'.

That was autumn 1986, and by February 1987, this Question was dead – killed so that O'Neil could forge a new, Zen-martial-arts version more in line with his own liberal politics than Steve Ditko's conservatism. Here another factor enters the intertextual mix. O'Neil was an established name with a distinctive style – less of a powerhouse in 1980s comic books than Alan Moore, but a major figure nonetheless – and he had been given relatively free rein on a new title. All the other aspects of influence surrounding the Charlton characters – their origins and previous incarnations, the importance of *Watchmen* and *Dark Knight Returns,* the post-Crisis reboot and the 'mature audiences' market – are filtered into *The Question* through O'Neil's auteurism, much as Batman had been shaped in very different ways by Moore and Miller's distinct approaches to character and narrative in *The Killing Joke* and *The Dark Knight Returns.*

So while the opening narration of this issue 1 may read as an attempt at Miller's hard-boiled prose or a variation on Rorschach's journal style –

> He has been waiting a while now, listening to the hiss of tires on wet pavement and the drone of voices from inside the small building – curses, mutters, an occasional bark of laughter. Waiting for the tension to build, feeling the knot of excitement in his belly tighten and the muscles beneath his clothing tense.[96]

– its source is in fact far older in origin. O'Neil's writing for the 1970s *Detective Comics,* indeed, would have influenced Moore and Miller in their earlier careers.

> Hear the wind screeching through the canyons . . . feel the sting of chill rain and sniff the sulfurous odor rising from the sodden earth. . . see the twists of pale lightning split the sky . . . this is the Batman . . . without hesitation, his superbly trained muscles react, launching him across the yawning emptiness.[97]

O'Neil's attitude towards Moore's recent work is dramatically visualized in issue 17, through scenes that also offer a vivid illustration of the broader relationship between *Watchmen* and the superhero genre of the late 1980s. The Question, in civilian guise as Vic Sage, picks up something to read on his flight. Bizarrely, it seems he glanced no further than the cover before boarding. 'Check it out', he muses, relaxing in his seat. '*Watchmen,* by Alan Moore and Dave Gibbons. Looks like some kind of comic book.'

> Whew. Heavy stuff. Not like the comics I remember from when I was a kid. This one character, Rorschach – maybe a bit over the edge, maybe a little bigoted and he sure as hell is angry, but he does have moves.[98]

Vic Sage's voice-over is laid over a frame by Gibbons in 'Spider-Man Go Home!' mode, with Rorschach's back to us as he walks down a graffiti-lined, trash-strewn alley. Wondering whether his mentor could make him a mask like that, Vic sleeps and dreams of himself as Rorschach. Later, stranded in the snow, Vic remembers that this is how Rorschach died and collapses with the words 'Rorschach sucks'.[99]

On one level this is charmingly self-conscious, ironic meta-commentary. O'Neil knows, of course, that Rorschach was based on The Question, and that The Question was based on Mr A, and that the original Ditko characters were ruthlessly conservative, counter to his own beliefs. But more broadly, it illustrates the push and pull, embrace-and-reject dynamic that characterizes the Charlton/*Watchmen* relationship. Just as Moore and Gibbons, as we saw in the previous chapter, kept some aspects of the 1960s heroes and combined them with elements from elsewhere, so the 'post-*Watchmen*' Charlton group are distant cousins, not direct copies, of Nite Owl, Rorschach, Dr Manhattan and Comedian.

It would be impractical, if not impossible, to examine every title that DC revamped in the mid-to-late 1980s. A single issue from 1988 alone features advertisements for a 'reborn' *The Wanderers*, *Power Girl* 'back in her own story' after twelve years' absence, 'America's first major costumed comics hero' *The Phantom*, a 'New Format' *Flash Gordon* and *The Crimson Avenger*, an obscure figure from 1938's *Detective Comics*, returning 'from out of the shadows of time'.[100] Next month the advertisements announced 'DC Does It Again! Now It's the Atom's Turn! Following the success of DC's revitalizations comes *Power of the Atom*.'[101] Clearly, the company was prepared to pump out modern takes on old heroes until the well ran dry – and an editorial from President and Publisher Jeanette Kahn presents *Watchmen* and *The Dark Knight Returns* as prompts for this trend.

Every once in a while, a comic book will be published that seems to create a new genre in its wake. *Dark Knight* did that, of course, and *Watchmen*, too.

> There are now a number of books that participate in the grim vision of the world so persuasively portrayed for us by Frank Miller, Alan Moore and Dave Gibbons.[102]

The use of 'grim' by the head of DC Comics, at the height of the 'revitalization' process, confirms that the term was not simply imposed in retrospect by fans and journalists but employed as an in-house marketing strategy at the time. However, as we've already seen, any turn towards 'darkness' post-*Watchmen* was complex; its influence was nuanced and mixed in with multiple other factors. *Peacemaker* and *Captain Atom*'s traumatized protagonists retained a brash, cartoonish quality; *Blue Beetle* harked back nostalgically (perhaps through *Watchmen*) to 1960s *Spider-Man*, and *The Question*'s noirish detection owed as much to its writer's legacy of 1970s *Batman* as it did to Rorschach, while the Zen philosophies were all O'Neil.

We cannot analyse a whole universe. But by surveying a selection of the other DC revamps, outside the Charlton character line, we can gain a convincing sense of its patterns. Most noticeable is the overarching, overwhelming concept of return and rebirth which had proved such a success in Moore's 1980s career. Take *Deadman* as an example: Boston Brand is presumed dead (really dead) from poisoning but recovers on the first pages of his 'All-New 1st Issue'. 'We both know that you were murdered months ago – but here in Nanda Parbat, you're alive and almost well!'[103] The trope was firmly established as a trend by 1988. In that year, *Martian Manhunter* discovers his true heritage, regaining his original alien form and learning that – like *Miracleman* – his memories are false, based on pulp fiction ideas of Mars. *Power Girl* similarly realizes that she is not Superman's cousin but 'granddaughter of an Atlantean magician who lived 45,000 years ago',[104] with false memories of living on Krypton. Teen superheroes *The Wanderers* are dead in space at the start of their first issue in June 1988 but swiftly cloned and given cool new costumes and edgy names like Aviax and The Elvar.[105]

DC's long-standing icons were, of course, not immune to this revisionary treatment. *Man of Steel* not only rewrote Superman's past on Earth, erasing the 'Superboy' stories of the pre-Crisis period, but also offered a new vision of Krypton before the infant Kal-El was born: our first sighting of the protagonist is as a 'matrix from the gestation chambers'.[106] *Wonder Woman*, in turn, began before Diana's birth, exploring the culture of her homeland Themyscira; the heroine was only named on page 25 of 32. Even classic pulp heroes were pulled out of retirement: *The Shadow*, scripted and drawn by Howard Chaykin, returned after thirty-five years' absence as a debonair figure striking fear into mid-1980s crime – 'it's been an awfully long time'.[107]

We should note, though, that this *Wonder Woman* origin was published in February 1987 – the same month as *Watchmen* issue 6 – while *Man of Steel* appeared the year before. Similarly, despite the apparent parallels between The Shadow's vengeful proclamations and the baleful tone of Rorschach's journal – 'It's time to further rid the world of its vipers – and as for the citizens of this metropolis – God help the guilty'[108] – the former was published first, in May 1986, so its hard-boiled style was more likely inspired by Frank Miller or, indeed, by the original radio incarnation of the character ('The weed of crime bears bitter fruit! As you sow evil, so shall you reap evil!').

In a foreword to *Wonder Woman* 1, artist George Pérez identifies his debt not to Alan Moore but to John Byrne and Frank Miller:

It was the fall of 1985 as I gleefully stalked into DC Comics' offices . . . *Crisis* was done, finished. [. . .] But then I heard the talk. The talk of big things happening. Of new beginnings. John Byrne had been commissioned to revamp and revitalise Superman. Frank Miller's *Dark Knight* was inspiring the company to consider new directions for Batman. And of course, I knew *Wonder Woman* was also scheduled for an overhaul. After all, Marv [Wolfman] and I had 'de-evolved' her in the last issue of *Crisis*.[109]

In this context, *Watchmen* looks more like the effect of an ongoing trend to revitalize characters both new and old, familiar and forgotten, rather than a root cause. The truth is that it was both. *Watchmen* was commissioned partly because of the broader enthusiasm for revamps at DC prompted by the long-planned *Crisis*, on the back of Moore's acclaimed *Swamp Thing* and his cult status as auteur, but there is no doubt that it also shaped the direction and expression of some relaunched titles and encouraged DC to explore all their available properties, however obscure, for revisionist potential. *Man of Steel* and *Wonder Woman* would have restarted anyway, but *Watchmen* demonstrated that the same trick could be pulled with also-ran characters recently purchased from other companies, and Moore's success encouraged experiment: after all, most of the new titles were four-issue miniseries, trial runs to see what worked. The matrix of influence is complex, and it varies from one title to another.

We can see this variation in the new titles that appeared after *Watchmen* had completed its run. The relaunched *Flash* of 1987 – itself a kind of rebirth, as the former Kid Flash takes on his dead mentor's identity – acknowledges that a super-speedster would constantly burn off calories and has the protagonist wolfing down burgers and Baby Ruths – an innovative notion along the lines of Moore's 'real-world' approach, applying logic and a vague kind of science to long-standing fantasy characters. There are striking, sparkling little phrases in the narration – 'In the Rockies, my fears crystalise into snow'[110] – and something of Moore's precise, unflinching prose in captions like 'I hit him twenty-five times in two seconds. My ring leaves little lightning imprints all over his face. I feel something snap in my knuckle and hit him twelve more times before I feel any pain.'[111]

Again, though, the influences are too complex to be summarized simply as 'post-*Watchmen*'. When Flash spots a fight while sprinting down 'the rail corridor through Central Wyoming,'[112] but is twenty miles away before his brain can process what he's seen, we are in the same territory as the 'man who moves so fast that his life is an endless gallery of statues' – Moore's approach to superhero comics as imaginative science fiction, a serious exercise in 'what if?' But the gritty chunks of combat narration – 'Grab gun. Jam on safety. Sickening sound. The pain throbs like a turbine'[113] – are closer to Miller's tough-talking Batman ('Good thing I brought the gun. Magnum load has to be – hits me like a freight train')[114] than Moore's verbose prose-poetry. Finally, the brand of the Flash, established in 1940, carries its own inherent values about family, loyalty, legacy and responsibility that provide the story with its heartbeat; a *Flash* comic could never be as cynical as the Comedian without undermining what the central character has meant for several decades.

Other titles from the period confirm the same pattern. Howard Chaykin's relaunched *Blackhawk* from March 1988 includes a remarkably Moore-style four-page sequence of dynamic panels in a 3-by-4 grid, opening with a pull back from black to show the glint in the eye of a lion, who then paces and pounces within the frame.[115] Powerfully suggesting movement – almost like a storyboard for an animated MTV video – these pages recall the nuclear dream sequence from *Watchmen* chapter 7, extended into an even more ambitious showpiece. However, they also use sound effects in diverse fonts as part of the graphic design – more like Miller in this respect than Moore, who cut all sound from *Watchmen* – and must be seen in their overall context. This is a Howard Chaykin comic and his confident, boorish flair is stamped all over it, from the lantern-jawed heroes and hourglass *femmes fatales* to the fast-paced dialogue with its unfinished sentences – 'Your dough's in the glove com-' 'Wha--!?!!'[116] – the media chatter interrupting every page, and even the title: 'Blood and Iron' here, 'Blood and Judgement' for his *Shadow* revamp of two years earlier.

Catwoman (1988–9), despite its unashamed debt to Frank Miller's *Year One*, also attempts to borrow some literary gravity from *Watchmen* with its showy opening quotations from St Thomas Aquinas, Rudyard Kipling, psychoanalyst Karen Horney and William Blake's 'The Tyger' – also used by Moore for the 'Fearful Symmetry' chapter of *Watchmen*.[117] J. M. DeMatteis's new *Martian Manhunter*, launching in May 1988, had the same idea, and titles one of its chapters 'Burning Bright', the second line after 'Tyger! Tyger!'[118] DeMatteis's origin for the manhunter J'onn J'onzz (revealed here to be not his real name) inevitably has to engage in some way with *Watchmen* chapter 9, in which Moore and Gibbons toured an accurately depicted Mars landscape. It weaves its own independent take through the conceit that J'onn's implausible memories of home – a planet crowded with warriors and wondrous species – are all artificial, based on Edgar Rice Burroughs fiction. Following the story reveal that Mars is in fact 'beautiful-but-barren',[119] Mark Badger's artwork approaches the faithful topography that Dr Manhattan and Laurie toured in *Watchmen*, but it owes more to the wilder, more expressionistic styles of late 1980s fan favourites Dave McKean and Bill Sienkiewicz than Gibbons's dutiful craftsmanship.

Similarly, while the rhythms of DeMatteis's captions – 'I'm a Pralah-beast, from the Mountains of Passion! I'm a Sho'keer, from the Valley of Sand'[120] – are reminiscent of Moore's scene-setting and storytelling in the interstellar episodes of *Swamp Thing*, his depiction of the Martian Manhunter includes another significant ingredient of his own. DeMatteis was also co-author of *Justice League International* (1987 onwards) which cast some of DC's second-string heroes in a superpowered soap that sometimes verged on sitcom (the Manhunter in this title is addicted to Oreo cookies, thanks to Captain Marvel). In the midst of all the poetry, then, J'onn's co-workers from the League crop up bickering, whining and wisecracking. Even Blue Beetle is here, complaining that 'for once, I can't think of a single joke'.[121] Again, while we can recognize an acute awareness of *Watchmen* that shapes, even overshadows other comics from the period, they all retain their own distinctive elements too.

Finally, consider Mike Grell's *The Longbow Hunters*, described by Jones and Jacobs earlier as 'one of the bloodiest and cruellest comics yet published'. An update of the classic hero Green Arrow, overlapping with the last months of *Watchmen*, it certainly seems on one level to be emulating what worked for Moore, to the extent that we could tick off the similarities. Green Arrow aka Oliver Queen has not been reborn but relocated from his former home, Star City, to Seattle to start a new life – a shift from a fantasy metropolis to a real city, with actual landmarks and a mappable geography like *Watchmen's* New York. Oliver lives with his girlfriend, Dinah Lance, who is also the superheroine Black Canary, above their shop 'Sherwood Florist' (remember Moore's penchant for puns). While they usually wear civilian clothes, Black

INFLUENCE AND INTERPRETATION 83

Canary brings out her former leotard-and-fishnets costume in private for Oliver, prompting him to carry her immediately up to their bedroom. 'I didn't know you still had that outfit', he remarks appreciatively. 'I never throw away the old stuff', she coyly replies.[122] (Later, she is brutally attacked, her helplessness sexualized as she hangs from a warehouse ceiling with her shirt ripped open.)[123]

In bed, Oliver suffers a mid-life crisis. 'Maybe I've been stricken with my own mortality', he muses, half-naked. 'I'm going to be 43 years old this week.' Dinah acknowledges that their shared superhero lifestyle is a risky addiction: 'You put your life on the line every time you put on that mask. That's part of the attraction . . . the thrill . . . the danger. I feel it too. More than you might think . . . it's in our blood.'[124] Oliver looks back nostalgically to the past, admiring a Robin Hood painting which to him represents 'a time when things were simpler, life was sweeter . . . They're gone, aren't they? The memories are still there, but those old days of glory are gone for good.'[125] We flash back as he speaks to his origin sequence, involving a shipwreck and a deserted island; his dialogue to Dinah becomes a voice-over narration. In what Dinah affectionately calls his 'dungeon', we later see that Oliver has thrown out his old, trick arrows and decided to get back to basics, honing his skills with a bow again. And just in time, because an assassin is in town, working through a kill list of former enemies. 'Wolczek is dead! Four of the others, too! I checked. I tell ya, someone is killing us off. Somebody knows!'[126]

Look back to *Watchmen*, and a mysterious assassin is killing off masked adventurers. 'Somebody knows', Rorschach records in his diary.[127] Dan and Laurie, after a meal at the Gunga Diner, go back to his townhouse, above his basement full of gadgets. Naked that night, Dan admits he's troubled by the news: 'It makes me feel so powerless. So impotent . . . I can just feel this anxiety, this terror bearing down . . . it's a stupid, mid-life crisis.'[128] Laurie changes into her short superhero dress for the first time in years, and soon afterwards, Dan regains his sexual appetite. 'Did the costumes make it good?' Laurie asks,[129] and they agree that they can't quit their 'dangerous habit' for crimefighting.

There are other similarities, both specific and general. When Dinah is away and Oliver sleeps alone, his shirtless, despondent pose in the half-empty double bed[130] is reminiscent of Dan's as he turns on his side, arm stretched across the pillow, knowing Laurie is just down the hall: 'Hell and damnation'.[131] *The Longbow Hunters* leans deliberately into 'mature' content: Oliver is shown leaping nude out of a bath, and Dinah is drawn tastefully topless, while the violence is graphically depicted, including a scene in which Oliver breaks a perp's fingers.[132]

On the face of it, then, this looks like an example of a superhero revamp heavily influenced by *Watchmen* and more broadly by Moore's approach to the genre. Even the opening narration, arranged over scenes of a sex worker approaching customers in Pike Place Market, echoes Moore's prose style:

> The hunters are dying off. Oh, you can still see them . . . if you know where to look . . . Born to the concrete jungles the way their primitive ancestors belonged to the forest, they seek the same things – food, shelter, comfort. As in any hunter/gatherer society, there are those who have worked out a system of barter . . . you have something I want . . . I have something you want. There are all kinds of hunters. Some hunt for sport. Some hunt to survive. And some just like to watch things die.[133]

Compare with Moore's *Green Arrow* story, 'Night Olympics' from 1985, which also opens with a tour of the grimier parts of the city, chooses a metaphor – in this case, sports – and stretches it to the limit, establishing a rhythm through the repetition of key words and phrases.

> The crowd was big and noisy, a technicolor stampede. It was a good gate, like every other night. There was no torch-bearer, and no lighting of traditional fires . . . nonetheless, a clear signal was given.[134]

> Afterwards, all that remained was the soothing of injuries . . . and the awarding of laurels. There was no torch-bearer . . . and no lighting of traditional fires. Nonetheless, a clear signal was given.[135]

This would certainly be a persuasive reading, but it would not be entirely complete or accurate. As we saw with the other late 1980s titles, there are fascinating similarities but also key differences.

On a fundamental level, unlike the independent, self-contained world of *Watchmen*, *The Longbow Hunters* fits into an established fictional universe and is therefore aware of its position in DC's history, both long term and recent. It includes a visual reference to the 1971 cover showing Green Arrow's ward Speedy taking heroin, and the storyline takes place within ongoing continuity: part of its job is to set up the possibility of sequels.

Miller's influence is also apparent. *Watchmen*, of course, does not feature Green Arrow, but *The Dark Knight Returns* does, and *Longbow Hunters*, with its sardonic 'Too slow, old man'[136] over an image of the ageing Green Arrow, references one of Miller's recurring lines about the veteran Batman, 'Lucky old man'.[137] Oliver's tough-guy line to a perp who protests 'I got rights': 'Yeah. You have the right to remain silent', as he pierces the man's ear with an arrow,[138] is also clearly inspired by Miller's Batman: '– I got rights –' 'You've got rights. Lots of rights . . . but right now you've got a piece of glass shoved into a major artery in your arm.'[139]

These points aside, no reader would ever mistake *The Longbow Hunters* for *Watchmen*. Just as Howard Chaykin put his unmistakeable, brash and flashy brand onto everything he touched in the late 1980s, so *Longbow Hunters* is a showcase for Mike Grell's visual storytelling. His default approach in this book, using watercolours and black ink outline, is regularly interrupted by frames in softer chalk and pastel, without the black; sometimes these indicate flashbacks or memories, but Grell also switches to black and white sketches on grey paper in the middle of a conversation, with no narrative motivation except a possible shift in emotional intensity.

When Black Canary asks, 'What's missing, Oliver?', for instance, leaning over him in bed, we see a sensual, sketched portrait of her from his point of view;[140] this could be explained in terms of his romanticized image of his girlfriend, except that Grell depicts Oliver, elsewhere, with the same flattering light and line, the texture of rougher paper showing through under white and blue chalk strokes.[141] His reminiscence about the good old days prompts a close-up portrait of his handsome, grinning face, in the same style.[142] Moore and Gibbons worked closely together to create a consistent world which stuck to its own rules of visual representation just as it followed through on the implications of its fictional history: Grell, while also telling a story and exploring a character, uses the comic as a portfolio, almost a sketchbook at times, taking advantage of new printing and paper quality to showcase the range of his artistic skills. A book that, in selective summary, sounds very much like a *Watchmen* copy turns out to feel extremely different in its execution.

I have discussed a dozen titles earlier, and from that sample alone, the truth is clearly more complex than often assumed. Some comics were relaunched with new aesthetics and origins before *Watchmen* could have had a significant effect, prompted by the company clean-up of the *Crisis*. Some were too established and iconic to be dramatically affected by *Watchmen*, retaining their own distinctive tone, motifs and brand – any Captain Marvel who still exclaims 'Holy Moley!', as he does in 1987's *Shazam! The New Beginning*,[143] has not strayed too far from the wholesome 1940s original. Byrne's *Man of Steel*, too, remained clean-cut, upbeat and straightforward; the grimmer 'Death of Superman' storyline did not appear until 1992.[144] Others were shaped by an auteur-creator, whether the overwhelming presence of Chaykin and Grell or the subtler touch of O'Neil. Some adopted aspects of *Watchmen* but combined them with other sources and strands. Just like *Watchmen* itself, they borrowed from the vast archive of superhero history and, beyond that, from popular (and sometimes 'high') cultural texts and tropes.

Was this, then, a case of misinterpretation and misreading, as Moore claims and as many comic-book critics and historians seem to believe? Is there evidence from this survey that the titles of the late 1980s, in their attempt to capture *Watchmen*'s success, only recognized its supposed cynicism pessimism, its scattered depictions of sex and nudity and its bursts of brutal violence? Yes, in part . . . but mostly no. *Watchmen*'s influence on the superhero comics of the late 1980s was important, but it was not dominant: it was far from the only factor that shaped the genre at the time, and its effects were partial. Rather than a misreading, it would be more accurate to identify a *mixed* reading, a complex matrix within which *Watchmen* was undeniably a significant text.

What if we shift our focus ahead a few years? The revisionist, 'mature' approach that had proved so successful with *Watchmen* eventually manifested in the indie, edgy DC Vertigo imprint in early 1993, edited by Karen Berger and including a revamp of obscure figures like Steve Ditko's *Shade the Changing Man*, the misfit team *Doom Patrol* and the protagonist from 'I Was the Man with Animal Powers' from *Strange Adventures* 80 (a deep cut from September 1965). Certainly, Moore's work for DC, followed by his falling out with the company, had prompted the company to actively recruit other UK writers – Jamie Delano, Peter Milligan, Neil Gaiman, Grant Morrison – in what was called the 'British invasion'.[145] Moore, while supporting and promoting some of the individual writers – Delano and Gaiman particularly benefited from his mentorship – was dismissive of the trend, seeing them as

> retreads of *Watchmen*. People trying to graft dark sensibilities upon characters that had never been designed to carry those kinds of sensibilities. Any poor wretched innocent Golden Age character that hadn't just washed up on Vertigo for a period – it was pretty certain that they were going to be re-imagined as a sort of dark, psychopathic monster from the edges of human rationality.[146]

But if we trace a line of influence back from Vertigo, it leads us not so much to *Watchmen* but to *Swamp Thing*,[147] which had continued under writer Rick Veitch after Moore's departure, and then branched off into *Hellblazer*, following the occult adventures of magician John Constantine. *Hellblazer* author Jamie Delano adopted Moore's prose style – initially, at least – with an explicit nod to *Swamp Thing* in the main character's narration and perhaps a hint of Rorschach's journal.

The thin, Sunday afternoon drizzle greases the tired streets. Ignoring the queasiness which quakes my stomach like an uneasy swamp . . . I turn up my collar against the toothless gnawing of the early November wind . . . the streets are hardened arteries leading to the city's dead heart . . . a streetlamp winks its sickly, yellow eye as I pass – footsteps echoing from sullen buildings.[148]

Neil Gaiman's *Sandman*, which became a cultural phenomenon, grew out of his *Black Orchid* three-part series, which in turn had obvious roots in *Swamp Thing*'s mythology of plant-based superheroes. Like *Hellblazer*, *Sandman* was initially based in the horror genre – again, far more like *Swamp Thing* in this respect than *Watchmen*. Of the six initial Vertigo titles, then, three – *Hellblazer*, *Sandman* and of course *Swamp Thing* itself – had evolved directly from Moore's pre-*Watchmen* work for DC.

The clearest example of late 1980s *Watchmen* imitation, ironically, was not released under the DC banner at all. In September 1988, Fleetway, publishers of *2000AD*, launched *Crisis* – the title was, of course, no coincidence – which included the story *New Statesmen*, by John Smith and Jim Baikie, who had previously collaborated with Moore on *Vigilante* and *Skizz*.[149] From the name onwards (and the opening quotation, this time from Sir James Frazer's *The Golden Bough*), *New Statesmen* was unashamedly a *Watchmen* variant: an uneasy team of government-enhanced humans trying to investigate an attempted assassination and track a conspiracy which ultimately led back to one of their own, the charismatic golden boy Phoenix.

There were Nite Owl-style characters like the troubled Burgess, wrestling with his conscience and sexual preferences, haunted by his role in government-sponsored violence – the massacre at 'Tariq Alley' was itself a very Moore-like pun, referencing journalist and activist Tariq Ali – and vulgar, cynical killers like Vegas, in the Comedian mould. There were cinematic zoom sequences,[150] television interviews, purple prose – 'The past rushes in, a riptide lethal with glass'[151] – and even scene transitions across visually similar compositions:[152] a shameless and comprehensive plundering of Moore's techniques. Each chapter was backed with a text supplement – an extract from a gossip magazine, a page of film reviews, an interdepartmental memo – providing further insight into the detailed world and its history. *New Statesmen* is perhaps the closest example of a wholehearted attempt to capture *Watchmen*'s approach and execution.[153] Ironically – perhaps because it threw the reader into its complex narrative with no guidance – it was almost entirely forgotten soon after publication and is now as obscure as the Golden Age characters dredged up from history for a post-Crisis revamp. As a commentator concluded in 2012:

> Things that were hot, post-graphic novel revolution: limited series. Painted comics. British writers. Bloody violence. Character deaths. Morally ambivalent protagonists. Straight up nasty protagonists. First-person captions. Sex and sexual deviance. Real-world political angles. Corruption in high places. Pseudoscience. Literary techniques. Literary allusions. Superheroes, still. Downbeat endings.
>
> In a perverse sense, it's mightily impressive that *New Statesmen* managed to tick all of the boxes above without making any impression on a comics public hungry for all those things. *Green Arrow: The Longbow Hunters* got more props for being an adult comic than *New Statesmen* did. Published twice, in *Crisis* in the UK (with accompanying publicity tour) and in a five-issue US miniseries, and collected into a trade paperback with the weight of a graphic novel when trade were rare, it sank without a ripple. It's about as well-regarded, and well-remembered, now as it was at the time.[154]

If anything, *New Statesmen* was too post-*Watchmen*: too blatant in its riffs and rip-offs, too cynical in its appropriations, too obvious in its influence. The more successful of *Watchmen*'s successors lifted selectively from Moore's stylistic box of tricks and used them in conjunction with others, blending the approach that had become his trademark with other distinct influences, from a well-established character brand (the consistent tone and themes of Flash and Superman comics) to recognizable authorial voices and tropes (O'Neil, Grell, Chaykin, DeMatteis).

New Statesmen's costumed conspiracy narrative was also overshadowed by an earlier release from its parent company, Fleetway. In August 1987, *2000AD* broke its tradition of focusing solely on science fiction with the introduction of its first metahuman, *Zenith*. *Zenith* was authored by Grant Morrison, whose work from the period includes *Doom Patrol*, *Animal Man*, *Batman: Arkham Asylum* (1989) and *Kid Eternity* (1991) and whose entire career is seen by some as a decades-long rivalry with Moore.

But Morrison's dynamic with Moore is too complex to relate here and will deserve a chapter of its own. While the spiky history between the two creators began even before *Watchmen*, during Moore's run on *Miracleman*, and their sometimes antagonistic professional relationship – called by some a feud, even a war[155] – continued throughout the 1990s and 2000s as a background narrative, it reached a climax in 2014 with the release of *Pax Americana*, Morrison's *Watchmen*-style take on the original Charlton characters. And by that point, what '*Watchmen*' meant – to the general public at least – had changed dramatically.

3

Adaptation and fidelity
Zack Snyder's *Watchmen*

It was said to be unfilmable,[1] and the repeated, failed attempts to get a *Watchmen* movie off the ground only tended to confirm that idea. Though it was optioned in 1986, with a script by Tim Burton's *Batman* screenwriter Sam Hamm – which took radical liberties with Moore's original story, from opening scene to plot-twisting climax – the Fox studio had given up on it by 1991. It was picked up by Warners and assigned to director Terry Gilliam (*Monty Python, Time Bandits, Brazil*) with a rewritten script by his *Brazil* collaborator, Charles McKeown. Gilliam finally announced in 2000 that it could not be faithfully reproduced: 'The problem with Watchmen is that it requires about five hours to tell the story properly, and by reducing it to a two or two-and-a-half hour film, it seemed to me to take away the essence of what *Watchmen* is about.'[2]

Moore, who had turned down an early offer to write the script himself, agreed that it was a doomed experiment. Despite the parallels between his own comic-book devices and cinematic techniques like shot type and camera movement, the experience of engaging with the story would be too different. 'With a movie, you are being dragged through the scenario at a relentless 24 frames per second. With a comic book, you can dart your eyes back to a previous panel, or you can flip back a couple of pages. Even the best director could not possibly get that amount of information into a few frames of a movie.'[3]

Between 2001 and 2004, the project went to Universal, then to Revolution Studios, with David Hayter as writer and director. This time, *Watchmen* got as far as a full scene of Dan and Rorschach talking in Dan's kitchen (adapted from chapter 1 of the comic), which offers interesting comparisons with the equivalent in Snyder. In both cases, discussions collapsed. In June 2004, Paramount tried its hand with *Watchmen* and within the space of a year, the movie was attached to directors as diverse as Michael Bay, Darren Aronofsky (for a weekend) and Paul Greengrass, before being abandoned once more. It was picked up by Warners again in 2005, and Hayter's screenplay, praised by Moore as 'as close as I could imagine anyone getting to *Watchmen*',[4] was retooled by Alex Tse. Zack Snyder was approached and attached to the project in 2006, on the back of his Spartan war epic *300* (2006), an adaptation of the 1998 graphic novel by Frank Miller and Lynn Varley.[5]

In the meantime, two very different superhero properties served indirectly as test cases for a *Watchmen* movie, indicating that the mainstream audience was ready for its distinctive, reflective and 'realistic' take on the genre. We should remember that, at this point, the genre itself was still at an early stage of its evolution into the dominant popular mode of the 2010s and early 2020s.[6] What would become the Marvel Cinematic Universe began with *Iron Man* in 2008. Christopher Nolan's 2005 reboot *Batman Begins* took a 'dark', 'gritty' slant but deliberately ignored and attempted to erase all memory of its previous, campier history, quite unlike *Watchmen*'s engagement with the Silver and Golden Ages of its costumed characters. Otherwise, superhero movies were relatively sparse. The 1990s saw isolated success for *The Crow* (1994) and *Blade* (1998) alongside three films in the increasingly patchy *Batman* franchise, which ceased in 1997. The *X-Men* trilogy (2000, 2003, 2006) stood alone on its own terms, as did the self-contained *Spider-Man* films (2002, 2004, 2007); in both cases, the third episode was far less critically successful than its predecessors and stalled the series until the 2010s.[7] Another relaunch, *Superman Returns* of 2006, failed to fully capture

ADAPTATION AND FIDELITY

the charm of the earlier Christopher Reeve *Superman* (1978) and its sequels, while *Daredevil* (2003), *Catwoman* (2004) and *Fantastic Four* (2005) fell flat.

Ironically, a family animation and a TV show came closer to *Watchmen*'s tone and approach than these genre movies. *The Incredibles* (2004), despite its cartoony CGI style, captured the spirit of Dan Dreiberg and Laurie Juspeczyk, a middle-aged couple of former superheroes squeezing into their old costumes to come out of retirement; in addition to flashback interviews of the heroes' younger glory days, echoing *Watchmen*'s alternate history of Minutemen and Crimebusters, there was a knowing in-joke about the danger of capes – recalling the demise of *Watchmen*'s Dollar Bill, whose cloak was fatally caught in a revolving door. As Jackson Ayres notes, the parallels 'disclose the pervasiveness of Moore's work in the superhero genre'.[8]

The TV show *Heroes*, debuting on NBC in 2006, nodded to *Watchmen* with the episode title 'Seven Minutes to Midnight' (13 November 2006) and borrowed more broadly from its concept of real-world heroes coming together to stop a conspiracy that will lead to the destruction of New York.[9] In Episode 19 (23 April 2007), mastermind Mr Linderman justifies the explosion, explaining that even if half of NYC is killed, it would only constitute 0.7 per cent of the global population, and the tragedy will unite the world in peace. 'That's an acceptable loss by anybody's count . . . this tragedy will be a catalyst for good, for change.' It was similar enough for the *New York Post* to declare '*Heroes* Pulls the Rug From Under *Watchmen*', surmising that Snyder would be galled to see such a central plot development aired while he was working on his own adaptation. 'Fans have waited two decades to see *Watchmen* put on-screen. The last thing Snyder wants is for people to think they already have.'[10]

Two other texts deserve attention before we move on to Snyder's *Watchmen*. July 2008 saw the online release of an unusual hybrid, *Watchmen: The Motion Comic*. Taking readers through the story panel by panel, chapter by chapter, with all voices performed by Tom Stechschulte, the motion comic used focus pulls and rostrum camera movements across the space to highlight aspects of Gibbons's art, smoothed the transition between frames and added minimal animation such as hands lifting cups and cigarettes, feet splashing down into puddles and the fluid ink shapes of Rorschach's mask. What changes does this make to our engagement with and understanding of the characters and narrative? Unlike a conventional film adaptation, it includes almost all the original's artwork and dialogue, and the pace is glacial enough for us to take in every detail. However, a comparison of the opening pages alone shows that the experience is quite different.

Most fundamentally, the motion comic immediately loses a key dimension of the comic-book page. While we usually read from top left to bottom right, allowing each panel to replace the last almost as if they were frames in a film strip – and with a slow transition from close-up to long shot like page 1 of *Watchmen*, we are invited to interpret this as a cinematic pull back – we also, inevitably, see the entire page at the same time. Jim Collins, in his discussion of *The Dark Knight Returns*, uses the terms 'syntagmatic' and 'paradigmatic' for this distinction. Conventionally, he suggests, we interpret comic-book frames sequentially, in a process through which 'the preceding images did not disappear' as they would in film but 'were pushed back by the forward thrust of the narrative'.[11] In *Dark Knight Returns*, he proposes, 'the entire page becomes the narrative unit, and the conflictive relationship among the individual images becomes a primary feature of the "narration" of the text.'

> The end result is a narration that proceeds syntagmatically across and down the page, but also forces a paradigmatic reading of interrelationships among images on the same page or adjacent pages, so that the tableaux moves the plot forward but encourages the eye to move in continually shifting trajectories as it tries to make sense of the overall pattern of fragmentary images.[12]

We can experience the first page of *Watchmen* both as a slow ascent, panel by panel, and as a complete layout showing us all the images at once. The final image is, therefore, not a dramatic reveal: we can see Detective Joe Bourquin looking down at the street as soon as we open the page. Surprises, in comic books, are usually kept for the first image after a page turn, often as a splash.

ADAPTATION AND FIDELITY 95

On pages 2 and 3, John Higgins's colours tint the flashbacks to Edward Blake's murder in shades of red and orange, which stand out immediately from the more 'realistic' colours of the present-day investigation. They do not simply signal a shift into the past (an 'elsewhen' in the same location) but present a visual pattern on the page: when frames 1, 3, 5 and 7 on a grid are bathed in red, we see them at once. Their layout forms a crude face that combines an echo of Blake's grimace with the brutal symmetry of a Rorschach blot. Immediately, then, the comic-book form allows Moore, Gibbons and Higgins to introduce imagery and concepts that will underlie the entire story: the opening pages begin to train the reader in *Watchmen*'s approach to storytelling.

Overlapping captions from the detectives' dialogue serve, as we saw in my first chapter, as a commentary to the scenes of Blake's murder: 'I think you'd have to be thrown' appears over the image of Blake being lifted over his assailant's shoulder, and more knowingly, 'Ground floor comin' up', referring to the elevator, captions the explosive moment where Blake is flung through a window.[13] Again, this is our first, blatant example of a key storytelling technique, which will be employed more subtly later in the narrative: I discussed earlier the way that the *Black Freighter*'s voice-over obliquely comments on Rorschach's presence in the background of a chapter 5 scene.

By contrast, the motion comic pulls back slowly and smoothly from the close-up of the smiley-face badge to a long shot from the roof, translating Moore's cinema-inspired technique into, ironically, an attempt at a more filmic visual experience that loses any sense of the comic-book page as a whole. The movement back is accompanied by dramatic, foreboding music in the *Batman* movie mode, sound effects such as dripping, splashing, passing vehicles and footsteps, and Schtechshulte's narration, which inevitably provides a specific 'voice' for Rorschach, complete with accent, rhythm and intonation, rather than allowing us to create our own internal version based on the character's vocabulary, the idiosyncratic journal font and the ragged, ink-spotted yellow captions (which also appear on-screen). While his vocal interpretation of Rorschach is entirely serviceable, Schtechshulte's later portrayal of Sally and

Laurie is inevitably less successful and risks breaking the viewer's immersion in the fiction, especially in love scenes where he voices both the male and female partners.

Even though the motion comic's pace may seem stately and its presentation wordy, it edits the original from the first page onwards. Rorschach's narration ends halfway through, with 'I'll look down and whisper "no"', omitting his rants about Truman, lechers and liberals and cutting the connection between his final line, 'nobody can think of anything to say', and Bourquin's banal comment 'Hmm. That's quite a drop.'[14] In a comic book, the speed of the opening track from gutter to roof is as slow as our reading of Rorschach's journal; the motion comic, perhaps mindful of the viewer's attention span, completes it in forty-five seconds. Moore and Gibbons allow us to experience the page's upward motion while also taking our time over the details of each frame and the lengthy captions; the adaptation hurries us along, confining us to a narrower engagement.

Pages 2 and 3 involve equally significant changes. The detectives' dialogue is stripped down to keep the pace, losing some of their dry jokes; even when the words appear in speech balloons on-screen, Schtechshulte does not read them all ('That would take either two guys' becomes 'That would take two guys'). As media scholar Drew Morton notes, the detectives' speculation about Blake's death shifts from voice-over narration commenting on the red-tinted flashbacks to present-day dialogue, with the flashbacks 'as diegetic inserts, without captions or dialogue'.[15] He suggests that this 'preserves the staccato rhythm of the original panel breakdown', but we should remember that on the comic-book page, the rhythm is up to the reader. Most of the captions over the flashback panels are short, pithy phrases ('I think you'd have to be thrown') encouraging a brief engagement with the frame, but two of them, at twenty-six and twenty-eight words apiece, imply a slower duration. In the motion comic, these scenes last two seconds.

Similarly, the motion comic decides which details are foregrounded, through focus pulls, zooms and pans; at the start of page 2, rather than seeing both detectives in shot, we start on Fine framed from the knees upward, with Bourquin a blurry figure nearer the 'camera', and then switch our attention to Bourquin as his image sharpens. The motion comic team, as Morton suggests, seems to have 'felt the need to . . . make the already-moving tableaus even more dynamic', introducing shallow depth of field and combining elements of comic books, animation and live photography in a curious remediation.[16] This has the unfortunate side effect of enlarging Dave Gibbons's simpler, sketchier background details into full-screen images that were never meant to be examined at such levels of magnification; the animation of smoke and the addition of spot sound effects like crackling cigarettes are a dubious bonus.

In this opening scene, the changes may make little difference to our understanding of story and character. But at times, the motion comic's manipulation of the original image obscures key aspects of mise en scène: when Dan leaves Hollis's apartment, for instance, a little later in chapter 1, the animators were so concerned with making the 'We Fix 'Em!' sign swing and creak that they ignored the importance of 'Obsolete Models A Specialty' below it: a comment on both retired crimefighters which is barely legible in the motion comic. Note too that the supplementary material at the end of each chapter is simply dropped; pages of an autobiography, or magazine interviews, clearly lacked the potential for dynamic motion. An apparently faithful adaptation, then, proves to be its own, strikingly different version of *Watchmen*. The same is true, as we'll see, of Zack Snyder's live action film.

Snyder's *Watchmen* was not, it turned out, upstaged by the finale of *Heroes*. Some of its dramatic thunder was stolen, though, by a last-minute intervention from an entirely surprising source. Directed by Harry Partridge, with an opening 'Happy Harry' logo recalling Rorschach's favourite dive bar, *Saturday Morning Watchmen* was released the day before the release of Snyder's movie and rapidly went viral.

Unlike the motion comic, this one minute, twenty-five second short commits entirely to the form of animation – specifically, 1980s kids' animation. It implies an alternate past where *Watchmen* had become a regular Saturday morning series and, within its brief span, provides a richly comic, affectionately detailed intersection between the 'dark' culture of late 1980s graphic novels and the lighter world of their cartoon counterparts.

References to contemporary animation are swiftly and deftly incorporated into the world of *Watchmen*. Ozymandias's pet Bubastis becomes a cowardly assistant ('looks like the Reds are polluting the city lake! What'll we doo-oo-o-oo?') of the Scooby-Doo variety. Nite Owl, the leader who loves to 'party down' and munch pizza, is based directly on 'party dude' Michelangelo from the opening credits of *Teenage Mutant Ninja Turtles* (Murakami-Wolf-Swenson, 1987) right down to the reflective dance floor where he shows off his moves. Rorschach is 'friends to the animals', gently petting dogs – a wry nod to his slaughter of two Alsatians in the original – while the 'pretty butterfly' he claims to see in Dr Long's ink blots flutters past. Nite Owl grumpily interrupts, 'Yeah, when he's not clowning around', in an echo of the turtles' wisecracking dialogue: in the opening credits of the 1980s cartoon, Raphael complains 'Gimme a break' when the song lyrics accuse him of being 'cool, but rude'.

Silk Spectre, fittingly given the gender stereotypes rife within 1980s media, is depicted in the style of pop-romance animation *Jem and the Holograms* (Hasbro, 1985–8), performing onstage against a sparkling, pastel background; Dr Manhattan, who 'can give you cancer and will turn into a car', is in the mould of shape-shifting *The New Shmoo* (Hanna-Barbera, 1979–80), while glimpses of 'Ozy and Bubastis' hunting ghosts and monsters confirm their connection to *Scooby-Doo* (originally Hanna-Barbera, 1969–70). As the offhand reference to cancer suggests, *Saturday Morning Watchmen* takes a gallows humour approach to its subject, cheerfully sanitizing aspects of the original as if for a younger audience, while hinting over the kids' heads at their more sinister aspects. Comedian, Laurie's father in the original story, is revealed as a fan with an inappropriate crush ('If I could only get that kiss!'), Laurie reads to three versions of Jon in bed (in *Watchmen*, this encounter is sexual) and Blake crashes through a window only to be caught by Ozymandias, who gives the viewer a winking thumbs up. Those winks, reproduced in the cartoon's version

ADAPTATION AND FIDELITY

of *Watchmen*'s iconic smiley face, are knowingly directed at fans of the original. Dave Gibbons loved it.[17]

And the following day, finally, the *Watchmen* movie opened, some twenty-three years after it was first optioned. Promoted as the screen version of 'the most celebrated graphic novel of all time', with a portentous trailer – 'In 2009 . . . everything we know will change' – and a difficult history, it landed not exactly with a thud but not with a triumphant fanfare either.

'*Watchmen* flops', announced *Business Insider*, shortly after the film's release.

Ouch! So much for that $70 million debut. *Watchmen* still managed to finish in first place opening weekend, but its three-day total is only $55.6 million, way below what box-office experts were predicting, even after Friday's disappointing finish. $56 million is nothing to sneeze at for a normal film, but given the expectations for this one, and how much money it has to make to break even, this isn't great. In fact, it's even below the opening weekend total for Zack Snyder's last film, *300*.[18]

Reviews were grudging and ratings middling, with an average 65 per cent on *Rotten Tomatoes*. 'Great book, mediocre adaptation', said Richard Roeper; Joe Morgenstern at the *Wall Street Journal* described it as 'an alternate version of *The Incredibles* minus the delight'.[19] Alan Moore, declining to watch the movie, dismissed it as 'more regurgitated worms',[20] and his absence from the process, one journalist noted, put ' Zack Snyder in the awkward position of reverent disobedience, as if building a temple to honour an absent god'. Snyder, 'imitating the conventions of another medium . . . seems only half aware that every adaptation must be some kind of betrayal – or remain a shadow of its source, like a pattern sketched in the dust of a dead planet'.[21]

Adaptation as betrayal – the dilemma around 'fidelity' to the original source – is a much debated topic in the academic field of adaptation theory. Robert Stam noted in 2005 that 'the conventional language of adaptation criticism has often been profoundly moralistic, rich in terms that imply that the cinema has somehow done a disservice to literature'.

Terms like 'infidelity', 'betrayal', 'deformation', 'violation', 'bastardization', vulgarization' and 'desecration' proliferate in adaptation discourse, each word carrying its specific charge of opprobrium . . . the standard rhetoric has often deployed an elegiac discourse of loss, lamenting what has been 'lost' in the transition from novel to film, while ignoring what has been 'gained'.[22]

Drawing on the post structuralist theory discussed in my first chapter earlier (Barthes, Bakhtin, Kristeva, Derrida, Deleuze and Guattari), twenty-first-century scholarly approaches to adaptation have tended to embrace its intertextual nature, treating the source text and its translation into another medium as entries in a wide-ranging and diverse cultural dialogue, rather than a simplistic 'dyad' of original and copy, bound by notions of fidelity. The 2020 film *Emma.* directed by Autumn de Wilde would therefore be considered not just in relation to Jane Austen's novel *Emma* of 1815 but also Douglas McGrath's *Emma* movie of 1996, the ITV series of the same year with Kate Beckinsale as Emma, the BBC *Emma* of 2009 starring Romola Garai, the sequel novels *Emma in Love* (by Emma Tennant) and *Perfect Happiness* (by Rachel Billington), both published in 1996, and the free adaptation *Clueless* (Amy Heckerling, 1995). It only needs one modest step further to include in this matrix Austen's other novels such as *Pride and Prejudice* (1813) and its many film and television adaptations, and in turn Helen Fielding's *Bridget Jones* series, directly inspired by Austen, which was itself adapted into a series of successful films starring Colin Firth, best known for his role as Mr Darcy in the 1995 BBC series. While the *Watchmen* textual matrix was not yet this complex in 2009 – it developed dramatically over the next ten years – Snyder's film could certainly have been considered from other angles, rather than simply in terms of how closely it had reproduced the comic-book series on-screen: I will propose another perspective at the end of this chapter.

But as Deborah Cartmell and Imelda Whelehan observed in 2010, while academic adaptation theory may have moved past the narrow insistence on 'fidelity', the broader, popular discourse of movie production and reception has not.[23] Film adaptations are still regularly reviewed in terms of how faithful they are to their source; and to be fair to those reviewers, this angle is often set up in advance by the films' marketing and promotion. See for instance the trend of including the original author's name in a film title – *Bram Stoker's Dracula* (1992), *Mary Shelley's Frankenstein* (1994), *William Shakespeare's Romeo + Juliet* (1996) and indeed *Frank Miller's Sin City* (2005), adapted from his neo-noir crime comics. Moore's absence was, of course, an issue for *Watchmen*, and Gibbons had to step in.

Snyder and his team, aware of the stakes involved in translating 'the most celebrated graphic novel of all time', stressed the film's reverence for the original through the trailer, which included close renditions of iconic visual moments such as Blake crashing through the window, Osterman being torn apart by radiation and the Owlship rising from its underwater hiding place. Although Moore scorned the project, Dave Gibbons was welcomed to the set, and his cheerful interviews before the film's release provided priceless publicity.

Everything is done exactly like the comic book . . . to see the movie was a bit like seeing the stock frames that I'd drawn as the comic book come to life again, because Zack has stuck so very closely to the panel compositions and a lot of the designs, although the designs have been tweaked up to make them work in movie terms. It's very, very reminiscent of the comic book.[24]

Clearly, the priority was to reassure fans that *Watchmen* was in safe, careful, reverent hands, and Gibbons's approval lent valuable authority to Snyder's project.

I introduced myself to him at the UK premier of *300*, and right from the very beginning we kind of hit it off, and I really had that gut feeling that he was going to do it properly. And I must say everything that I've seen since has only increased my confidence. He does completely get it. I'm absolutely sure of that.[25]

It's deeply ironic, then, that the film stood accused for the unprecedented cultural crime of *too much* fidelity. The reproduction of key visual images, which had worked for Snyder's previous release *300* – adapted slavishly from Frank Miller's graphic novel – and indeed for Miller and co-director Robert Rodriguez with their *Sin City* movie, now seemed excessive in some ways, insufficient in others.

'*Watchmen* is too faithful to Alan Moore's book', *The Guardian* suggested soon after the film's release. 'At times this labour of love seemed like a shot-for-shot adaptation of the comic, with as little as possible squeezed out during its lengthy running time.'[26] *The Atlantic* described it in May 2009 as 'as devout and frame-by-frame a reworking as could be imagined' but suggested that it 'labors a little under the burden of its fidelity to the original'.[27] This criticism followed *Watchmen* doggedly, well beyond its ten-year anniversary. 'The *Watchmen* movie proves you can be faithful to a comic and still miss its whole damn point', complained *AV Club* in 2019, a decade after the film's release.[28] 'Zack Snyder's *Watchmen* Shows The Limits of Faithful Adaptations', argued *The Escapist* magazine in the same year: 'the film is . . . a reminder that the value of an adaptation lies in more than just superficial fidelity. Film is a different medium than comic books, and the art of adaptation is more than mere translation.'[29] In 2021, *SyFy.com* was still musing that '*Watchmen* was perhaps too faithful to the "unfilmable" comic'.

> Snyder's approach, which was basically just to make an exact copy of the graphic novel with one notorious exception . . . also showed the perils of giving fans what they want – or maybe just what they think they want.
>
> Snyder tried to stay as true to the look and feel (and even the story) of the comic as possible, even using the book itself as a storyboard. It got to the point that certain angles of shots were exactly what they were in the comic, leading to the sense that Snyder was just trying to precisely replicate the graphic novel itself.[30]

The common argument is that Snyder's 'fixation on direct translation kept him from applying any deeper insight to the text';[31] that without the supplementary material, with their backstories reduced for time, the characters have less humanity and offer limited engagement. Though it seemed to be made for fans, Will Leitch in *SyFy Wire* recalled that half the *Watchmen* fanbase 'hated how much it felt like a Xerox'd, uninspired copy of the original'[32] – noting that they also resented a change to the ending (that 'notorious exception' earlier) that, again for reasons of time,[33] replaces the fake extraterrestrial squid with reactors that duplicate Dr Manhattan's energy.[34] As another journalist, Kaleem Aftab, commented soon after the film's release, 'The failure of this very faithful adaptation highlights the fact that to capture the spirit of a comic book, a film must do more than bring a collection of still frames to life.'[35]

In the remainder of this chapter, I ask three key questions. Was Snyder's *Watchmen* faithful to the original? Could it possibly have been faithful? And was it even intended to be faithful?

Robert Stam proposes that 'fidelity in adaptation is literally impossible. A filmic adaptation is automatically different and original due to the change of medium.'[36] He provides a fascinating example to demonstrate that 'the "automatic difference" between novel and film is evident even in fairly straight-forward adaptations of specific novelistic passages by "realist" directors'. John Ford's *Grapes of Wrath* was a realist production of a realist novel, adapted 'in what most would regard as a "faithful" rendition' months after the novel's publication, 'yet even here the "cinematization" generates an "automatic difference"'.[37]

Stam compares the two versions of a scene where Ma Joad is examining her memorabilia and points out that, for instance, Ford has to provide actual photographs to illustrate Steinbeck's mention of 'photographs', that the reference to 'a newspaper clipping' requires Ford to choose a newspaper and mock it up with 'specific headlines, illustrations, fonts, none of which is spelled out in the original'. Nothing in the novel describes Ma Joad sitting in front of a fire, 'the reflections of which will flicker over her face', or the point-of-view editing that will alternate between the objects she examines and her emotional reaction. There is no mention of music in Steinbeck, yet Ford provides a slow accordion rendition of 'Red River Valley'. As Stam convincingly concludes:

> Even if the text *had* mentioned 'Red River Valley' that would still have been quite different from our actually hearing it performed. And even if the passage *had* mentioned both the music and the firelight, and the light's flickering over Ma Joad's face, that would still not have been anything like our seeing her face and hearing the music *at the same time*.[38]

It could be argued that comic books are inherently closer to film than the written word; after all, Snyder used pages from *Watchmen* as a basis for his storyboards. However, an examination of the motion comic – even more closely related to the comic-book page – has already revealed key differences behind these visual similarities. Looking more closely at these two versions of *Watchmen* shows them to be radically distinct, even in shots that, superficially, look like direct replicas.

Take the first few seconds of the scene where Rorschach visits Moloch, finds him dead and is trapped by the police – the ending of *Watchmen* chapter 5. Snyder's storyboards include panels of Gibbons's art, and yet the scenes that result are leagues apart, their difference obvious even from the first seconds. Page 23 of the comic opens with three panels: first a red-tinted image of a puddle with the Rum Runner logo reflected, then Rorschach's foot descending – the panel now in more naturalistic blues – and Rorschach's foot splashing in the puddle, again with red and orange dominating. These three panels break a simple action into its parts: the effect is very much like looking at subsequent frames from a film, except that, as noted earlier, a film would propel us through those frames at its own speed. On the page, we can linger over the details of Gibbons's art – a Gunga Diner flyer, discarded newspapers, the ripples and splashes – and appreciate at length John Higgins's ability to highlight reflections on water with a limited colour palette. The change to red tint might seem inexplicable at first, but we can relate it back to a previous scene in chapter 2, where a flashback to Moloch's bedroom was alternately

ADAPTATION AND FIDELITY

rendered in purples and greens, and a sickly orange.[39] The colours, we quickly deduce, convey the flashing neon light of the Rum Rummer tavern next to Moloch's building. In this context, the pace of those three panels must, strictly speaking, take a matter of seconds – light on, light off, light on again – from which we get a sense of Rorschach's steady walking rhythm. The remaining panels on this page show Rorschach at the top of the building's steps, then opening the door, then in the hall and then the kitchen – the first and the third image in naturalistic light and the second and fourth artificially illuminated by yellow neon. In turn, this must tell us that Rorschach broke Jacobi's lock in the space of a moment and moved swiftly through his house. We absorb all this information, and more – the graffiti of embracing lovers against the wall in the background, the Gordian Knot trademark on the lock in the foreground – through a process of reading forward, referring back and taking in the layout of the page as a whole.

In the film, the first three panels are faithfully rendered. The puddle, the reflection, even the angle of Rorschach's boot and the rhythm of its descent almost precisely match what we see in the comic book. And yet the experience is quite different. That movement is over in three seconds, as quickly as the on-off of a flashing light. It is gone almost before we realize what we've seen. A 'cinematic' sequence in a comic book can successfully convey motion, but the reader is able to play it (and replay it) at variable speeds, while also seeing it as part of a larger, static arrangement of images – a recreation of that sequence in cinema flashes past to be replaced immediately by a new spectacle. In this case, Snyder gives Rorschach a more dramatic entry to Moloch's house and adds a voice-over, no doubt intended as gritty *noir* but sounding more like the plodding narration that weighed down the first cut of *Blade Runner*: it explains plot details that the comic-book reader could pause and check by referring back to previous chapters.

As with the motion comic, hearing an actor play Rorschach replaces any internal voice we had developed with specific cadences and pronunciations – here, the growl of Jackie Earl Haley, in the style of Christian Bale's Batman. While it could be argued that this choice is obvious for a New York vigilante, Moore's own recording of Rorschach's voice is strikingly different and undeniably effective: halting, adenoidal, slightly wet, it is immediately the monologue of a disturbed individual (albeit from Northampton, rather than New York).[40]

And while Gibbons's art is detailed, with clues and symbols concealed throughout its pages, he is also able to reduce that detail when the story calls for it. In the tense action sequence that follows Rorschach's ambush by the police, Gibbons strips out any distractions, showing us only what we need in order to understand the basics and keep the pace moving. Much of the mise en scène is lost to shadows in the dark house, while the regular flashing of the neon sign highlights the props Rorschach collects as makeshift weapons. In the combat scenes, Gibbons employs heavy blacks, almost in the Frank Miller mode; these images are easy to process, with figures picked out by Higgins in simple, contrasting colours.

Inevitably, in a live action film – even in an age of digital manipulation and CGI – the very nature of photography and its means of capturing the world[41] means that we are regularly presented with incidental details absent even in the most 'realist' superhero art. However tightly a director controls the image, it will inevitably include unforeseen folds in clothes, fastenings, stitches and the texture of different fabrics; a close-up of a character will capture the pores in skin, the pulse of veins, the idiosyncratic twitches and creases of every face. Background details may creep into any long shot – a rogue extra, an accidental reflection, a prop out of place, an element that escaped notice. Every object that is meant to be visible in a set will have been considered for its connotations and deliberately positioned; every ripped poster on the walls of *Watchmen*'s alternate 1985, every newspaper or pamphlet in its gutters, had to be designed and printed, then authentically dirtied and distressed. Every piece of graffiti was commissioned, every police uniform carefully sewn. While an artist like Gibbons has absolute mastery over everything in the frame, Snyder had to construct a scene from real objects and film what is there in front of his camera.

ADAPTATION AND FIDELITY

In this case, Snyder built an intricate set as part of his effort to recreate *Watchmen*, and understandably, he wants viewers to see it. Moloch's building is situated in a red light district (literally, in the original), and our first glimpse of the police shows them standing in front of signs for 'Video Booths' and 'Ann's Bar'. Minutes later, as Rorschach struggles against the cops, the camera whirls past shop fronts and seedy cinemas labelled 'Kinky of Paris', 'Totally Nude Girls' and 'Super Porno Sex Combo Movie'. 'Enola Gay and the Little Boys', a nuclear-themed show that features in the comic, is also in shot, testifying to Snyder's fan-pleasing recreation of Gibbons's artwork.[42]

Yet even without any of this showy dressing, the fact that Snyder is photographing real people in real costumes inevitably changes the nature of the image. We may notice that Steve Fine has faint scars on his cheeks, and that Rorschach's coat has a slight oily gleam when it moves under lights. These details, like the beads of perspiration around a young cop's mouth, the battered brown finish of Moloch's banisters and the peeling paper on his walls, provide additional information that Gibbons would struggle to include in his already crowded frames, even if he wanted to. They are the product of photography, and as such they echo Roland Barthes's remarks, in *Camera Lucida*, about the aspects that strike him in still images.

> Here, on a torn-up pavement, a child's corpse under a white sheet; parents and friends stand around it, desolate: a banal enough scene, unfortunately, but I noted certain inferences: the corpse's one bare foot, the sheet carried by the weeping mother (why this sheet?), a woman in the background, probably a friend, holding a handkerchief to her nose. Here . . . leaning against the wall of a house, three Sandinists, the lower part of their faces covered by a rag . . . one of them holds a gun that rests on his thigh (I can see his nails); but his other hand is stretched out, open, as if he were explaining and demonstrating something.[43]

Similarly, men in a series of nineteenth-century photographs surprise Barthes with their long fingernails, prompting him to wonder about the cultural context surrounding this style. 'Photography can tell me this much better than painted portraits.'[44] 'Since the Photograph is pure contingency and can be nothing else (it is always *something* that is represented) . . . it immediately yields up those "details" which constitute the very raw material of ethnographic knowledge.'[45] From a photograph of 'Mayday 1959' in Moscow, Barthes learns 'how Russians dress (which after all I don't know): I *note* a boy's big cloth cap, another's necktie, an old woman's scarf around her neck, a youth's haircut.'[46] These details were all incidental to the picture; their inclusion was accidental but inevitable, due to the nature of photography, which simply opens its lens and records what is before it.

Barthes introduces the term *the punctum* for this element that 'rises from the scene, shoots out of it like an arrow, and pierces me'; certain photographs are 'in effect punctuated, sometimes even speckled with these sensitive points; precisely, these marks, these wounds are so many *points*. [. . .] A photograph's *punctum* is that accident which pricks me (but also bruises me, is poignant to me).'[47] The faint imperfections visible on the skin of Detective Steve Fine, perhaps recalling Comedian's deeply scarred cheek and pre-empting the reveal of Rorschach's battered, bullied features, add an unforeseen but touchingly human element to the character.

Snyder, surprisingly given its visual potential and the sense of timing that it offers, eschews the device of the flashing Rum Runner neon sign that structures this scene in the comic – reducing the colour scheme only to cold shadows, rather than alternating them with warm illumination – and instead creates rhythm through editing. He adds a sequence where the police count down from three before they slam a hammer into Rorschach's door and uses standard conventions of action cinema to ramp up the tension: we cut between close-ups of a cop's lips mouthing the countdown and details of gloved hands hefting the hammer, preparing for impact. The soundtrack – bass drum like a heartbeat, suspenseful strings and foreboding deep brass – further tightens the dramatic tension. Moments of action are emphasized with musical stings. Natural sound is exaggerated into whooshing flame and punches that land with a thumping crack; every movement creates a whipping rush of air, ironically giving the scene a sense of larger-than-life 'comic book' effects. Steve Fine's 'I hope you're ready, hero' is meant to be sardonic, but Rorschach's slo-mo leap through the window is accompanied by a dark fanfare that again would not be out of place in a *Batman* movie.

Snyder's individual tastes and techniques are in evidence here, as I'll discuss later. The falling hammer blow is rendered in slow motion, as is Rorschach's use of hairspray as a flamethrower; in the original, he lights it while almost hidden at the corner of a frame and releases it in a single panel, but here the match strike is displayed in extreme close-up and gouts of flame sweep slowly across the screen in five separate shots. Fire, in Snyder, tends to be filmed at leisure and depicted with love.

In the comic, Rorschach's demise is inglorious, in keeping with Moore's 'realist' approach to superheroes. If an agile, tough man leapt from a third-floor window, he would not perform a graceful, gymnastic landing; he would, as Moore suggests, be more likely to crash into a garbage can and find himself unable to stand. That man, despite his wiry strength and inventive street-fighting skills, would not be able to fight off a squad of armed police; they would, as Moore shows, be likely to boot him in the face and beat him with nightsticks. Snyder makes a different choice and has Rorschach landing in an effective breakfall, growling 'come on!' and engaging the police in a spirited, noisy and acrobatic combat for several seconds before he is overpowered.

These are artistic decisions. The sequence could have been shot without music, its pace governed by the flashing orange light and its details restricted only to what Moore and Gibbons depict on the page. But even so, as we saw, it would not – could not – have been entirely 'faithful'. We can apply the same approach to any scene from the film. Even if the opening encounter between Ozymandias and Comedian had been reduced to the glimpses of brutally one-sided combat that we see in the comic, rather than Snyder's extended, speed-ramping clash of muscular titans whose blows smash through walls, the iconic image of Blake crashing through the window would not have been equivalent to the original, precisely because of the duration and movement implied by 'crashing'. Snyder's Blake is raised up over his opponent's head with a rush of air, is propelled forwards and then travels backwards in slow motion, the camera following him through the window frame as he flails and plummets. We have seen a blood drop land heavily and splash, with exaggerated significance, on his badge; we take in the tacky luxury of his wallpaper and décor, the ribbed softness of the dressing gown he will die in, the three rifles mounted on his wall next to a Vargas portrait of a former lover. The violence of the moment is juxtaposed with the rich vocals and soaring strings of Nat King Cole's 'Unforgettable', punctuated by the rhythmic thuds and cracks that typify *Watchmen*'s fight scenes. Rather than a drawing of an imaginary vigilante, we see the solid form of actor Jeffrey Dean Morgan (albeit padded out with prosthetics and aged with make-up), his teeth outlined by blood and his features a mask of gore as he mutters thickly, 'Mother, forgive me.'

Moore and Gibbons, by contrast, only show a man frozen in mid-air, arms outstretched, with shards of glass in a static arrangement around him as his yellow badge smiles blissfully just to the left of his horrified face. We might be tricked into thinking that we have seen a faithful reproduction of this frame in the film, but the comparison only works – and even now, it hardly works, as Snyder has again stripped away the crimson colour scheme that makes Gibbons's image so nightmarish – if we select a single frame from the movie and place it side by side with the comic. Snyder's adaptation is not faithful, because it could not be faithful, because of the fundamental differences between cinema and comics.

The question remains whether it really aimed to be faithful and what other factors may have been involved in shaping it. One answer lies in the film's most original (and most regularly praised) sequence, the opening montage that takes us through *Watchmen*'s alternate history. Entirely absent from the comic, and in a sense serving the purpose of its chapter-ending supplementary material, this five-minute title reel showcases a series of shots that move at various speeds, from barely slowed (the leaves rushing rapidly over Rorschach's scrawled calling card) to almost static (bullet casings arc leisurely through the air from a villain's machine gun, as Comedian holds him in a headlock). The camera dollies and pans across the scenes, but there are no cuts. These are tableaux, moving pictures, and as such, they already seem to comment self-reflexively on the process of adaptation – bringing still images to life. Significantly, the pace increases as we move forward through time, so the first tableau of Nite Owl clobbering a crook appears at first to be a photograph – the hero's grimace remains unchanged for the full duration of the shot – while the last, a mob firebombing a TV store, is virtually at normal speed. We start with stills and end with a movie. Snyder is effectively showing us what he aims to do and how he aims to do it.

This interpretation is confirmed by the fact that so many of the moving tableaux animate an iconic still image. The 'Minutemen 1940' scene shows us the Golden Age heroes getting into position before their portrait, which appears regularly throughout *Watchmen* as a photograph. Silhouette's clinch with a nurse is a same-sex twist on 'V-J Day in Times Square', the photograph by Alfred Eisenstaedt published in *Life* in 1945. Sally Jupiter's retirement dinner is based, in its composition and lighting, on Leonardo da Vinci's *The Last Supper*. Comedian's secret assassination of JFK is a recreation of the Abraham Zapruder footage. A television screen in Sally Jupiter's home shows footage that closely resembles Malcome Browne's 1963 photograph of Buddhist monk Thích Quảng Đứccan's self-immolation.[48] Marc Riboud's 1967 image of anti-war protester Jan Rose Kasmir presenting a flower to a line of armed soldiers is extended into a more mawkish sequence where a hippy girl tentatively places her flower in a gun barrel, which then fires at the protesters. Neil Armstrong's 1969 portrait of astronaut Buzz Aldrin on the moon's surface is replayed here with Dr Manhattan holding the camera.

Other still images recur throughout. The first shot includes the cover of Batman's first issue on the wall alongside posters for opera *Die Fledermaus*, carrying the vague implication that Nite Owl prevented the murder of Bruce Wayne's parents. A military plane passes the camera, backlit by a nuclear explosion, its fuselage painted with a Varga-style pin-up of Sally Jupiter. Andy Warhol presents his silk screens of the second Nite Owl. The most recent group of superheroes, called The Watchmen in the movie, assembles for a new photograph, with portraits of their predecessors in the background. In every shot, finally, the titles appear as solid yellow letters that cast shadows and are caught in reflections, like comic-book captions solidified into real objects.

This title sequence is clearly intended as a mediation about remediation and the nature of the image – film, TV, photojournalism, painting both classical and modern, comic books and their graphical text. But it is easy to miss the most important aspect: the dominance of the camera. The Nite Owl shot is only fully visible because of the slowed-down flash of a journalist's camera; similar flashes illuminate the subsequent shots of Sally Jupiter with a squad of cops, Comedian with the armed criminal, the Minutemen in 1940, Silhouette's kiss, Dollar Bill's death, Sally's retirement, Mothman's confinement to an asylum, the murder of Silhouette, Dr Manhattan meeting JFK, Warhol's silkscreens, Ozymandias outside Studio 54 in the 1970s and the final team portrait. Cine film apparatus also appears in the Zapruder and Warhol scenes. The early shots in the sequence are effectively silent: we hear only Bob Dylan's 'The Times They Are A-Changin'', with occasional gunfire, explosions and, significantly, the burst of those camera flashes on the soundtrack; in the 1960s, dialogue starts to creep in, through the raised voices of Sally and her husband and the television's comments on the monk's immolation. The campus shooting includes speech through a megaphone; the moon scene includes Armstrong's supposed remark 'Good luck, Mr Gorsky'. The final shot is accompanied by a soundtrack of shouts, cheers and broken glass as it restores cinematic conventions, bringing us back up to speed and preparing us to return to the film itself.

This accomplished video essay, then, has an agenda and an argument. Cameras are visible in the majority of shots, often crucial in lighting the scene and revealing details, and immediately stressing the importance of this medium: compare to the Marvel Cinematic Universe convention of opening

ADAPTATION AND FIDELITY 113

with a montage of comic-book frames, in deferential tribute to the original. Snyder's moving tableaux are spectacularly framed and composed, their artful slow-motion movement instantly 'superior' to the familiar images they recreate: they are richer, deeper, more revealing. The Silhouette shot gives us the before and after of a story, unlike the V-J Day photo; the JFK footage is smoother and clearer than Zapruder's. As the sequence evolves and film and television cameras enter the historical milieu, Snyder also adds atmospheric sound and dialogue and speeds up his pace. By the end, the photograph, comic-book drawing, cine film and black and white television have all been superseded by his film camera. Like a superpowered incarnation of Soviet filmmaker Dziga Vertov's *kino-glaz* or 'camera eye' in the 1920s,[49] it has shown us what it can do, what it can see, what it can offer, and demonstrated that those visual pleasures are beyond the reach of other media forms. It can simulate them all and do what they do, but better.[50]

In this context, what if we considered Snyder's *Watchmen* in relation to cinema rather than comics? Some of its references are clearly and specifically to the superhero movie genre. Nite Owl and Ozymandias's costumes, for instance, are not the cloth, metal and spandex of Gibbons's designs but moulded plastic armour reminiscent of Joel Schumacher's *Batman*. Snyder's explanation rambles, but it makes the point.

Nipples didn't just show up on that costume cuz we thought it was cool. It's because we want to say yeah . . . frickin' Joel Schumacher made a bunch of superhero movies. It's crazy. And that's part of the language now, though, of cinema. But like you can see it in like Nixon's war room. It's like, we did, it's so *Strangelove* it's ridiculous. We were in there going we're going to get sued for this, this is crazy. And you know when Rorschach walks down the streets of New York, it's *Taxi Driver*. And you have to do that, with that stuff . . . we tried to, we definitely tried to reference as much sort of superhero cliché, movie cliché as we could without it becoming self-aware.[51]

Clearly, his intentions have not always been understood. He has rejected the criticism that his action scenes look like video games – 'Well, maybe it's *supposed* to look like a video game'[52] – and his use of music is apparently more tongue-in-cheek than usually supposed. On Leonard Cohen's 'Hallelujah' in *Watchmen*'s love scene, he explained:

> I originally had the Allison Crowe version of that song, a version I've always loved, but in the end it was just too romantic. Everybody thought that I meant it. They thought the love scene was serious ... For me it is incredibly ironic, even with that version of the song it is incredibly ironic. I don't care what version of 'Hallelujah' is on, in that love scene it is ridiculous, but in a great way.[53]

Compared to his contemporaries such as Christopher Nolan, Snyder's work has not been afforded the benefit of extensive critical analysis. David Ehrlich, in *IndieWire*, offers a rare appraisal of the director as a potentially 'misunderstood myth-maker', assessing his central themes as 'what it means to be a hero in a fallen world', obsessions 'with power and its corruption', 'our relationship with authority' and the Hero's Journey: visually, he deals in 'baroque pop spectacles' with a 'hyper-muscular flex'.[54] Paul Ridd, writing for the BFI, echoes this assessment. 'Snyder's films certainly indulge in sensory overload and cathartic bloodlust. Yet his deconstruction of warrior mythology has unfortunately gone rather unexplored.'[55]

We can trace a path through Snyder's films from his 2004 debut to *Watchmen* and beyond. *Dawn of the Dead*, his first feature, also aimed at realistic immersion in a fictional world, and Snyder's production team built a detailed set within an abandoned mall, complete with fully stocked stores containing invented products – useful preparation for constructing *Watchmen*'s alternate New York with its range of imaginary brands from Mmeltdowns to the Gunga Diner. The plot, centred around an urban zombie attack, has multiple parallels to *Watchmen*: a motley team of survivors, each representing a distinct cultural type and moral position – the gun-happy conservative, the geeky, liberal leader, the plucky, resilient nurse, the grizzled veteran cop – is forced to work together to face a crisis. As in *Watchmen*, there's a fight in a decorative water fountain (compare to Ozymandias versus his hired assassin), a nightmarish sequence of shipwreck and bloated bodies (see *Tales from the Black Freighter*), a constant media commentary from TV screens and portentous religious overtones ('When there is no more room in hell, the dead will walk the Earth').[56] Even the cast overlaps, in the form of Matt Frewer, the former Max Headroom actor who plays Moloch in *Watchmen*.

While Snyder develops a grammar of slow motion and close-up focus on details in *Dawn of the Dead*'s action scenes – as in the Rorschach sequence discussed earlier, he relishes improvised weaponry and lingers on roaring montages of fire – he has not yet introduced his trademark speed ramping; that followed in *300*, along with his increased use of CGI and, consequently, closer control over the film's palette, environment and character motion.

Watchmen can be seen as the logical next step from his previous two films, taking elements from both. It combines a fascination with body horror and the muscular human physique, with what the body can achieve and what it looks like when torn apart; it takes pleasure not only in speed-ramping spectacle and CGI but also in physical set building and the creation of an immersive environment. Like its two predecessors, *Watchmen* draws on the slick language of music video and, more broadly, the aesthetic of advertising through which Snyder originally developed his style. All three films indulge brutal violence in rapidly cut visual sequences punctuated with over-the-top sound effects; *Dawn of the Dead*, like *Watchmen*, also uses a folk song over its titles (Johnny Cash in the former, rather than Dylan), with a main score by the same composer, Tyler Bates. Although *300* offers more obvious comparisons – it was certainly this film Warners had in mind when they approached him to direct – *Watchmen* is a middle ground between Snyder's computer-aided close reproduction of a comic-book page, complete with implausibly ripped bodies and balletic violence, and his previous creation of an immersive, real-life environment for a group of disparate, misfit characters fighting in the face of apocalypse.

We can only speculate about the motives behind his next film, a fully animated adaptation of a children's story, *Legend of the Guardians: The Owls of Ga'Hoole*, which returns to aspects of his by then established style and thematic concerns – power, mythology, heroism, explored through acrobatic combat and speed-ramped action – but with an entirely avian cast. Clearly not afraid of following obvious connections, given that he commissioned the band Owl City to provide the soundtrack to a movie about owls, it's tempting to wonder whether Snyder was inspired by *Watchmen*'s Dan Dreiberg and his passion for ornithology.

Was *Watchmen* meant to be 'faithful'? Yes and no. It engages closely with the original text, but as I've shown, it cannot possibly reproduce it, except for a frozen second when the film resembles a particular frame; and as the bravura title sequence suggests, its purpose is not solely to copy still images on a printed page but to transcend them through the dynamic power of the contemporary cinematic camera eye. It intersects with Moore and Gibbons's text, of course, but it also brings with it Snyder's preferences and techniques, evident in his previous and indeed subsequent films. As such it is not a translation that aimed to be exact, and failed; it is a dialogue between authors, a process of give and take, an exchange. A text, as Bakhtin proposed, continues to live and be shaped 'through conflict and conversation with other texts, always in process';[57] as such, it could be argued that Snyder's intervention, despite its mixed reception from fans and critics, kept *Watchmen* alive, alert, current and controversial in a new millennium, rather than allowing it to rest as a celebrated but static nostalgic object of the 1980s. Certainly, we can wonder whether *Watchmen* would have become such an active franchise in the 2010s without Snyder's film. We explore two more examples of this ongoing, critical and artistic dialogue in the next chapter; this time, both of the creators engaging anew with Alan Moore's work operate within Moore's own medium of comics.[58]

4

Influence and interpretation
Grant Morrison and Kieron Gillen

In November 2020, Grant Morrison adopted non-binary pronouns – the singular 'they' – as 'a badge of honour'.[1] While this can make for complicated and ambiguous grammatical constructions, I will respect them here: the linguistic suggestion of plurality in a singular individual is also fitting. Morrison has deliberately adopted various public personae during their career, often inserting them into their own work – a fey intellectual in the 1980s (*Animal Man*), a shaven-headed bullyboy in the 1990s (King Mob in *The Invisibles*), a magician, guru and rock star creator in the 2000s.

The supposed rivalry between Morrison and Moore, fuelled by their sniping comments about each other and the frequent parallels between their work, combined with the irresistible image of two self-styled British magicians – one English, one Scottish, one swamped in hair, the other bald as an egg – has led commentators to imagine an epic battle between them or, as Elizabeth Sandifer has chronicled, perhaps tongue-in-cheek, the *Last War in Albion*.[2]

Certainly, there are remarkable overlaps in their careers, dating back to the early 1980s when Morrison, impressed by Moore's *Marvelman* (aka *Miracleman*) for *Warrior* magazine, sent in an unsolicited script of their own. It was bought by the editor but then, according to Morrison, spiked by Moore, who later quashed his chances of writing *Miracleman* on a regular basis.[3] Morrison had, as they report it, written respectfully to Moore to ask for his approval to continue the ongoing story.

> And he sent me back this really weird letter, and I remember the opening of it, it said, 'I don't want this to sound like the softly hissed tones of a mafia hitman, but back off.' And the letter was all, 'but you can't do this,' you know, 'we're much more popular than you, and if you do this, your career will be over,' and it was really quite threatening, you know, so I didn't do it.[4]

Moore claims no memory of this letter and suggests that it is entirely Morrison's invention;[5] it does sound unmistakeably like his style, but on the other hand, Morrison's published work has extensively demonstrated that they can do a fine impression of the Alan Moore voice, as we'll see later in this chapter. This is typical of the 'feud' between the two, interpretation of which depends heavily on which of these provocative writers we believe about minor events from decades ago. Much of this history is uncertain.

Far less in doubt is the fact that *Zenith* was prompted by *Watchmen*. 'We announced to the world that Zenith was intended to be as dumb, sexy, and disposable as an eighties pop single: Alan Moore remixed by Stock Aitken Waterman.'[6] Stylistically and thematically, as well as chronologically, *Zenith* Phase One, as the first arc was called, is a 'post-*Watchmen*' comic: packed with cultural references and media commentary, with an alternate UK backstory of superhuman development and three ageing heroes coming out of retirement to face a new threat, it applies Moore's 'what if' logic to a lazy, arrogant teenager with incredible powers and realizes that he'd be more interested in maintaining his luxury lifestyle than fighting villains. 'I mean, what d'you think I am? Some kind of boxer or something? Why should I get my head kicked in for you?'[7]

It opens with a sequence following Zenith's drunken plunge from above the clouds to his Docklands apartment – what in cinema would now be handled with a drone or CGI and in comic book terms looks like a music video version of the stately crane shots in *Swamp Thing* and *Watchmen*. A voice-over from

INFLUENCE AND INTERPRETATION

breakfast TV seems to comment on the action, with an interviewee suggesting 'we were on a collision course . . . with disaster' just before Zenith crashes feet first into his flat, with the title 'Dropping In'.[8] The key elements are very similar to *Watchmen* chapter 1 – a juxtaposed narration over showy 'camerawork', a conversation that refers cleverly to what we're being shown, even a hero crashing through a window – but *Zenith* literally shifts them into fast reverse: the camera zooms down rather than up, and the hero (a naive beginner, not a cynical veteran) crashes in rather than out, all in the first two pages. The chapter titles are snappy and unpretentious cultural references compared to *Watchmen*'s: 'Blow Up', "Fear of Flying', 'Enter the Dragon' rather than 'The Abyss Gazes Also' and 'Look on My Works, Ye Mighty . . .' (Morrison made up for it with the 1989 *Batman: Arkham Asylum*, subtitled 'A Serious House on Serious Earth', from Phillip Larkin).

Phase 1's final battle against a Lovecraftian Old God, one of the Lloigor, is resolved through a post-hypnotic command: the words 'Tyger! Tyger!', from, of course, the William Blake poem that was quoted in *Martian Manhunter, Catwoman, Watchmen* and Moore's *Green Lantern* story from 1986.[9] The Lovecraft mythos played an increasingly important role in Moore's work – see *The Courtyard* (2003), 'What Ho, Gods of the Abyss!' in 2007's *Black Dossier* and *Neonomicon* (2010) – culminating in the twelve-part *Providence* (2015–17). Morrison, similarly, employed cosmic-demonic entities as the overarching threat in several works from 1987 onwards:[10] they expand to dominate *Zenith* Phases III and IV and reappear in variant forms as the Shichiriron in *Kid Eternity* (1991), the Archons in *The Invisibles* (1994–2000) and the Gentry in *Multiversity* (2014–15).[11] Morrison and Moore's shared interest in occult magic and transcendent states leads to visually similar scenes in *The Invisibles* (from May 2000) and *Providence* (July 2016) where figures move through space, trailing their own afterimages like time worms.[12]

Naturally, Morrison's work incorporates many other influences too. *Zenith* Phase I is equally shaped by Peter Milligan and Brendan McCarthy's lesser-known title *Paradax!* (1987), which indulged the technicolour misadventures of a hip and flippant anti-hero; McCarthy designed the main characters of *Zenith* in the same flamboyant, fashionable style, which owes very little to *Watchmen*'s classic and more stolid superhero wardrobe. *Zenith* Phase III, which calls a whole army of half-forgotten British comic book heroes out of retirement for a cosmic war, is clearly Morrison's take on the *Crisis* – they had already responded to it in *Animal Man* – but it also strongly recalls scenes from *Captain Britain*, where some of the same vintage characters, like Robot Archie from the 1950s comic *Lion*, are briefly swept up in battles they barely understand.[13] Phase III's scenes of massacre and destruction are, perhaps inevitably, similar to those in the *Miracleman* chapter 'Nemesis': Moore and Totleben had provided a definitive vision of the hell that supervillains could wreak on a city and its people.

Phase IV is structured very much like an extended version of Moore's *2000AD* tale 'The Reversible Man', as narrator Dr Michael Peyne moves backwards through his life from old age to childhood – 'I'm just coming out of puberty. I stopped shaving this morning'[14] – but its central concept is also borrowed from the Monty Python sketch 'Bicycle Repairman', in which everyone is superpowered except for one mundane (and therefore exceptional) average human.

Morrison acknowledges that they began their career by admiring Moore's approach and attempting to replicate it. We can see the evidence in their first *Future Shocks* for *2000AD*, starting in 1986, which lift ideas directly from Moore's *D.R. and Quinch*,[15] in their 1987 *Zoids* with Steve Yeowell[16] and also in their Kid Miracleman story, finally published in 2014, with captions like 'The days of the revelation were come upon the world and something unclean was abroad. Something venomous was walking the quiet roads and the lonely pathways, something cold and far from human.'[17] After kicking punkily against what they saw as *Watchmen*'s 'pompous and concept albumy'[18] pretension in *Zenith*, Morrison again deliberately copied Moore's prose style in their first work for DC as a pragmatic professional strategy to give the company, and its readers, what Morrison thought they wanted.

INFLUENCE AND INTERPRETATION

Issue 1 of *Animal Man* (September 1988) opens with 'Screaming . . . the monkeys screaming . . . rattling the bars, hammering the wire mesh, playing their cages like tuneless instruments...an orchestra of cages . . . a headful of screaming monkeys'.[19] Later, a woman remarks of her husband that 'he only shoots blanks', and we cut to a man raising and racking the slide of a hunting rifle, bringing down a bird with a single bullet.[20] In issue 2, Animal Man loses his arm[21] in a shock sequence very much like the slow-motion revelation that Evelyn Cream's head has been decapitated, in *Miracleman*'s second volume.[22] The issue closes with a splash page of the hero lying in a very Dave Gibbons alleyway, surrounded by painstakingly detailed litter: empty boxes, eggshells, a broken comb and alternate-earth burger packaging from McDougie's.[23]

With issue 5 though, Morrison began to do their own thing, and their own distinctive, career-long theme of meta-comics that break the fourth wall was introduced in 'The Coyote Gospel' – a surprisingly moving fable based on the question 'what if Wile E. Coyote was real?' – leading up to the moment in *Animal Man* 19 when the protagonist turns to the reader, wide-eyed and horrified, declaring, 'I can see you.'[24] Note, though, that even this issue, which is followed by Animal Man's climactic encounter with his creator, Grant Morrison, cannot fully escape the influence of *Watchmen*: the final pages focus on a wall calendar for September showing an owl swooping in for its prey, the image splashed with blood. Dan Dreiberg has an owl on his calendar for October; November is 'a hawk taking a sparrow in flight. Ominous kinda picture, huh?'[25] Given that *Animal Man* 7 had introduced a villain called the Red Mask whose chest emblem was the Rum Rummer logo,[26] and killed him off in a sequence exactly replicating the first page of *Watchmen*,[27] while issue 10 had Animal Man stripped down to muscle and bone precisely like Dr Manhattan, with the caption 'why does it feel so familiar?',[28] it is safe to say that either Morrison was deliberately referencing Moore's most famous work throughout their first DC superhero arc or that *Watchmen* remained a heavy presence in their creative subconscious.[29]

Morrison and Moore's careers developed quite differently in the 1990s, 2000s and 2010s – Moore took greater risks with independent publishing, hybrid genres and sometimes self-indulgent personal projects, while Morrison found their metier producing intelligent self-reflexive (and again, sometimes self-indulgent) superhero content for the big companies and for the most part stuck with it. There are further distinctions between their approaches – Morrison's obsession with magically aware comics is not quite the same as Moore's consistent return to the idea of a shared fictional space, while Moore's hippyish roots contrast with Morrison's punk and mod tendencies. Moore's one-man worship of Glycon the snake god and Morrison's attempt to encourage a collective 'wankathon' among readers of *The Invisibles* occupy different schools of magic. What they do share is a nostalgia for superhero history, a fascination with formal experiment and a surprisingly sentimental approach to character.

Some commentators have drawn further parallels between their later work as evidence of an ongoing feud. Morrison's true crime meditation *Bible John* (1991) can be loosely compared to *From Hell* (which began in 1989) for instance, while Zatanna's wanderings around the 'Imaginal World' in *Seven Soldiers* (2005) can be read as a pastiche or parody of the Immateria in Moore's earlier *Promethea*.[30] Even Morrison's anti-hero King Mob, which they used as their own persona while writing *The Invisibles*, was inspired by the *Watchmen* panel showing 'King Mob's Ape Mask'.[31]

Morrison, on the other hand, has caustically noted that it would be easy to play the other side of the game and argue that their *Doom Patrol* 53, in the Stan Lee/Jack Kirby style, inspired Moore's similar *1963* project at Image Comics, one year later[32] – that the larger story arc in *League of Extraordinary Gentlemen: Century* 'cannot help but recall' the similar 'apocalypse/moonchild plotline running over three time periods in *The Invisibles* fifteen years previously' and that Moore's 'Supremacy' for retired superheroes rips off the comic book limbo Morrison had previously introduced in *Animal Man*.[33] On this last point, compare for instance *Supreme* 41, from August 1996, in which

INFLUENCE AND INTERPRETATION 123

an out-of-continuity version of the character finds himself 'in limbo . . . it was just like I'd been written out', with *Animal Man* 25, from 1990, in which the hero is told 'It's limbo . . . you were written out' – but consider also that this issue of *Supreme* was also drawing on a more distant source, Alan Moore's own *Miracleman* in *Daredevils* issue 6, from June 1983, in which the hero first meets alternate universe variants of himself.[34]

All of this leads us to *Pax Americana*, a one-issue chapter of Morrison's 2014–15 worlds-colliding meta-comic series *Multiversity*. They showed me the original artwork for the series before publication, in Summer 2014, and leafing through Quitely's delicate pencils while discussing the details with Morrison – 'Is that Etrigan the Demon?' I ventured. 'No', the author laughed, 'It's Abin Sur!' – was one of the most memorable cultural experiences of my life. But if *Pax Americana* has a moral, it is that loving a work of art does not prevent you from critiquing it.

In Morrison's words,

> it tells the *Twilight Zone*-ish story of a man's life in a series of backward jumps through time – from his assassination as US President on the first page to the traumatic boyhood event on the last page that explains everything we've just read in the 38 pages in between. It's set on Earth-4 of the Multiverse of alternate worlds and it's a kind of political-philosophical-thriller thing featuring the superheroes DC acquired from Charlton Comics back in 1983. The Charlton originals helped inspire the protagonists of *Watchmen*, of course, so we thought it would serve symmetry to put Captain Atom, the Blue Beetle, Nightshade, and the Question into a highly formal, *Watchmen*-style deconstructionist murder mystery story they can call their own![35]

While this was Morrison's first full engagement with the Charlton characters – who, as they say, were currently occupying 'Earth-4' of DC's complicated multiverse – they had previously introduced the character Captain Adam, who was described as a 'quantum' variant of Superman from a different reality. First appearing in Morrison's *Final Crisis: Superman Beyond* (October 2008),

Adam was a glowing blue figure with a hydrogen symbol on his forehead, his abilities and demeanour clearly based on Dr Manhattan. In *Pax Americana*, the thin disguise is dropped, and he is simply called Captain Atom, or Allen Adam.[36] There is a subtle linguistic joke when he tells President Harley to call him Adam, and the president replies 'Atom'. We cannot be sure whether he is agreeing with or correcting the suggestion: the two words look different on the page, of course, but spoken in a US accent would sound almost identical.[37]

Far earlier, in 1991, Morrison had created 'The Fact', a faceless detective in a trench coat and hat,[38] who returned as an obvious Question analogue in the 1996 miniseries *Flex Mentallo: Man of Muscle Mystery*. *Flex Mentallo* also marked Morrison's first collaboration with artist Frank Quitely, who would work with Morrison on *JLA: Earth-2* (2000),[39] *We3* (2004) and *All-Star Superman* (2005–8). Of these, *We3* is most directly relevant to *Pax Americana* in its bold experiments with form, which break down the flow of character movement into multiple, exceptionally detailed mosaic images. 'They experience time and motion differently', a scientist explains of the cybernetically enhanced animal protagonists[40] – something equally true of Dr Manhattan and Captain Atom.

In 2014, Morrison presented *Pax Americana* explicitly as a *Watchmen*-style treatment of the original Charlton characters, in terms that, perhaps subconsciously, convey their ambivalent, love-hate relationship with Moore's work. Morrison has portrayed themselves, sometimes in the same interview, as both Moore's harshest professional critic – 'I was the first person to say Watchmen wasn't very good – in fact, the only person to ever say that' – and as a long-term fan ('I love his work. Well, there's a lot of it I don't like, but of course, he's great').[41]

It's meant to be like *Watchmen* in the way that the Rutles are like The Beatles. There's no sidestepping it. That's what it's about. It's about *Watchmen*. It's about that type of storytelling. It's about the very tight, closed, controlled universe that's created for something like *Watchmen*.

INFLUENCE AND INTERPRETATION
125

As a critique of *Watchmen*, I think the critique is there was well. The narrative techniques and the formal devices are so in-your-face it's practically like setting off fireworks, isn't it? It's almost an affront to critics, I would think, because it's so in-your-face. But I guess that also makes it easier to pick at.

But otherwise, I also want to honour *Watchmen*, which is an amazing artistic achievement, by doing something that's at least trying as hard as *Watchmen* to pack the panels with meaning and connection.[42]

Although it opens as unmistakeable tribute – a close-up on the cover that leads into the first panel and a title lifted from a longer, poetic quotation (in this case, a work by Delmore Schwartz) – *Watchmen* was, inevitably, not the only influence on *Pax Americana*. The central characters, of course, are from Charlton – Question, Nightshade, Peacemaker and Captain Atom – but the cast is slightly different. Some of the lesser-known heroes from those defunct comics make a rare appearance here – Sarge Steel and Judomaster's kid sidekick Tiger have cameos – while one key character from Moore and Gibbons is absent. We will see him again later. Another figure in *Pax Americana*, Yellowjacket, was the first ever Charlton Comics character and had never before appeared in a DC title.[43]

Nightshade, who of course became Laurie/Silk Spectre, is restored by Morrison to a role closer to the Charlton original as daughter of President Eden (Senator Eden, in the 1960s comics)[44] and seemingly younger than Laurie during the main action of *Watchmen*. In place of Adrian Veidt's media empire, *Pax Americana* has Blue Beetle lusting after the kind of merchandise we see Ozymandias developing in *Watchmen*. 'Screw anonymity. Roll on Blue Beetle toys, games, and millionaire playboy status.'[45] Nightshade has her own perfume, futureBOMB, and The Question, in his civilian identity Vic Sage, hosts a TV show called *Black and White World*, a reference as much to the binary right and wrongs of Steve Ditko's Objectivism (which he transferred to his character Mr A) as to Rorschach's mask and mentality.[46]

This version of the Question is, in Morrison's words, 'a little bit like Rorschach but absolutely nothing like Rorschach':[47] his uncompromising philosophy has evolved into an eight-stage colour-coded system based on a theory of 'spiral dynamics', which is echoed in the eight-panel grid that dominates the comic, and in turn by the image of an 8-shaped looped Moebius strip (formed by a superhero domino mask), which also suggests the symbol of infinity (nothing ever ends). In addition to the colour spectrum, the number connects to musical octaves and from there to the pseudo-science of 'vibrations' that supposedly separate the alternate worlds within the DC Universe. The Question's calling card, branded as usual with a question mark, is scribbled over here to transform the punctuation into another 8. Morrison further explains the figure 8 image in terms of never-ending cycles, relating to their own specific 'revamp' of *Watchmen* and more broadly to the retelling involved in all popular narratives. These stories, they say, are

> designed to be told over and over again. If you were an Aboriginal kid or a tribal shaman, that's what you'd do, you'd participate in the recycling of old stories, the 'revamping' of characters and scenarios, the explaining away of plot holes. Some to the job with more skill than others, but if you work with Marvel, DC or other companies' pulp fiction characters, you're basically repainting pictures of the ancestors on cave walls.[48]

While this sense of repetition, and the fact that *Pax Americana*'s ending takes us back to its beginning, echoes *Watchmen*'s looped structure with its message that nothing ever ends, Morrison also refers, perhaps less consciously, to previous images and ideas from their own work over the last few decades, just as Moore did himself in *Watchmen*. Like Moore, their individual authorship (or scriptor-ship, to return to Barthes's term) is an act of curation from a vast archive of earlier sources, and patterns emerge from their characteristic use of that material.

The image of an ouroboros, or snake eating itself in a perpetual loop, is central to Morrison's *Batman Incorporated* (2011–13), which also introduced a covert operations agency called Spyral. A cave drawing of Batman's symbol concludes Morrison's epic *Final Crisis* (March 2009). Driver 8, a character from Morrison's *Doom Patrol* (first appearing in issue 30 of March 1990), wears a cap that, tilted, turns the number into an infinity symbol. In 1989's *Arkham Asylum*, Harvey 'Two-Face' Dent has undergone a similar process to the *Pax Americana* Question, weaned by a therapist from his trademark coin to a dice, giving him six options, and then to a Tarot deck. 'That's seventy-eight options open to him now, Batman. Next, we plan to introduce him to the I-Ching. Soon he'll have a completely functional judgmental facility that doesn't rely so much on black and white absolutes.'[49] As we saw earlier, even when an author explicitly attempts to pay critical tribute to *Watchmen* – and even when that author's approach and interests closely parallel those of Alan Moore – their own personal style and themes seep into the mix, intentionally or otherwise, along with mosaic bits and pieces of other influences.

Harley, the son of a comic book creator, strongly resembles comic book artist Wallace Sage from Morrison and Quitely's *Flex Mentallo* in certain scenes, while the breakdown of dynamic movement into several panels – like a superhero version of Eadweard Muybridge photographs – recalls Morrison and Quitely's *We3*; but that painstakingly detailed, second-by-second cinematic action also recalls the 'decompressed' style[50] associated with the Warren Ellis and Bryan Hitch comic *The Authority*, which Morrison worked on very briefly in 2006–7. The sequence where the president calls in the Peacemaker as his secret weapon almost precisely mirrors, in turn, a transition from Miller's *Dark Knight Returns*, where the White House exterior, framed with railings, cuts to the American flag in close-up (and then segues to Superman's chest logo).[51] As one commentator notes, 'It's a fleeting nod, but it's enough to let us know that *Pax Americana* isn't just interested in homaging *Watchmen*, it's looking at the legacy of all the eighties revisionist superhero comics.'[52] That figure 8, in this context, takes on a further meaning.

Watchmen itself, then, is woven through this new and complex matrix, rather than easily located at its centre. The Question is pursuing a murder mystery – here, who killed Yellowjacket? – his conspiracy theories here pushed to a more extreme and ridiculous level, as the hero disappeared decades ago. 'Captain Adam gone almost a year. Four prominent scientists. Four unsolved murders. You know how close I am to tying all of this in a bow with the Yellowjacket case?'[53] As in *Watchmen*, his colleagues shoot down his paranoid investigation – "There is no "Yellowjacket case". 'He disappeared. We've talked this into the grave' – but it turns out, ultimately, that Question was right. Yellowjacket, aka comic artist Vince Harley, we discover in the final scene, was accidentally shot by his son, who grew up to be President Harley. Blue Beetle's spiky exchanges with Question are literally another alternative universe take on the Nite Owl-Rorschach dynamic; just as the late 1980s DC series discussed earlier presented them as bantering buddies, and *Watchmen* amps up the awkwardness, so *Pax Americana* offers a no-holds-barred verbal battle of barbed comments, many of them based on the characters' depiction in *Watchmen*, rather than Charlton or the DC mainstream.

'You made compromises you can barely live with', Question hurls at the Beetle. 'Anxiety attacks, an ulcer, erectile dysfunction'.

'And you're so deep in the closet, you pay rent in Narnia', Beetle snipes back, playing on fan rumours about Rorschach.

The Question's treatment of petty crooks is clearly inspired by Rorschach, right down to the torture traps, as are his pithy remarks, scrawled here on calling cards: compare 'White Trash – Black Outlook' to Rorschach's punning taunts 'Tall order' and 'Fat chance'. His guttural, Gollum-like noises – 'Hrrf', 'Hnnk', 'hff-snt', 'ngg!' – are right out of Rorschach's vocabulary, as is his casual sexism ('"FutureBOMB" by Nightshade. More like "Hooker's Handbag"'). Like Moore, it seems that Morrison found the Rorschach analogue a guilty pleasure (Moore, as we saw in the first chapter, distances himself from the character now, after making him, in Morrison's words, 'slightly repugnant, yet lovable')[54] and the other characters are given less space and time to develop. They serve a purpose in the plot, and nod to *Watchmen*'s tropes and props, rather than holding centre stage. Nightshade, for instance, has a brief scene with her elderly mother, as Laurie does at the start of *Watchmen* chapter 2, and her globe-shaped perfume bottle resembles Nostalgia by Veidt. Blue Beetle is subject to a lecture from the Question about the ethics of pouring money into gimmicks and gadgets instead of funding charities – a challenge more usually raised around Batman.[55] The *Pax Americana* team-building scene,[56] with costumed heroes posing awkwardly against a blank background, clearly echoes the first Crimebusters meeting from *Watchmen* chapter 2, right down to Nightshade/Laurie at the bottom of the tableau, and Peacemaker/Comedian's interruption from the right of frame. 'Somebody had to say it, might as well be me.'

The relationship of all these scenes and exchanges to *Watchmen* is ambiguous; they are obviously meant to repay the attention of fans who remember *Watchmen*, but rather than explicitly parodying, they play more like pastiche, storytelling in the style of – 'a neutral practice of such mimicry', in Fredric Jameson's words, 'without any of parody's ulterior motives, amputated of the satiric impulse'[57] – or even a form of affectionate tribute, fitting in terms of Morrison's ambivalent attitude towards Alan Moore. Jameson's further description of pastiche as 'blank parody, a statue with blind eyeballs' is especially appropriate in terms of the classical bust of Janus at the centre of *Pax Americana*.

By contrast, the extended sequence where President Eden leads his daughter Eve (Nightshade) around the Pax Museum is a merciless satire of Moore's mid-1980s tendency to match his dialogue cutely to accompanying images. Eden's every remark comments pedantically on what he is doing in that frame: 'We've turned a corner', 'One door closes . . . another opens', 'Unless we take steps to prevent the decline – everything goes into reverse', 'What we need now is a convincing exit strategy'. In this context, Moore's image of kettle steam blocking Laurie's face as she refers to 'shadows in the fog'[58] and Dan's 'we're both leftovers' as we focus on a discarded box of fast-food chicken seem equally clumsy.[59]

Eden's speech ends with 'Can you take a leap of faith with me?' and cuts to a shot of the Question vaulting through space. After a couple of weak puns – 'Get a grip!' as the Bug is lifted by a magnetic crane, like a fairground grabber machine – Morrison relents, the parody accomplished, and focuses more on formal narrative devices. Here again, Morrison and Quitely take *Watchmen*'s framework and push it, setting themselves the challenge of achieving even more complex symmetries and patterns than Moore and Gibbons managed in 1986. One of their showpieces involves the fragmentation of the grid from a row of four panels to eight, to sixteen, to thirty-two, to sixty-four – now just miniature icons of an eye, a flag, a dove, a star, a smiley – to what seems an impossible 256, the comic book reduced to its absolute minimum as a tiny row of dots. In another, three stories take place in the same location across three different time periods, indicated by Nathan Fairbairn's colours depicting day, evening and night.

As a final example, a gorgeous vista of a bridge and its reflection shows us Eden and Captain Atom in conversation both above the water and mirrored in it, the images joining into a loop; Morrison even scripted and sketched the movements of a bird and dragonfly, almost hidden in the scene, whose twinned flights form another figure 8. It's a technically complex, brilliantly executed scene, its achievement only paling slightly when you compare it with the similar spread in Alan Moore's *Promethea* 15, with two characters conversing around a Moebius strip, and remember that the original was published in August 2001.

'One of my critiques of *Watchmen*', said Morrison,

> is that I feel that the formulaic devices, while they fascinate me, and they do fascinate me because they're so perfectly deployed – there's not a line out of place in it – but in the service of trying to talk about reality, I don't think reality is like that. As the president himself says when they're walking through the gardens of Captain Atom, 'These gardens are a masterpiece of design and organization. Life, by contrast, seems a puzzle, a maze of contradictions.'[60]

The paradox there is that, as Morrison implies, their own characters are trapped by the same formal devices – worse, perhaps, as this is a more intricate

INFLUENCE AND INTERPRETATION

cage, built around the model established by two other creators in 1986. When Captain Atom remarks 'What? Sorry, I'm in the future –' and then, in the next scene, corrects himself '– no. I got that wrong. it's now. The future is somewhere else', he is doing so partly because Dr Manhattan announces, in *Watchmen* chapter 12, 'Excuse me, Rorschach. I'm informing Laurie ninety seconds ago.'[61] When Beetle challenges Question, 'What's that? What's in your hand?', seeing his former colleague pull out a remote control, he does so partly because Dr Manhattan asks Ozymandias, 'What's that in your hand, Veidt?',[62] as the mastermind produces a TV remote. The characters seem involved in a puppet show, following their set routines and delivering rehearsed lines with occasional variation.

This is, on one level, the point of *Pax Americana* – that life, for the protagonists, follows a pattern – 'an underlying structure hidden in plain sight', which only Harley and Atom can see. Possession of this knowledge allows them to flip through time as if it was a comic book, seeing other people's thoughts – 'transparent, weightless in little clouds' and returning to earlier points in the story. Yet inevitably, none of them escape their formulaic roles. They go through their paces, improvising slightly within the character template set by *Watchmen* almost three decades before and Ditko two decades before that; even the overarching device of comic books as meta-metaphors is yet another reworking of the idea Morrison first introduced with *Animal Man* 19, back in 1990. Morrison has built a brilliant prison, as complex and elaborate as the crystalline structure Manhattan raises on Mars; but it seems to restrict not just the characters but also Morrison's own authorial originality and creativity. Like Captain Atom's pet dog, which he dissects in order to see how it works, *Pax Americana* is cleverly constructed but devoid of warmth and life.

'It is brilliant,' one reviewer laments, 'and in that brilliance, it is maddening, it is frustrating, it is broken and fractured to pieces, it is unlovable. I admire this comicbook. I respect this comicbook. But I cannot love this comicbook.'[63] In classic Superman comics, Kandor is a perfect shrunken city, protected by a glass dome. That is Morrison's achievement in *Pax*: they and Quitely have constructed an incredible miniature *Watchmen*, hermetically sealed and self-contained, with little figures running around inside.

A prison – or, to return to Harold Bloom's theory from chapter 2, a *misprision*, as Bloom reminds us that the two words have similar meanings. '"Misprision" for Shakespeare, as opposed to "mistaking", implied not only a misunderstanding or misreading but tended also to be a punning word-play suggesting unjust imprisonment.'[64] (Note that the image of bars and railings recurs throughout *Pax Americana*, including of course the blank 'gutters' that evenly divide the grid of panels). Yet Bloom does not use the term as condemnation; he sees 'misprision' as a form of active interpretation, an attempt to engage with what has come before and to respond creatively to the powerful influence of previous writers. Bloom is interested 'only with strong poets, major figures with the persistence to wrestle with their strong precursors, even to the death'.[65] His examples are along the lines of Shakespeare and Marlowe, Shelley and Wordsworth, but Moore and Morrison clearly fit the dynamic.

The relationship is complicated by the fact that, as we saw, Moore's 1980s work is in no way original and does not pretend to be. Geoff Klock, writing long before the release of *Pax Americana*, explores *Watchmen* in terms of Bloom's theory and sees it as equally indebted to the sources that preceded it. '*Watchmen* betrays an intense anxiety over the return of the dead, the return of the comic book history Moore's *kenosis* disabled, rising for revenge.'[66] *Kenosis* (taken from the Greek; a theological term for emptying oneself) is one of Bloom's 'revisionary ratios' or strategies for dealing with previous work,[67] and Klock applies it to what he sees as *Watchmen*'s 'emptying out of the tradition'[68] – its undermining of grand superhero tropes, its frumpy sadness and lack of glamour. Dan's podgy stomach and his memory of breaking his arm the one time he used an exoskeleton suit provides one example; the revelation that a single-minded street vigilante like Rorschach would be too devoted to his 'mission' to eat hot food, wash his clothes or tidy his apartment is another.

INFLUENCE AND INTERPRETATION   133

Klock, in turn, details the multiple instances within *Watchmen* of the dead returning – the corpses in the pirate story, the 'old ghosts' of Hallowe'en, the Egyptian theme of Ozymandias' offices, with its implication that cadavers would rise –[69] to demonstrate what he sees as 'its position as a receptacle for the dead . . . supported on a raft of the dead'.[70] Klock interprets Manhattan's line to Ozymandias – 'nothing ever ends' – as an acknowledgement that *kenosis* is never complete. Ozymandias, and through him Alan Moore, 'faces the realisation of comic book continuity: the chain of revision can never end. One misprision will follow upon another'.[71] *Watchmen*, a revision and reworking of its own precursors and influences, will become a precursor and influence in itself, towering over what followed. And of course, that came true, and Morrison's work is the prime example.

Pax Americana's grandly ambitious attitude towards *Watchmen* is not a self-deprecating 'emptying out' or *kenosis*. Of Bloom's six categories, it more closely matches *apophrades*, not simply the fear of the dead returning (which Klock identified in *Watchmen*) but the actual return of the dead. And if Bloom's terms may seem overscholarly and obscure, note that comic book reviewers also picked up on this theme, without any reference to Ancient Greek tradition. '*Pax Americana*,' observed the *Mindless Ones* blog in 2014, 'betrays an intense excitement and anxiety over the return of the dead, the return of comic book history'.[72] Klock reminds us, in his discussion of *Watchmen*'s relationship to its buried corpses, that 'Rest In Peace' is not a blessing like 'sleep well' but a prayer to prevent their return;[73] the phrase appears in *Pax Americana*, too, but with the acknowledgement that coffins cannot be kept shut. 'The super-hero is dead', Eden tells his daughter. 'Rest in peace. One door closes, Evie . . . another opens.'

To Bloom, the 'later poet' – that is, Morrison –

holds his own poem so open again to the precursor's work that at first we might believe the wheel has come full circle . . . but the poem is now *held open* to the precursor . . . and the uncanny effect is that the new poem's achievement makes it seem to us, not as though the precursor were writing it, but as though the later poet had himself written the precursor's characteristic work.[74]

What this means in practice, then, is that *Pax Americana* is held up to *Watchmen* to the extent that it both absorbs the preceding text like blotting paper and also, through a time-twisting retcon, makes it feel almost as though Morrison had written the 1986 series in the first place. This is, indeed, what Morrison seemed to be aiming for. 'A whole new story which asks "what if Watchmen had been conceived now . . . with the Charlton characters themselves, rather than analogues?"'[75] The wheel has come full circle: the copy has seemingly become the original, and the pattern of influence is reversed. Again, if Bloom's high cultural theories seem distant from superhero comics, note that Elizabeth Sandifer explores exactly the same idea in her 'Last War in Albion' column:

> Given . . . the fact that *Watchmen*, with its rejection of the idea of endings and its own looped structure, whereby the final panel echoes the first, is similarly ambivalent about the precise sequence in which causes and effects need occur, it is just as reasonable to treat *Pax Americana* as an influence on *Watchmen* as it is the other way around.[76]

While this thought experiment is playfully extreme, it certainly seems the case that we cannot go back to *Watchmen* after *Pax Americana* and read it in exactly the same way. Rorschach's hard-ass, tough guy patter is now filtered through Morrison's absurdly performative, possibly closeted Question and looks more like an overcompensation or cover-up. It is hard to return to Moore's clever captions about fog and leftovers, matched to images of kettle steam and abandoned food, and not recall Morrison's grindingly obvious dialogue about turning a corner, finding an exit and taking steps. The 2014 parody sticks to the 1986 text, encouraging us to read it as ridiculous – perhaps preventing us from ever taking it entirely seriously again. And so we turn and return from one to the other: instead of oppositions, the two stories are part of a fluid circuit skating a figure 8 between decades.

Where does this leave the Morrison of *Pax Americana*? Trapped in a short circuit of anxious influence, switching between the past and the future, using Moore's precursors – the Charlton characters – to write a post-*Watchmen* story; weaving in and out of *Watchmen*'s complexities in an effort to create more elaborate structures, caught between the two polarized roles of Moore's ardent fan and harshest critic. In exposing the prison of *Watchmen*'s formal structure, Morrison becomes trapped with the characters inside it. By arguing for the stale familiarity of Watchmen's central cast – 'surprisingly conventional Hollywood stereotypes', according to *Supergods*[77] – Morrison reduces them to even flatter figures, copies of copies, cardboard cut-outs reciting borrowed slogans. (If Laurie is undeveloped, what is Eve Eden? Barely a shadow against a wall.)

Morrison sought to 're-think and update' *Watchmen*;[78] 'whether he explicitly stated it or not, *Pax Americana* is to be Grant Morrison's *Watchmen* Redux'.[79] In trying to provide the final word on *Watchmen*, Morrison opened it up again for our examination; in trying to replace *Watchmen*'s take on the Charlton heroes with a more authentic version ('with the Charlton characters themselves, rather than analogues'), Morrison reminded us of and referred us back to the originals, to rediscover their greater depth and nuance. In trying to impose on Moore's best-known achievement, Morrison rewrote it on a smaller scale, super-condensing it into something formally brilliant but stripped of feeling.

After years of subjecting Moore's masterpiece to snide remarks from the side of the stage – 'the *Watchmen* characters were drawn from a repertoire of central casting ciphers to play out their preordained roles in the inside-out clockwork of its bollocks-naked machinery'[80] – Morrison finally had the chance to engage with it through practice. Though they announced that *Pax Americana* was their *Citizen Kane*,[81] *Pax* – a little mechanical model of *Watchmen*, a Kandorian version of Moore's greatest work – is almost the opposite of Orson Welles's original, groundbreaking debut. Like Dr Manhattan and Captain Atom, Morrison sees the patterns but cannot escape them; they have an objective, architect's view of the prison but they are also its subject, a fellow convict alongside their characters.

But Morrison does see the bars and the structures, or most of them – as we might expect from someone who began a career-long exploration of fourth wall breaking in 1990, with *Animal Man* looking wide-eyed out of the page at the reader. Some of the paradoxes at the heart of *Pax* were signalled by Morrison in their summary of the comic:

> the Moebius strip continues. Like the overblown logic of a pulp comic where the only hope for America is to kill America's most beloved leader. But even that misguided hope is trapped inside, alongside the promise of something better. What's left remains incomplete, a figure eight circling back on itself. The superhero ideal put into service of politics and message, strangled by its inability to break free from its own tropes and inevitable patterns, eight panels at a time.[82]

Indeed, the central paradox is not just contained within the text – inherent in the looping ouroboros of the narrative – but flagged up in one of its precedent sources, from decades before. The initiating prompt for *Watchmen* was a simple murder mystery: 'Who Killed the Peacemaker?' *Pax Americana* is built around a more complex slogan. The first issue of *Peacemaker*, from March 1967 (and of course, the Latin word *Pax* links directly to his name, highlighting his central, symbolic role), has the cover caption 'A Man Who Loves Peace So Much That He Is Willing to Fight for It!'[83] The line was later toughened up into 'Willing to Kill for It', and it launches the first scene of *Pax Americana*, where Peacemaker assassinates President Harley in order that Captain Atom can resurrect him and 'redeem the ultimate villain. And restore symmetry to a broken world.'

To Morrison, this concept is part of an application of the Charlton characters to 'modern' (2014) society and politics. 'I suppose,' they said, 'it's about America and specifically about America's self-image as the world's policeman. It tried

INFLUENCE AND INTERPRETATION 137

to make a mind-devouring narrative Moebius strip out of the complicated, contradictory idea of using violence to enforce "peace".[84]

Morrison has dealt explicitly with this kind of complex opposition before, visualizing and personifying the dynamic in the benign Superman and his violent counterpart Ultraman, in a chapter of the 2008 series *Final Crisis*. Identifying an energy source powered by conflicting ideas, Captain Atom comments, "'Dualities'? No. There are no dualities. Only symmetries . . . I am beyond conflict.' Bringing Ultraman and Superman together into an explosion of opposites, he comments, 'Hate crime. Meet selfless act.'[85] *Pax*, we might note, combines and collides two different sides of Morrison's approach to *Watchmen*: Harshest critic. Meet ardent fan.

But there is another idea at work, which Morrison does not acknowledge. Note that their stated aim was to bring *Watchmen* and Charlton up to date with the current political and cultural moment. 'It might also cast a jaded eye on how lessons learned from the leftist, deconstructionist "realistic" superhero stories of the 1980s were assimilated and re-tooled to create post-9/11 Marvel Studios-style "realistic" super-soldiers and champions of the Military/ Industrial complex.'[86]

That his story features George W. Bush (whose office ended in 2009) and a spectacular replacement for the destroyed World Trade Center (the 'Freedom Tower' began construction in 2006) can be explained partly through the choppy chronology of the narrative and partly by the fact that Morrison had been planning this issue since 2009. But the arresting opening sequence of President Harley's assassination, shown in grotesque detail, recalls the Zapruder footage from Dealey Plaza in 1963. It has little connection to contemporary politics and is there for a more fundamental, mythical reason. It is the end of the murder mystery explained on the final pages, where we realize that President Harley, as a boy, shot his father – who was secretly Yellowjacket – dead with his own gun. Whether the shooting was entirely accidental or a case of mistaken identity is never clear, but Harley grows up with the grief and guilt and makes a plan with Captain Atom that the only way he can redeem himself and bring peace to the nation is by arranging his own assassination, then his resurrection. We see the killing clearly, but it is left ambiguous whether Atom will be able to bring the president back.

Now consider Bloom on *apophrades*, in the chapter where he elaborates on the device of 'the return of the dead'. He quotes a poem by Wallace Stevens, *Esthétique Du Mal* from 1945 (itself an echo of the earlier Baudelaire's *Les Fleurs Du Mal*):[87]

> It may be that one life is a punishment
> For another, as the son's life for the father.[88]

The echoes are striking. 'Only a superhero can redeem the ultimate villain', by killing the son to punish him for murdering his own father, years before. Bloom goes on:

> The mature strong poet is peculiarly vulnerable to this last phase of his revisionary relationship to the dead. This vulnerability is most evident in poems that quest for a final clarity, that seek to be definitive statements, testaments to what is uniquely the strong poet's gift (or what he wishes us to remember as his unique gift).

Bloom's example is Shelley, who leaves his work 'open again to the terror' of Wordsworth and the influence of his precursor; the poem is 'The Triumph of Life', Shelley's last major work before his death. We might remember that four years earlier, Shelley had published 'Ozymandias', the poem that gives a title to *Watchmen*'s climactic chapter: 'Look upon my Works, ye Mighty, and despair!' That poem itself describes a monument abandoned in the desert sand, a 'colossal Wreck', its head broken off and lying nearby – like the Janus statue in the centre of *Pax Americana* – and it speaks of a great achievement that has fallen into ruin, a crystal castle collapsed into the red terrain of Mars, or in the anxious mind of a creator, a career capstone, loudly proclaimed like a *Citizen Kane* – 'Look upon my Works!' – but ultimately forgotten or overshadowed. Of course, though, by reporting on the forgotten statue, the poem brings it back to our attention, restoring it: what might seem a bleak portrait of fallen vanity and arrogant folly actually becomes a form of tribute.

These are the complex, interlocking and looping contradictions that structure *Pax*, perhaps the single text that best encompasses Morrison's approach to Alan Moore. Beneath all the clever references, Morrison chose to construct a story about killing the father, twice – the JFK-like 'father of the nation' and his father, comic-book creator Vince Harley – and then trying to atone for those deaths through sacrifice or resurrection. We are left uncertain as to whether President Harley can be brought back to life, but the reverse sequence of the opening pages, the Zapruder film played backwards, effectively rebuilds him in horrific detail – blood flowing upwards, his jaw reforming and brain matter gushing back into his broken mouth – until he rises with an uncanny grin from the dead.

Remembering that Frank Quitely's real name is Vince, like the comic artist father in the story, and that both Quitely and Gibbons are influenced by Moebius (real name Jean Giraud), like the strip that runs through the story, we might also be tempted to wonder whether Morrison is aware of the linguistic inheritance in their own name, 'Moore's son'. Once more, if this seems a far-fetched stretch into self-regarding academic spirals, consider the 2015 blog review of *Pax Americana* from *Mindless Ones*. It is worth quoting at length to demonstrate that these ideas were noticed by and incorporated into contemporary popular journalism, written and read by fans.

> The problem is that Morrison seems to think of himself as the Mozart to Moore's Salieri, but Moore actually is as good as his reputation, and got there first. Morrison will always be second-place, and this casts a shadow over all his work.

> At any other time, Morrison would be regarded as the greatest writer working in comics. The fact that there is another person with a claim to that title, who works in the same areas, who got there first, and who might be better than him is possibly the single most important thing to keep in mind when reading his work.

140   NEVER-ENDING WATCHMEN

> *Pax Americana* starts and ends with a father being murdered. At the start, the symbolic father, the President. At the end, an actual father.
>
> The whole thing is designed to show that Morrison could do *Watchmen* just as well, and that even if he couldn't *Watchmen* wasn't something that was worth doing anyway. And what's left is something that only works, that only makes sense, with *Watchmen* having a canonical status. It's a work that can never be read by anyone who doesn't already know *Watchmen*, just as singing 'no Beatles, Elvis, or Rolling Stones' only works if your audience know who those people are. Morrison can try to smash the idol that is Moore, but all he does is produce a work that reinforces Moore's status.[89]

The author of that piece, Andrew Hickey, concludes with another poem about parents. This one is from Phillip Larkin, whose 'Church Going', in a neat symmetry, provided Morrison with the title for his first prestige Batman book: 'They fuck you up, your mum and dad. They may not mean to, but they do.' And, Hickey, adds, 'If your mum and dad fuck you up, you have to kill them, of course. At least, you have to kill your dad.'

Pax starts with a man who loves peace so much, he's prepared to kill for it, and a president prepared to die in order to absolve himself for killing his father, decades before. The Morrison of *Pax* was, in public at least, a man who loves *Watchmen* so much that he's prepared to destroy it, who hates it so much that he writes it an elaborate love letter. If this comic enacts the 'death of the author', it is hard to tell which author is being assassinated: perhaps both, in a murder-suicide ('If I Kill You . . . I Die!') or even deicide, the crime that began Morrison's *Final Crisis*. Remember that Barthes wryly describes conventional attitudes towards interpretation in terms of receiving 'the "message" of the Author-God'. Morrison is even more scathing in their account of Moore's authorship:

> The God of *Watchmen* was far from shy. He liked to muscle his way into every panel, every line. He strutted into view with his blue cock on proud display, and everywhere you looked, the Watchmaker was on hand to

INFLUENCE AND INTERPRETATION   141

present his glittering structure for our approval and awe, just as Manhattan erected his own flawless crystal logic machine . . . the God of *Watchmen* could not hide and begged for our attention at every page turn.[90]

Now turn to Bloom on 'Apophrades or The Return of the Dead'. Bloom describes the powerful precursor-poet as 'God the Father', who imposes on those who follow him the 'terrible double bind of two great injunctions: "Be like Me" and "Do not presume to be too like Me"'.[91] Morrison has already acknowledged that Moore is an 'Author-God', and these injunctions also ring true in relation to his influence. Moore, we recall, would 'have liked to have seen more people trying to do something that was as technically complex as *Watchmen*, or as ambitious, but which wasn't strumming the same chords as *Watchmen* had strummed so repetitively'. When he finally unleashed his opinions on Morrison in 2014, they were blisteringly harsh but followed similar lines as his earlier, milder opinion on those who copied his 'chords'. Morrison 'had decided to connect himself with my name by simultaneously borrowing heavily from my work and making studiedly controversial statements about me in comic-book fanzines'.

> What I at first believed to be the actions of an ordinary comic-business career plagiarist came to take on worrying aspects of cargo cultism, as if this funny little man believed that by simply duplicating all of my actions, whether he understood them or not, he could somehow become me and duplicate my success.[92]

We could read *Pax Americana* as Morrison's self-sacrificial apology for those attacks on Moore – it is worth noting, too, that Quitely's layout drawings of President Harley show him bald, like Morrison, and that only the final version disguises him with hair[93] – except that this act of tribute, critique and contrition seems not to have significantly altered Morrison's approach to Moore's archive of earlier work. As one blog notes,[94] while Morrison has ceased to comment in interviews on his supposed rival, the more recent *The Green Lantern* from 2018, despite its definitive title, seems indebted in several details to Moore's throwaway one-off shots from thirty-five years ago, such as the six-page 'Mogo Doesn't Socialise' from May 1985. In that modest strip – 'I just tried to do a better than average *Green Lantern* back up story', he later explained[95] – Moore mentioned 'Leezle Pon, a superintelligent smallpox virus'; Morrison, in their high-profile monthly title, introduces 'Floozle Flem, a super-intelligent all-purpose virus'.[96] Is this tribute, parody, copy, unconscious influence or unlikely coincidence? Perhaps this immensely talented writer simply cannot escape the structures of Moore's 1980s work, whether they respond by swiping from, sniping at or celebrating it; perhaps for some reason Morrison chooses to stay within this strange cage of their own creation.

It would take another creator, from a younger generation, to try to break comics out of *Watchmen*'s prison. Kieron Gillen, born in 1974, was too young to be caught up in a sense of peer rivalry or jealousy around Alan Moore; he was only twelve when *Watchmen* was published (Morrison was twenty-six and, as he tells it, already an established professional)[97] and did not read the book in its entirety until he was twenty-one, waiting in a McDonald's one morning for an American embassy visa.[98] There was no point in trying to compete or catch up with Alan Moore by that point, in 1995. The immediate drama was over; the 'post-*Watchmen*' period was almost ten years old. 'By the time Gillen came to consciousness as a dedicated comics reader, *Watchmen* would have been a given rather than an event', observes academic Eliot Borenstein.[99]

According to Gillen's own origin story,[100] he obtained the visa and then spent a miserable year in the United States with no company except *Watchmen* and some philosophy texts: he read, and reread, *Watchmen*. But while deeply inspired, Gillen didn't try to follow Moore's example immediately. He developed a reputation in games journalism, then wrote the simple gag strip *Save Point* for the PlayStation official magazine in the early 2000s with Jamie McKelvie. Their creative styles developed in tandem through Gillen's first committed comics project, *Phonogram* (2006–16), and then *Young Avengers* for Marvel in 2013, which is around the time that I met him with McKelvie, and he told me his next project was even more explicitly about superheroes

INFLUENCE AND INTERPRETATION   143

and pop music. We were both at the Nine Worlds convention in Summer 2014, where he first gave his speech – fuelled by adrenaline on this occasion, later refined, redelivered and filmed at GOSH comics in London – that aimed to analyse, celebrate and re-evaluate *Watchmen*.

Next came the superhero pop epic, *The Wicked + The Divine* (abbreviated trendily to *WicDiv*), again with McKelvie, which ran from 2014 to 2019; and then in January 2019, Gillen's *Peter Cannon: Thunderbolt* was released. Peter Cannon was, for reasons of copyright and ownership, the only major Charlton character not featured in *Pax Americana*: and for the same reasons, he is the only Charlton character featured by name in Gillen's five-part series, which was published by Dynamite Entertainment. There had been various half-hearted attempts to revamp and re-release Cannon before. He appeared very briefly in the *Crisis*, his face obscured – perhaps fittingly, he was attempting to commit suicide[101] – then in a twelve-issue series from 1992 to 1992 and a ten-issue run from 2012 to 2013. They were all unsuccessful and forgettable. Gillen's is quite different. As Borenstein wryly observes, in Kieron Gillen, 'Peter Cannon finally found his Alan Moore. Well, technically, he'd found an Alan Moore before, but this one was going to let him keep his name.'[102]

Prior to engaging directly with *Watchmen* in *Peter Cannon*, Gillen had – like Morrison – nodded to and pastiched it throughout his previous work. Unlike Morrison, though, these references tend towards direct homage and quotation, rather than wholesale borrowings or critical response. '*Watchmen* was always a big influence on *WicDiv*, and this is me trying to do something as intricate as *Watchmen* across 50 issues.'[103] Gillen's extensive blogs also indicate his deeply embedded debt to the Moore/Gibbons epic. 'I'm the Watchmaker', he says of his own approach to writing in 2018.[104] His awareness of *Watchmen* as a towering predecessor can be painfully self-conscious. Of *The Wicked + The Divine*, he says, 'I like to think our comic is a riposte to Rorschach's I'm Not Trapped In Here With You – You're All Trapped In Here With Me.'[105] He compares a scene in issue 34 to 'the joy of Rorschach searching the wardrobe in the first chapter of *Watchmen*;'[106] a scene in issue 22, where the heroes collectively agree to lie about a murder – 'It was self-defence . . . it's what we were saying it was' – clearly recalls the moral dilemma faced by Nite Owl, Silk Spectre and Rorschach at the end of *Watchmen*.[107] The *Wicked + The Divine* 38 includes the line 'A liferaft of bodies',[108] which Gillen foregrounds in his commentary, knowing his readers will connect it with *Watchmen*'s pirate story.[109] Of issue 26 he muses:

> It's not the first time we've done a Nine Panel Grid in our work, but it's certainly the longest. And if we're doing Nine Panel, it brings it back to *Watchmen*, which means that we should highlight that. Hence, the title altering to THE WATCH, which obviously has all kinds of connotations.[110]

It can hardly be an accident, in this context, that Gillen and McKelvie's rave-hedonism god Dionysius wears a smiley badge.[111]

Gillen's subsequent project, *DIE* (December 2018–September 2021) – which, incidentally, also featured H. P. Lovecraft and his Cthulhu creatures – had a character in the first issue boasting about a new role-playing game: 'This is RPG-*Watchmen*!'[112] Clearly, Kieron Gillen had not escaped the shadow of Alan Moore by the time he wrote Peter Cannon: indeed, he both admitted to and embraced the influence. Unlike Morrison, too – unlike almost everyone else in the contemporary comics industry, including Dave Gibbons – Kieron Gillen was still on good terms with Moore at the time of writing and regarded him as a friend.[113] His talk on *Watchmen* was linked from the official Moore Facebook page, endorsed by Leah Moore; Alan Moore contributed to Gillen's *24 Panels* (2018), a charity volume to support survivors of the Grenfell Tower fire, and has praised Gillen's work in interviews. 'It's something you have trouble actually fitting inside your head' was Gillen's response. 'Moore's my single biggest influence in comics. I have difficulties dealing with the idea that Alan has read any of my stuff, let alone likes it.'[114]

As with every other take on *Watchmen* we've encountered so far, there are many other elements in the mix. Gillen saw *Peter Cannon* not as solely a commentary on *Watchmen* but on *Watchmen*'s legacy, with each chapter reflecting the approach and tropes of a different author: the widescreen cinematics of Warren Ellis (*The Authority* again), the self-reflexive address (or 'weird pop formalist', in Gillen's phrase)[115] of Grant Morrison, the 'cynical violence' of Mark Millar[116] (*The Ultimates, Old Man Logan, Kick-Ass*),[117] the indie autobiography of Eddie Campbell's *Alec*[118] and finally a fully-fledged grappling with *Watchmen* itself, although its presence runs through the entire story. 'Dancing with my biggest influences, in every way, was definitely a reason to do this comic', Gillen stated upfront.[119]

Inevitably there are other factors involved,[120] including Gillen himself: rather than trying to erase his presence, he filters the other creators through his own interpretation as reader/author and in his typically apologetic, self-reflexive way, he admits that too.

> As I progressed, I realized that each issue was (at the core) a riff on a certain strand of post-*Watchmen* superhero comics. With the playful dimension skipping, I was thinking this as the Morrisonian weird-pop issue, and that school [. . .] Except now, when I sit back and look at this beast, I realize that's not really true. It's not Morrison. It's me.[121]

Gillen's decision to make Cannon's servant, Tabu, into his former boyfriend is just one example of his own distinctive – in this case, actively LGBT-allied – approach. ('I've done a lot of queer cast books. Making Peter Cannon and Tabu lovers seems the most obvious Kieron-Gillen-Move imaginable.')[122] The cross-universe sequences are based on very similar dimension hopping in Gillen and McKelvie's *Young Avengers,* with blank frames acting as portals to other worlds.[123] Of course, the Charlton Comics source material plays a part, too. The slogan 'I must. I can. I will' is adapted from Peter Cannon's first appearance in January 1966 – 'I can do it . . . I must do it . . . I will do it!'[124] – and the villain's origin sequence is rendered authentically in the cruder, more luridly colourful style of 1960s comics.

More broadly, the idea of heroes fighting hopelessly against a superior enemy, Gillen acknowledges,[125] echoes Marvel's galactic epic *The Infinity*

Gauntlet, in which Captain America and his colleagues were wiped out, one by one, by Thanos.[126] Of course, this story was itself adapted into the blockbuster *Avengers: Infinity War* (2018), and so the scene in *Peter Cannon* now resonates with that sense of desperate heroism from Marvel's Cinematic Universe. Like *Watchmen* itself, then – like *Pax Americana* – *Peter Cannon* is self-consciously and diversely intertextual, its multiple influences channelled and corralled by its scriptor's personal tastes and concerns.

It would be neat to suggest that Gillen transforms *Watchmen* from a prison to a prism, shining new light through its crystalline structure that splits it into diverse, colourful parts, with each issue representing one of the various strands it inspired. Although comic-book critics have been unable to settle on any title for whatever phase followed the 'Dark Age', one persuasive suggestion was the Prismatic Age. In contrast to the narrow, cynical and perhaps repressively macho grim'n'gritty mood – which, as we saw, was always a simplified version of a more nuanced truth – the early twenty-first century is characterized as a more playful period of analogues, of radiant, rainbow possibilities, where everything goes and all continuities and universes are possible.[127] This 'Age' was already considered to be nearly over by 2012 – 'we are probably at the tail end of it', wrote academic Andrew Kunka that year[128] – but that would put *Peter Cannon* in position to survey it retrospectively, while it was still recent.

Ironically, though, Gillen gently swerved that label: 'I quite like "The Prismatic Age," the idea that it was the age of analogues . . . but for me, it was the Paramilitary Age. All the superheroes were basically in the army.[129] (Recall Morrison on how superheroes 'were assimilated and re-tooled to create post-9/11 Marvel Studios-style "realistic" super-soldiers and champions of the Military/Industrial complex'.) It's this aspect, which he also associated with his own work on *Young Avengers*, that Gillen aimed to capture in the 'Ennis' and 'Millar' chapters of *Peter Cannon*.[130]

'Ellis' is signified by full-page spreads of destruction and ensuing 'bullet violence': Gillen uses the phrase as dialogue and claims that Ellis enjoyed the pastiche.[131] The Morrison influence is confirmed by a character staring

INFLUENCE AND INTERPRETATION 147

out of the page, declaring 'I see you'. Both – like the 'Millar' chapter – retain the same visual style. The 'Campbell' chapters, however, prompt a complete change in aesthetic, adopting a near-perfect simulation of the indie original, with artist Caspar Wijngaard switching to scratchy black and white inks and Hassan Otsmane-Elhaou providing free-floating, often lowercase lettering. ('Only super-heroes can afford to live in color', as Moore's *In Pictopia* put it.)[132] The opening frame makes the debt explicit: 'Peter Cannon would never have forgiven himself . . . for leaving Peter Cannon concussed at the turnpike.' The original, over an almost identical landscape of silhouetted road signs, passing cars and scrubby Letratone grass, reads, 'Danny Grey never really forgave himself . . . for leaving Alec MacGarry asleep at the turnpike.'[133] Moore had wanted to 'take a group of . . . superheroes, and suddenly drop them into a realistic and credible world'.[134] Gillen, through Campbell's kitchen sink style, demonstrates another, perhaps more convincing, way of approaching 'realism', as the *Watchmen* heroes are temporarily recast as normal people in a pub called the Clock.

So what does Gillen do with *Watchmen*? First, he regularly reminds us of its presence as his guiding text, through references both subtle and obvious, textual and visual. The first page is a close-up of a lifeless face with a diagonal streak of blood across the forehead, just above the eye: an explicitly violent 'Millar' take on Moore and Gibbons's smiley badge symbol. Peter Cannon's superhuman crew is made up of Charlton characters through a *Watchmen* filter: a Blue Beetle/Iron Man type in red ant armour, a patriotic American bully boy, a walking weapon called Nucleon with Dr Manhattan speech balloons, a raggedy obsessive called The Test and a woman, Baba Yaga, whom Gillen interestingly admits – as Moore did about Nightshade/Silk Spectre, thirty years earlier – proved to be a disappointing member of the team and the most difficult to develop.[135]

The plot is a never-ending *Watchmen* in both its broad strokes and its specifics. Thunderbolt, an evil alternate universe version of the heroic Peter Cannon, has been pulling Ozymandias's fake alien stunt repeatedly on multiple earths. Some have resulted in short-lived peace; many were destroyed. 'None have truly survived so far, but we are getting closer', Thunderbolt declares. 'But if I stop, I am a villain . . . but when I succeed, I will be a messiah who used a raft of corpses to carry all humanity to paradise.'

There are other near quotations along similar lines. When Pyrophorus, the red ant version of Blue Beetle, begs The Test to 'just . . . say nothing', Test responds, 'Of course, I'm joking. Never compromise. Even in the face of this fucking guy.' Thunderbolt raises his hand in the exact pose of Dr Manhattan obliterating Rorschach, and The Test becomes a blot on the wall. Visually, Gillen evokes the smiley face again through a circular table for a superhero meeting, seen from above and streaked, somewhat implausibly, with raspberry pulp: as he notes, this is effectively a reference to *Watchmen* through his own earlier 'The Watch' for *WicDiv*.[136]

More subtle is the fact that Thunderbolt's speech bubbles have the angular design of Dave Gibbons's 'present-day' *Watchmen* dialogue (as opposed to the Golden and Silver Age periods) and his account of evaluating the Nucleon/ Dr Manhattan of his world: 'I studied his limitations. A power fantasy. Simple, comforting morality. Little else.' Compare Ozymandias on Comedian: 'I studied his limitations: skilful feint; devastating uppercut; little else.'[137] This echo is far less obvious than the regular references to apocalypse being triggered 'thirty-five minutes ago' and works as a subconscious resonance for *Watchmen* readers, testifying to Gillen's fan engagement.

Gillen stresses that *Watchmen*'s successors were misguided in focusing on the comic's content – specifically its violence – over its form. 'Breaking fingers . . . it's one of the worst things to take as a primary influence from *Watchmen*.'

Of all the things *Watchmen* does, it is by far the least interesting, and the worst thing it did to the medium. It's not *Watchmen*'s fault, of course, as you can't help what people take from you . . . but what Moore described as a bad mood he had one year becoming a primary aesthetic for a long time is pretty depressing.[138]

His own take, therefore, plays extensively with *Watchmen*'s page layouts, adopting its nine-panel grid and then having Cannon simulate it in 'real life' through white paint outlines on the surface of his Los Angeles courtyard and an unrolled text banner in the *Watchmen* title font. Cannon's fall into the Campbell universe is structured and drawn very much like Comedian's plunge from his apartment but with white panels for windows[139] – 'that's quite a drop', Thunderbolt comments, quoting *Watchmen*'s first page – and his return is based just as closely on Rorschach's climb to that same broken frame. The title, again in *Watchmen*'s font, is 'For a New Society', taken from the John Cale LP whose track 'Sanities' provided the title 'A Stronger Loving World' for Moore's final chapter.

The stage is set for a crossover conflict of Peter Cannon versus Thunderbolt. What complicates and deepens this superhero combat is the fourth chapter, where, as mentioned, Cannon escapes to the indie-comic dimension of Eddie Campbell's *Alec* stories.[140] Here he encounters a 'real-world' version of himself – of course, this world is just as artificial in its way as *Watchmen*, *Pax* and but the rest of *Peter Cannon*, but it occupies a refreshingly different mode of realist conventions – and the other Charlton characters, devoid of powers and in similar roles. Danny works the night shift, John carries around photographs from New York (Manhattan) and Dr K is a doctor. 'We're trapped in here with each other. So we should make the best of it, hrm?'

Eddie is a comedian of sorts – a comic-book writer whose career fell apart in the early 1990s. 'It's an icy wasteland. Tundra.' These two characters introduce further layers of knowing intertextuality, as Dr K – Rorschach as therapist – looks very much like Alan Moore, and Eddie represents Eddie Campbell as well as Edward 'Comedian' Blake.[141] (Tundra was a comic book company that published Moore's independent work of the period, then folded.) Again, the least developed character is 'Lauren behind the bar. Her mum owns the place, and Lauren's meant to take over. She's been pulling pints since she was fifteen.' The 'only question' about Lauren, even in Gillen's reimagined *Watchmen*, is whether she woke up with Danny or John that morning.

What Peter Cannon takes from this interlude is a sense of humanity and humility. The hero who climbs back up Thunderbolt's skyscraper structures is not the same Cannon that left, two chapters ago, and again, the change is signified in formal terms. His narration retains the loose, handwritten captions from the Campbell universe. The superhero fight is relegated to off-screen action, with playful labels providing a commentary ('It's all kicking off! Amazing martial arts!'), and though Cannon pummels his rival into submission, he stops himself, fist raised, wipes blood symbolically over his eye and declares wearily, 'all of this? You did it thirty years ago.'

Thunderbolt represents, it is clear, the superhero mode that never moved beyond *Watchmen*. Given the chance to escape his prison palace by changing, he ends up imprisoned within the nine-panel grid and exploding from what Cannon calls 'unrelenting deconstruction'. By this term Gillen refers not so much to the theoretical approach associated with Jacques Derrida but, more casually, the process of 'taking apart' the superhero genre that is associated, in journalistic and fan discourse, with *Watchmen*.

The key line of this issue, perhaps of the whole series, is '"Better" is never static . . . it's a direction'. *Watchmen* was 'better' than other comics of its time, but as Moore had always said, it was never meant to provide a template for copies. It was meant to set a bar for others to beat. Gillen neatly incorporates the idea with Peter Cannon's reliance on 'ancient scrolls', a hangover from the original Charlton character. 'There are so many lessons from other scrolls . . . so many scrolls yet to be written.' *Watchmen*, of course, is now an ancient scroll in this context, from (over) thirty years ago, part of the canon. Gillen encourages his contemporaries to build a new 'Cannon', as his hero does, and even resists the temptation of a tribute on his penultimate page, where Cannon looks out at the viewer, Morrison style, and offers, 'I leave it entirely in your hands.' The final page reconsiders. 'That would be too obvious. Too easy. Nothing about "being better" is easy.' He breaks the frame and takes Tabu's hand, and it is the handwritten narration that concludes with 'Let's find out'.

INFLUENCE AND INTERPRETATION

Peter Cannon is intended as a form of therapy for the genre, a gentle polemic for the industry. Unusually, perhaps uniquely among *Watchmen*'s successors and imitators, it honours Moore's own stated intentions.

> The only thing I didn't like about *Watchmen* was the effect it had on the industry . . . what I'd seen *Watchmen* as being was something radically different that was taking lots of chances and trying to do something that had never been done before. So the idea of people doing things that were like *Watchmen* was a contradiction in terms. If it had been like *Watchmen*, then it wouldn't have been like anything else.
>
> *That's* the way to emulate your heroes, not by doing pastiches of their works, and I kind of hoped that after we'd done *Watchmen* people would have looked at it and not said 'Oh wow, we can do super-heroes but more violent and with more sex and swearing.' I really hoped that they would look at it and think, 'Hey, there's interesting story possibilities here; there's storytelling techniques that maybe we could adapt, or change a bit, or come up with some new ones.' We were trying to say that, 'Hey, you know, there's a world of possibilities out there. *Watchmen* is just us exploring one of those possibilities.' That there's a world of possibilities and everybody should explore their own.[142]

Gillen made an honest, heartfelt effort to break the superhero genre out of the thirty-year-old prison that *Watchmen* had unintentionally established. It didn't work, of course.

5

Prequels, sequels, supplements and remixes
The *Watchmen* multiverse

Fredric Jameson was clear about the distinction between parody and pastiche. Parody, flourishing during modernism when it could be used to mock the distinctive tropes of high stylists like D. H. Lawrence, William Faulkner and Gustav Mahler, had found itself 'without a vocation' during the postmodernism of the late twentieth century. There was, Jameson claimed, no longer any sense that 'alongside the abnormal tongue you have momentarily borrowed, some healthy linguistic normality still exists'.[1] To turn back to superhero comics, this argument implies that the dense, rich, sometimes overripe purple prose of Alan Moore's 1980s work could not be satirized, because there was no longer a linguistic norm against which it could be contrasted. In simple terms, you can't mock someone's abnormal habits if everyone has abnormal habits; and it was even more difficult in Moore's case, because so many comic-book writers had adopted his approach that his authorial tics and techniques had effectively become the norm.

To an extent, as we've seen, this is true. Moore's wordy prose of the *Swamp Thing*, *Miracleman* and *Watchmen* era for years became such a dominant trend within 'mature', 'dark' and 'sophisticated' superhero comics that it was absorbed and emulated as standard practice. The lines 'I'm a Pralah-beast, from the Mountains of Passion! I'm a Sho'keer, from the Valley of Sand' from Giffen's *Martian Manhunter* or 'the chill spring wind that blows this day blows ill indeed – carrying only the plaintive wail of congregating fire engines and the acrid smell of smoke and fugitive sparks' from Len Wein's *Blue Beetle* are not intended as mockery of Moore, or even as explicit tribute; rather, they serve as pastiche, 'a neutral practice' without 'ulterior motives'. They are blank imitation, 'the wearing of a linguistic mask'.[2] The approach was, no doubt, partly a pragmatic choice by the writers and their editors: when Moore was flavour of the month, it made commercial sense to adapt to popular tastes.

Few writers abandoned their individual style entirely to fit this new mood. Miller, of course, had already carved out a space of his own, with a hard-boiled, staccato storytelling voice. Chaykin established his own even brasher, flashier brand, both more shocking and more superficial than Miller's, and O'Neil retained the gritty, neo-noir, 'darknight detective' narration he'd pioneered in the early 1970s. Giffen's revamped *Martian Manhunter* hinted, under the lyrical captions, at the soap opera and sitcom vibe of *Justice League*. Morrison, even when deliberately trying to pass as a new Alan Moore, could never hide a playfully subversive attitude, and John Smith, a young writer trying quite openly to sell his work on the back of *Watchmen*, nevertheless produced something quite different in *New Statesmen*. However, it is fair to suggest that Moore's characteristic approach to 1980s comics – mixed in with some of Miller's – became an established norm, to the extent that the various writers adopting this style were not parodying it but rather writing within the conventions of the dominant mode.

Yet parody, *contra* Jameson, was still possible within postmodernism: look at Moore's own affectionately savage satire of Miller's *Daredevil*, in *Dourdevil* from 1983. Racist, ableist and crude by today's standards, this short skit signals its satirical nature through gross exaggeration of Miller's tough-guy mannerisms.

PREQUELS, SEQUELS, SUPPLEMENTS AND REMIXES 155

What are you, some sorta retard? Don't make me laugh! Noo Yawk is grim, and gritty, and realistic. There are big black buildings with little white squares on, and water towers, and manholes and lots of other gritty stuff. And giant black men. Hundreds of giant black men in vests and woollen hats carrying large radios.[3]

What distinguishes this from pastiche is the self-conscious absurdity and excess, in the linguistic affectations ('Noo Yawk'), the scenario ('hundreds of giant black men') and the wry reflection on the comic-book convention whereby skyscrapers are regularly depicted as 'big black buildings with little white squares on' (Mike Collins's artwork delivers an extra punchline by drawing the skyscrapers just as Moore describes them). In his first panel, the blind superhero Dourdevil lands on a dead dog next to an overflowing, littered gutter, near a group of sex workers – tropes that were, ironically, toned down a little in Rorschach's journal – and declares that the 'fur rug', perfume and music from a nearby boom box must mean he's in Hugh Hefner's Playboy Mansion.[4] It's as unsubtle as *Mad Magazine* and clearly quite different from, say, the captions in Mike Baron's 1987 *The Flash,* which slip neutrally into an emulation of Miller's style: 'Grab gun. Jam on safety. Sickening sound. The pain throbs like a turbine.'

In the 1980s, then, it was still possible to make a clear distinction between parody and pastiche: and indeed, Jameson's article on the subject was first published in 1988, the year after Baron's *Flash.*[5] But as the decades passed, that line became more difficult to draw. What do we make of Morrison's *Pax Americana,* expressly a tribute ('I . . . want to honour *Watchmen'*) with some scenes that seem to neutrally pastiche aspects of Moore's original and others that relentlessly mock it? The captions that ploddingly comment on every action – 'We've turned a corner', 'One door closes . . . another opens' – are not devoid of ulterior motive; they are send-ups of one of Moore's most celebrated storytelling devices.

And if *Mad* was once a reliable measure of satire, turn to 'Botchmen', the magazine's parody of *Watchmen* from February 2009.[6] In another neat irony, remember that Kurtzman and Wood's satire *Superduperman,* in *Mad* number 4, 1953, was a significant influence on Moore and Gibbons's approach, inspiring *Watchmen*'s rich background details and 'sight dramatics'. That circle of influence loops back here to complete a circuit, but the incidental details in the *Mad* satire are mild, throwaway jokes like a gross-out image of Laurie sneezing violently, Dr Manhattan wearing smiley boxer shorts and Rorschach's mask displaying the logo from Moore's *V for Vendetta.*

The laughs here are thin and the parody uncertain. Some of the jokes gesture towards a vague sense of adolescent rudeness: Rorschach becomes 'Wackjob', presumably because it kind of rhymes and has a schoolyard irreverence about it, while 'Ozcargrouchus' for Ozymandias might raise a giggle in kindergarten. The opening image of Rorschach holding a whoopee cushion and laughing at its flatulent noise ('Still a classic')[7] offers an almost apologetic, self-conscious clownishness, as if recognizing both the magazine's obligatory role as cultural jester and the half-hearted quality of its gags.

The creeping sense that this comic, billed as a parody, is only making a token effort at humour is compounded by its decision to rename Comedian as 'Funnyman' – more a synonym than a satire, surely – and the enigmatic title, in *Watchmen*'s font: 'CALL IT, FRIENDO'. The only apparent connection is to dialogue from Joel and Ethan Coen's movie *No Country for Old Men* (2007) in which psychopathic hitman Anton Chigurh (Javier Bardem) asks a gas station proprietor, 'What business is it of yours where I'm from, friendo?' and then subjects him to a coin toss for his life: 'Call it.' Behind the gas station counter, during this scene, is a prominently displayed package of smiley-face stickers.

Rather than light parody, this is a darkly obscure cultural echo – the type that we might find in *Watchmen* itself – and by the penultimate scene, *Mad*'s approach has abandoned its weak puns and slapstick for a more profound commentary. In the prison cell, one of Big Figure's gangster henchmen starts to question his own role in the text. 'There's always a direct, concomitant parallelism on each page of this book. The last page featured an owl mask. What does a prison riot have to do with owls?'[8]

PREQUELS, SEQUELS, SUPPLEMENTS AND REMIXES 157

Big Figure agrees, musing, 'How about this? The owl was considered an omen of death in many cultures, including Mayan and Aztec.'

'That's a little esoteric, don't you think?' responds the thug, and the two perps continue to debate the symbolic meaning of the mask – which they could only be aware of if they also somehow 'read' the previous page, featuring Dan and Laurie's costumed love scene – worried that 'the whole sequence falls apart' if they don't puzzle out the reference. Could it be a hint towards the goddess Athena and the fact that the whole narrative is a quest? 'But now you're conflating larger thematic concerns with specific visual cues', the sidekick points out. 'Maybe we're overthinking this.'[9]

Although the final page also squeezes in another schoolboy joke, as Manhattan announces that the cold of Antarctica will have a 'shrinking' effect on his anatomy, the author's interest seems to lie more in Rorschach's claim that 'our story is structurally complex. Mature artistic statement.' The result is a fascinating text that resists easy categorization: while it gently satirizes Moore's heavy-handed metaphors, there is also a distinct sense of admiring homage.

That author is Desmond Devlin, not a comic-book writer himself but a *Mad* stalwart, responsible for the magazine's *Harry Potter* and *Lord of the Rings* satires. The artists, however, come direct from comics, rather than *Mad*'s usual stable of cartoonists. Dave Gibbons and John Higgins provided a special Comic Con cover, and Glenn Fabry, a *2000AD* regular during *Watchmen*'s original publication, was assigned to interior art.[10] While *Mad*'s regular satires rely on caricature, Fabry's take on Gibbons – unsurprisingly, given that the two were contemporaries and collaborators – is religiously faithful and respectful, reproducing the composition and detail of key panels and the likeness of characters without distortion or exaggeration. Even the speech balloons have Gibbons's authentically angular structure. While there are, of course, departures from the original – Rorschach's mask displays a semicolon in one frame and exclamation mark in the next – they come across more as artistic experiment than fun at Gibbons's expense.

One frame, where Manhattan takes apart and examines the contents of a sandwich,[11] is remarkably similar to the image of Captain Atom disassembling his dog in *Pax Americana*, which was published several years after this comic: coincidence, no doubt, unless Morrison read *Mad*, but as we saw in the previous chapter, the increasingly complex network of the *Watchmen* matrix lends itself to this kind of speculative, looping logic of influence. Indeed, more than anything – certainly more than the standard *Mad* satire – 'Botchmen' reads like *Watchmen* as it might have taken place in a different parallel world, very much along the lines of *Pax Americana*, which takes place in DC's Earth 4, and Gillen's universe-hopping *Peter Cannon*.[12] At times, Fabry's version even, arguably, improves on the original; his Silk Spectre's body language and facial expressions are far more fluid and mobile than Gibbons's rather static female figures.

So while parody still exists, it is perhaps no longer as clearly distinguished from pastiche as it was in the 1980s; and 'Botchmen' is certainly not a clean-cut example of the form. Parody, surely, holds up a distorting mirror to the original for laughs; despite its crude title and the handful of juvenile jokes, 'Botchmen' gives us a surprisingly sophisticated and self-aware reflection. Its ambivalently satirical mirror offers a portal to a 'what-if' dimension, a *Watchmen* variation.

Although its final twist is that Ozymandias has sold the movie rights to Hollywood and produced tacky merchandise of his fellow crimefighters,[13] prompting Dan, Laurie and Rorschach to beg him 'zap me first!' in a series of mercy killings,[14] 'Botchmen' was never intended as a parody of Snyder's film. Originally published in 2009, it was relaunched on *Mad*'s website in 2012 in response to the announcement that DC was 'expanding on the classic series *Watchmen* with seven inter-connected prequel mini-series. Some of the industry's biggest names are involved, yet one name was conspicuously absent — ours!'

That prequel miniseries was *Before Watchmen* (2012). It was followed by a sequel, *Doomsday Clock* (2017–19), which was followed in turn by the entirely unrelated HBO TV series *Watchmen* (2019) and a separate comic-book limited series, *Rorschach* (2020). The 2010s were a remarkable decade in terms of the sudden expansion of a fictional world constructed in the mid-1980s: after a quarter of a century's relative stasis, that world went supernova. All at once, within a short space of time, Moore and Gibbons's self-sufficient, self-contained original story was given not just a new official history but also three new equally official (and often incompatible) futures.

This chapter examines those texts, alongside two previous expansions in other media: *The End Is Nigh*, the video game adaptation that accompanied Snyder's film (2009), and a far earlier role-playing game supplement from 1987, which has the rare distinction of being the one spin-off approved by Alan Moore. Both are prequels. Neither has any relationship to the other.

This is not a series of reviews, weighing up each story one by one and ranking their relative creative success. Rather, it critically examines these six texts – three comic-book series, one TV show, an RPG module and a video game – in terms of their approach to the 1986 *Watchmen*: what they do with it and what this means. How do these supplements insert themselves into and attach themselves to the original? How do they reassure audiences of their engagement with the *Watchmen* world and craft themselves as plausible continuations of the universe Moore and Gibbons created, despite (in most cases) Moore's express disapproval?

How do these various spin-offs, across multiple media, extrapolate from that original text? What unfinished or unresolved aspects of *Watchmen* do they pry open and draw out in order to tell their own new stories? And how, in doing so, do these spin-off narratives contradict each other – even contradict themselves – constructing clashing versions of the characters' histories and futures that cannot be reconciled into a single coherent whole? Finally, what does it say about contemporary storytelling, and, more broadly, about meaning-making, interpretation and truth in these early decades of the twenty-first century, that reading *Watchmen* has become a process of navigating between incompatible alternatives, with each reader choosing their own route from a range of available options?

Sequels, both authorized and unauthorized, are nothing new. As far back as 1614, Miguel de Cervantes was incensed by the publication of a second part to his *Don Quixote,* while he was in the middle of writing the sequel himself. In 1741, Henry Fielding published *Shamela,* a parody of Samuel Richardson's 1740 novel *Pamela* and a celebrated work in its own right. There were numerous unofficial follow-ups to Lewis Carroll's *Alice's Adventures in Wonderland* (1865) and over a dozen official continuations of *The Wonderful Wizard of Oz* (1900) by L. Frank Baum. Sequels to Jane Austen's novels began with the author's own playful musings to entertain her family but had expanded into a subgenre of their own by the 1990s, including Joan Aiken's *Mansfield Revisited* (1984) and *Jane Fairfax* (1990) and Emma Tennant's *Pemberley* (1993) and *Emma in Love* (1996). Lubomír Doležel observes that Daniel Defoe's *Robinson Crusoe* (1719) led to a 'never-ending series of "Robinsonades"', of which J. M. Coetzee's *Foe* (1986) is an outstanding example.[15] Following that linguistic model, and prompted by Virgil's epic poem *The Aeneid,* we might call *Watchmen* sequels 'Watchmaeneids'.

Prequels are a more recent phenomenon, often offering a different perspective and casting villains in a more sympathetic light: Jean Rhys's *Wide Sargasso Sea* (1966) revisits Jane Eyre from a postcolonial perspective, Gregory Maguire's *Wicked* (1995) explores the backstory to *The Wizard of Oz,* and John Updike focuses on the relationship between Hamlet's parents in *Gertrude and Claudius* (2000). In cinema, of course, we are now accustomed to official prequels by, or involving, the original author, such as George Lucas's trilogy revealing the origin of Darth Vader (1999–2005) and J. K. Rowling's *Fantastic Beasts* series (2016–22), set prior to *Harry Potter.*

'Yet more recent', adds Armelle Parey in an essay from 2019,

and possibly still a neologism, is the word 'coquel', which like 'prequel' is adapted from 'sequel' with a prefix that indicates its temporal relation to the plot of the source: coquels evoke events that are simultaneous with the source text. Unlike prequels and sequels that take up pre-existing

PREQUELS, SEQUELS, SUPPLEMENTS AND REMIXES   161

protagonists to take them beyond the time frame of a finished text, coquels tend to remain within the time frame of the source text but focus on more or less secondary characters, and their side or 'version' of the story.[16]

Parey includes in this group 'companion novels' such as Carol Shields's *Small Ceremonies* (1976) and *The Box Garden* (1977), later published together as *Duet* (2003): 'There is no sense of this second book being a sequel to the first,' Shields remarked, 'but a number of threads connect them.'[17] Phillip Pullman, in turn, categorized *The Book of Dust* (2017, 2019) as an 'equel' to *His Dark Materials*: 'it's a different story, but there are settings that readers of *His Dark Materials* will recognise, and characters they've met before.'[18] Technically, as *Watchmen* spans such a broad time frame, the role-playing adventures in *The Watchmen Companion,* the 1970s-set video game *The End Is Nigh* and much of *Before Watchmen* fall within its chronology, making these additions 'coquels' or 'equels' as much as prequels (*Before Watchmen: Dr Manhattan* concludes after Jon Osterman has left earth, taking it beyond the end of *Watchmen* and perhaps qualifying its final pages as a sequel).[19]

However, Parey makes a further distinction between 'autographic expansions' by the original author and 'allographic' work by different authors 'that return to a closed narrative world and time of a classic text and give a different slant on already told events'. She cites Geraldine Brooks's *March* (2005), which revisits Alcott's *Little Women* from the perspective of the girls' father, and Jo Baker's *Longbourn* (2013) – Austen's *Pride and Prejudice* from the point of view of the servants – and we might also consider Tom Stoppard's play *Rosencrantz and Guildenstern Are Dead* (1966), a retelling of *Hamlet* as seen by two minor characters. Of course, a great deal of unofficial fan fiction falls into this category.

When prising open a closed world by a different author, the new writer faces many challenges, such as balancing novelty with consistency, finding new territory while respecting the established landscape, and providing a new angle while, ideally, not factually contradicting the original.[20] As we'll see, many of *Watchmen*'s spin-offs fall short in this regard.

Another key challenge involves adopting the voice of the original author. As P. D. James wrote of her *Pride and Prejudice* crime mystery, *Death Comes to Pemberley* (2011):

I read all Jane Austen's novels at least once a year and the style has become so much of my inner voice that I thought I could write English which could be contemporary with Jane Austen without slavishly copying her. To get the language right was the greatest challenge of the book.[21]

The same applies, inevitably, to expansions of *Watchmen*'s world. We have seen that Alan Moore's writing in *Watchmen* constituted a distinctive style of its own; on one level, the poetic rhythms and esoteric imagery of Rorschach's journal and Dr Manhattan's cosmic narration, and on another, the tropes and tricks like overlapping, juxtaposed captions and images, visual echoes across scene transitions elaborate camera movements and the sight dramatics hidden in the crowded mise en scène. These details were of course articulated visually by Gibbons, who has his own distinct style: clean, clear and measured, with a draftsman's precision and consistency.

The *Watchmen* role-playing game source book and supplements were written by Ray Winninger and Daniel Greenberg in the late 1980s and enabled fans to explore Moore and Gibbons's world through the pre-existing *DC Heroes* system. Winninger explains in an introduction to *The Watchmen Companion* collection that although he pitched the ideas, Moore discussed and approved them during lengthy transatlantic calls.

I mine the comics and scripts for background details and pitch stories fleshing them out. What sparked off the police riots in the 1970s? What is Dr Manhattan doing in that government laboratory? What is the connection between the second generation of masked heroes and five-term president Richard Nixon? We like that last one and gradually hash it out. Alan is a *fearsome* brainstormer. The ideas *pour* out of him.[22]

PREQUELS, SEQUELS, SUPPLEMENTS AND REMIXES

The prose descriptions and dialogue in the role-playing game supplements make little attempt to mimic Moore's style – in contrast to many of the superhero comics published at the same time – but they retain a convincing sense of character. Captain Metropolis, opening a Crimebusters session, is fussy and formal – 'It's unfortunate that we are not meeting under more cheerful circumstances . . . let's share information and resources on this matter' – and the guidelines for players advise that 'Rorschach . . . will probably reluctantly agree' while 'The Comedian . . . might be obnoxious'.[23] These suggestions clearly extrapolate from what we see of the Crimebusters' abortive meeting in *Watchmen* chapter 2, where Captain Metropolis gives an awkward, overeager speech interrupted by Comedian's loud belches and 'bullshit'.[24] Daniel Greenberg's further instruction to the players that 'a distant bell tower ominously toils the hour'[25] captures Moore's sense of drama without aping his ornate language.

The unique aura of authenticity that surrounds the game is, in fact, not due so much to Moore's background support as to Dave Gibbons's direct involvement: he provides multiple illustrations, including new portraits of main and minor characters. The *Watchmen Sourcebook* reproduces extracts from *Under the Hood*, Moore's fictional autobiography of Hollis 'Nite Owl' Mason, alongside scraps, memos and letters written by Daniel Greenberg that fill in further gaps of the *Watchmen* universe: a Harlem newspaper piece about Hooded Justice's 'racist beliefs and attitudes',[26] a screenplay for a cheaply titillating Sally Jupiter movie, *Law in Its Lingerie*,[27] and exchanges between bank managers deciding Dollar Bill's superhero name (the possibilities include both Captain Americaman and The Mutilator, presumably a veiled comment on the 1980s superhero shift towards grim grittiness).[28] The format gives Winninger's creative ideas the same status and authority as Moore's.

This was the only *Watchmen* spin-off to benefit from Moore's collaboration and approval. Subsequent spin-offs had to work harder, and in different ways, to integrate themselves with the world of the original *Watchmen*.

The *End Is Nigh* video game takes an interesting approach to bridging the gap between its glossy graphics – CGI likenesses of Rorschach and Nite Owl, clearly based on the 2009 movie rather than the 1986 comic – and the original text. Its transitional cut scenes, in a fascinating strategy, resemble the motion comic in their simple movement, offer a crude emulation of Gibbons's style and borrow John Higgins's colour schemes (lots of garish orange and purples) but are, again, based on the movie's costume designs. These sequences – oddly reminiscent, too, of *Saturday Morning Watchmen* – mediate between a video game based on a movie through an animated cartoon based on a comic. The narration, including extracts from Rorschach's journal, strains for Moore's style, while Patrick Wilson and Jackie Earl Haley voice their characters from Snyder's film. The setting, however, is 1972, just before what would, in our universe, be Watergate.

'Raining again tonight', Rorschach narrates. 'Raining a lot lately. Like Heaven is trying hard to wash away all of New York's sins. Hn. Waste of time. Steel wool couldn't scour clean this city's soul.' 'Sing Sing, dead ahead!' announces Nite Owl, as the crimefighting duo approach a prison riot. 'Black as Moloch's heart down there', Rorschach growls in response. The pastiche of Moore's dialogue is, like the art style, not especially sophisticated.[29]

Moore had described Snyder's film as 'more regurgitated worms'. His view of *Before Watchmen*, the prequel series that followed three years later in 2012, was simpler and sadder. 'I don't want money. I want this not to happen.'[30] *Before Watchmen* had Dave Gibbons's support but not his active involvement; John Higgins provided two pages of art each issue for a pirate story, *The Crimson Corsair*, written by *Watchmen* editor Len Wein. Otherwise, the creators primarily belonged to a younger, post-*Watchmen* generation: Darwyn Cooke's first professional work was published in October 1985, Adam Hughes's in June 1987, Amanda Conner's in November 1988 and Jae Lee's in 1991). None of these artists make any attempt to adapt their own trademark styles to emulate Gibbons's original. They each have an instantly recognizable approach – Cooke's nostalgic, retro elegance, Conner's clean, cartoony expressivity, Hughes's cheesecake charm and Lee's delicate, acrobatic compositions – and Moore and

PREQUELS, SEQUELS, SUPPLEMENTS AND REMIXES 165

Gibbons's characters are transformed through their various lenses, even when specific images from *Watchmen* are directly adapted and redrawn.[31]

Before Watchmen includes nine-panel grids interspersed with wildly different layouts, nods towards juxtaposition of caption and image,[32] some inconsistent use of *Watchmen*'s block-letter chapter titles and end quotations,[33] some fixed-camera technique[34] and the occasional sequence based on visual echoes[35] but without any of the original comic's precise, systematic commitment to its formal conventions. This is a kaleidoscope approach, a many-voiced mosaic anthology that, even within its own pages, presents multiple visions of the same scene: the first Crimebusters meeting, for instance, recurs several times across the stories, rendered in a wide range of styles and from different perspectives. The project's attitude towards Moore and Gibbons is neatly conveyed in its opening pages, where Cooke provides eight painstaking panels of arching or circular images – a cradle, a tunnel, a sun, cogs, a puddle, a clock – matched with carefully constructed, pseudo-intellectual captions, before faltering and giving up.

'You hope that over time . . . over time . . . this is terrible.' And pulling back from the clock on the mantlepiece, we realize Hollis Mason is writing the epilogue to *Under the Hood*. He addresses his pet dog: 'I'll just have to face facts, girl. I'm no Tolstoy. Going for a deep, philosophical ending here isn't going to work. I guess we'll just have to stick to being ourselves, huh?'[36] Cooke deals with the anxiety of influence through a self-deprecating admission – Hollis isn't Tolstoy, Cooke isn't Moore – which reframes this failure as a down-to-earth, homespun directness and celebrates a different kind of 'authenticity'.[37]

Critical reaction to *Before Watchmen* was mixed, but it was successful enough to justify a sequel. Alan Moore, understandably, was not impressed. In January 2018, one month after the launch of *Doomsday Clock*, he declared that 'anybody who has anything to do with any of these shitty *Watchmen* travesties, even as a member of the audience, will be dragged screaming to hell by their nipples. Peace out.'[38]

Written by Geoff Johns and illustrated by Gary Frank, *Doomsday Clock* imitates and emulates *Watchmen* in almost every respect, from its exterior design to its formal conventions. Its logo runs in yellow capitals up the page; its monthly covers focus on a close detail, which is then repeated in the first panel of each chapter. Its pages are structured largely around the nine-panel grid preferred by Moore and Gibbons, with bold black titles that are revealed, at the end of each chapter, to be drawn from lengthier quotations; the back cover shows a clock ticking closer to midnight, with blood slowly dripping down the page. Each issue contains supporting material – newspaper clippings, menus, movie magazines and government documents – in the *Watchmen* mode. Gary Frank's art, though more finnicky than Gibbons's in its linework and benefitting from rich, smooth computer colouring techniques that were unavailable to John Higgins in 1986, is far closer to the original *Watchmen* than any of the more idiosyncratic approaches in *Before Watchmen*.[39] Even the lettering emulates Gibbons's hand-drawn style: compare in particular the anguished exclamations such as 'Aaauuuu!'[40] and 'Yiiaaaaagh!'[41] in both comics, with the pained cries wobbling inside their speech balloons.

Doomsday Clock opens with Rorschach's journal, that quirky handwritten font on the familiar ripped, yellowing paper, and gradually pulls back in a crane shot, echoing *Watchmen*'s page 1, from a sign proclaiming 'The End Is Here' (rather than 'The End Is Nigh') and away from a protesting crowd. The captions muse darkly, recalling Rorschach's 'dog carcass in alley' speech that opens *Watchmen*: 'We slit open the world's belly. Secrets came spilling out. An intestine full of truth and shit strangled us. Soon the bugs will be all that's left. And the cockroaches will go to war with the maggots, fighting over the scraps of the moderates.'[42] As the diary reveals, it is November 1992. Walter Kovacs has been dead for seven years, and a different man now wears the mask, adopting his trenchcoat, his hat and his shorthand style.

Rorschach's voice is, as we saw with the *The End Is Nigh* video game, one of the most obvious features to incorporate into a new *Watchmen* narrative, in order to convince readers (or viewers, or players) that they are re-entering

PREQUELS, SEQUELS, SUPPLEMENTS AND REMIXES

Moore and Gibbons's narrative world. *Before Watchmen*, inevitably, also attempts this narration, with typewritten journal entries from July 1977 – 'Times Square. Neon romanticizes its filth. Light of day makes its darkness worse. More brazen, arrogant. Hopeless' – and Geoff Johns clearly stakes a great deal on capturing that psychotic street poetry on the opening page of *Doomsday Clock*. Whether he convinces with his new Rorschach's tone and vocabulary is open to question, but his intention is clear. This is meant not as a creative departure – *Watchmen* seen through the prism of other styles and interpretations – or a copy of the original, but a continuation. Like the new Rorschach, Johns is taking on his predecessor's mantle, wearing the mask, doing the voice. As the back cover promises, or threatens, 'Nothing Ever Really Ends.'

Chapter 1 closes with a slow pull back from a man and woman talking. The sequence transitions over eight panels from a close-up of his expression to a very long shot of the two of them kneeling face to face. The parallel with *Watchmen*'s first issue, which pulls back from the smiley badge to an aerial view of Dan and Laurie on a restaurant rooftop, is again obvious and intentional. In both examples, the final line carries a poignant reflection, a conversation killer to conclude the chapter.

Watchmen:
'There don't seem to be many laughs around these days.'
'Well, what do you expect? The Comedian is dead.'

Doomsday Clock:
'I can't remember the last time you had a nightmare.'
'I don't think I've ever had one.'

Moore and Gibbons round up their first issue with a line from Bob Dylan; Johns and Frank use a quotation from Horace Smith's 'Ozymandias', a poem written in competition with Shelley's 'Ozymandias', published slightly later and overshadowed by the verse that gives Moore his penultimate chapter title,

'Look On My Works, Ye Mighty'. Is this an act of careful humility like Darwyn Cooke's – Johns inviting the comparison and accepting that he is the lesser poet – or is there arrogance even in the presumption that he could compete with Moore on the same territory?[43]

The same territory, or almost. Johns, in contrast to Moore, is deeply embedded within the DC/Warner entertainment complex, best known as a comic-book writer for *The Flash* and *Green Lantern* titles and equally involved in DC's broader film and television productions. Johns works comfortably within DC's mainstream continuity, and *Doomsday Clock*'s agenda – prompted by commercial imperatives as much as creative curiosity – is to merge *Watchmen*'s successful but separate storyworld with that broader universe.[44] The couple whose conversation closes chapter 1 are Clark Kent and Lois Lane, and the climax to the series is a face-off between Superman and Dr Manhattan.

The two remaining series, further expanding what *Watchmen* meant in 2019 and 2020, are quite different from those preceding them and indeed from each other. Damon Lindelof, showrunner of HBO's 2019 TV show – simply called *Watchmen* and billed as a 'remix' rather than a sequel – had previously described the original as 'the greatest piece of popular fiction ever produced'; his praise appears on the 2005 reprint of the graphic novel, where Lindelof is cited as co-creator of *Lost* (ABC, 2004–10), itself influenced by *Watchmen* in its non-linear storytelling, its approach to time and its character-focused flashback episodes.[45]

Moore's name is not included in the show's credits, though Dave Gibbons – who had by this point fallen out irreparably with Moore – lent it credibility through public gestures of support such as drawing Lindelof's protagonist Sister Night in his own style for the HBO Twitter account.[46]

Lindelof defended his project through the inventive claim that going against Moore's wishes was, in fact, very much in the spirit of 1980s Alan Moore. As such, he openly recognizes the relationship with a symbolic 'father' that underpins Bloom's theories about literary influence, and foregrounds the dynamic of rebellion and tribute that seems to shape so many of these recent

PREQUELS, SEQUELS, SUPPLEMENTS AND REMIXES

approaches to *Watchmen* as younger creators, indebted to Moore, now find themselves competing with or critiquing him.

> Alan Moore is a genius, in my opinion, the greatest writer in the comic medium and maybe the greatest writer of all time. He's made it very clear that he doesn't want to have any association or affiliation with *Watchmen* ongoing and that we not use his name to get people to watch it, which I want to respect. As someone whose entire identity is based around a very complicated relationship with my dad, who I constantly need to prove myself to and never will, Alan Moore is now that surrogate . . . I do feel like the spirit of Alan Moore is a punk rock spirit, a rebellious spirit, and that if you would tell Alan Moore, a teenage Moore in '85 or '86, 'You're not allowed to do this because Superman's creator or Swamp Thing's creator doesn't want you to do it', he would say, 'Fuck you, I'm doing it anyway.' So I'm channelling the spirit of Alan Moore to tell Alan Moore, 'Fuck you, I'm doing it anyway.'[47]

Set thirty-four years after the events of *Watchmen*, Lindelof's series lacks direct references to the original comic book to lend it authority – it cannot follow Snyder's example and reproduce specific panels to reassure fans of its fidelity – but conversely, its unshackling from the original gives it greater freedom to explore Moore's world. It adapts the comic book's storytelling techniques inventively, rather than trying to treat *Watchmen* as a storyboard and translate its panels directly into consecutive shots, as Snyder did.

The relationship between *Watchmen* and *Watchmen*, Snyder's 2009 movie and Lindelof's 2019 TV series, is initially ambiguous. On one level, as live action filmed representations of actors wearing costumes, they inevitably resemble each other more than they do the various comics, motion comics or video game. Lindelof even seems to give a nod to Snyder in his use of title credits.[48] Rather than Moore and Gibbons's black capitals against white, which were used so distinctively in *Peter Cannon* and *Doomsday Clock* to signify the *Watchmen* mode, Lindelof uses yellow text that acquires a CGI solidity within the scene, like the floating names that make up the opening credits of Snyder's film.[49]

However, the show soon introduces a rain of tiny squids, immediately separating its new continuity from that of Snyder's *Watchmen*, where Ozymandias used an energy device (with the acronym S.Q.U.I.D.) rather than an alien creation.[50] From this scene onwards *Watchmen* (2019) is not, clearly, a sequel to *Watchmen* (2009). How, then, does it establish its connection to *Watchmen* (1986)?

The opening scene throws the viewer into a black and white, silent movie depicting the adventures of Bass Reeves, a heroic Black deputy within the Western genre. Then, as it moves outside the cinema to the exterior of Tulsa, 1921 and the racist massacre on 'Black Wall Street', the tone shifts to sepia, signifying a sense of 'pastness'. This device is entirely absent from Moore and Gibbons's *Watchmen*, which uses the same colour scheme for each decade of its story; however, the technique is used in Moore and Bolland's *Killing Joke*, which switches to desaturated black and white for its flashbacks.[51]

Like *Watchmen*, *The Killing Joke* uses matches between similar images to bridge scene transitions, particularly when they move backwards and forwards in time. Chapter 2 of *Watchmen*, for instance, zooms in on Adrian Veidt's face at Blake's funeral and then match cuts smoothly to Veidt in close-up, seen from an identical angle, at the first Crimebusters meeting. Lindelof does the same in an early scene, dissolving from young Will Reeves walking down a dirt track in 1921 to car headlights approaching the camera down the same (or a very similar) road in 2019. These transitions become showier as the series progresses: in episode 4, a view through a telescope becomes a long shot of the moon, and in episode 7, a close-up of eyes dissolves to an image of stained-glass windows. Film historian David Bordwell, in an extended online essay, details various further examples of Lindelof's visual 'hooks', including 'graphic matches' (Laurie's face dissolves to the similar composition of a masked bust) and 'category matches' (a pocket watch cuts to a clock face), all of which echo similar moments in the original *Watchmen*.[52]

An early example comes in the first episode, where Lindelof cuts from a TV aerial shot of Dr Manhattan on Mars, standing in a circular crater and

PREQUELS, SEQUELS, SUPPLEMENTS AND REMIXES

destroying one of his palatial follies, to overhead (and under-the-table) shots of circular plates during Angela Abar's cooking demonstration, as she transfers (circular) yolks and explains the importance of separating them from the egg whites. Her voice-over cleverly comments on the activity in hand, on Manhattan's demolition of his castle and more broadly on the racial tensions that already inform the series: 'if we don't have walls, it all comes tumbling down. Now, those walls are strong, but they won't stay that way if just even a little bit of yolk gets mixed in with the whites. So, that's why we gotta separate them.' Angela smears the yolks together, and they form a smiley face.[53]

More subtly, during the squid shower, Lindelof offers an aerial angle, the camera looking down from directly above at Angela's car and pulling slowly back from the highway with its stalled traffic: an echo of the celebrated crane shots that open and close *Watchmen* chapter 1. The recurring visual and linguistic motifs from Moore and Gibbons's original are nodded to, in turn, through the bleeding cut over Will Reeves's right eye, the note he carries ('WATCH OVER THIS BOY') and an advertising blimp's announcement that 'The clock is ticking . . . tomorrow night, the countdown ends'. Perhaps most cleverly, Lindelof captures Moore's approach to comic-book pacing – the technique of starting each new scene at the top of a new page – in the timing of his own opening scenes. The silent movie starts at 00.10; Will Reeves leaves the cinema and enters the Tulsa massacre at 2.10. That scene ends at 5.10, and at 7.10 the title appears on-screen. Lindelof relaxes the rhythm at this point, but that regular beat is not forgotten: Dr Manhattan's first appearance is at 17.10.

Finally, Lindelof's use of mise en scène follows Moore and Gibbons's example of worldbuilding through 'sight dramatics'. An early shot in HBO's *Watchmen* foregrounds the *Tulsa Sun* newspaper, with the headline 'Veidt Officially Declared Dead' – less legible stories to either side detail a squid shower and a KKK attack on the Statue of Liberty.[54] In the classroom where Angela demonstrates cooking, barely visible posters inform kids about the 'Anatomy of a Squid' and 'Four Important Presidents', with Redford as the incumbent next to Nixon. We can find similar instances in *Watchmen* chapter 1, where a newspaper announces that Vietnam has become the fifty-first state[55] and another midway through the issue, harder to decipher, declaring that 'Congress Approves Lunar Silos'.[56] The Gunga Diner sign and Mmeltdown advertisements, of course, provide more subtle worldbuilding, as do Lindelof's US flags with a blue circular field of fifty-one stars and the overhead blimp's promotion of a new TV show, *American Hero Story* (itself a reference to the real-life FX series *American Horror Story*).[57] Lindelof's wordplay in the first episode – Angela's bakery is Milk and Hanoi, with the slogan 'We let Saigons be Saigons' – is entirely in keeping with Moore's penchant for puns.[58] More background details to the TV series are provided through an online source, 'Peteypedia', which serves the role of the endpapers in each chapter of *Watchmen*.

By the halfway point of his first episode, then, Lindelof has extensively demonstrated his approach to translating Moore and Gibbons's storytelling techniques; and again, freed from Snyder's obligation to follow the original text faithfully, he can adapt them more loosely and creatively, at a pace more suitable for television. Moore and Gibbons are able to place a newspaper in the background of a single panel and know that the reader could flick past it, then return to study it in detail; Lindelof leaves the Veidt headline visible on-screen for the best part of three seconds, matching it with a chilling electric note on the soundtrack that confirms its importance. (Snyder, arguably, pulled off the same achievement during his opening sequence, when he was liberated from the original material.)

Lindelof's post-*Watchmen* worldbuilding is based on a dynamic of sameness and difference: we are offered familiar nods to the original *Watchmen*, such as mentions of Vietnam, electric cars, Dr Manhattan and a racist group in Rorschach masks, but those masks are cheap, mass-produced reproductions, and Looking-Glass, the new cop character who wears a 'face' like Rorschach's, is hidden by a shiny reflection rather than a constantly shifting black and white pattern. Even Rorschach's opening speech is repeated but with a more explicitly bigoted political agenda. 'Cop carcass on the highway last night . . . soon the accumulated black filth will be hosed away. Soon all the whores and

PREQUELS, SEQUELS, SUPPLEMENTS AND REMIXES   173

race traitors will shout "save us."' And perhaps most fundamentally, Moore's *Watchmen* depicts a society where masked adventurers are illegal, while in Lindelof's, all cops are masked and some have superhero-style pseudonyms. As Moore said of Frank Miller's Batman, 'Everything is exactly the same, except for the fact that it's all totally different.'[59]

And lastly, *Rorschach*, written by Tom King with art by Jorge Fornés and Dave Stewart, published as a twelve-issue miniseries under DC's mature Black Label imprint in 2020–1. King arguably belongs to an even younger generation. Born in 1978, eighteen years after Grant Morrison, his first professional comic-book work was published in 2014, not just post-*Watchmen* but post-*Before Watchmen*. Unlike the HBO series, the Snyder movie, *Doomsday Clock* and every other official spin-off, King's *Rorschach* makes no obvious attempt to market itself as part of the extended brand. It eschews the yellow capitals and adopts a visual style more reminiscent of 1970s crime drama, with a nameless detective protagonist who looks like Columbo (originally 1968–78), a political thriller plot in the vein of Pakula's *The Parallax View* and Coppola's *The Conversation* (both 1974) and an aesthetic and colour palette highly reminiscent of David Mazzucchelli's work on Frank Miller's *Batman: Year One*, set roughly ten years before its publication in 1987. As Fornés said: 'Mazzucchelli is one of my favorite artists and yes, he absolutely influenced my work. I'm a huge fan of the look and feel of 80s comics, so I try to reflect that in my art.' His other key influences, significantly, are Miller and Ditko.[60] The dramatic use of sound effect typography as part of the image is also a Miller technique, entirely absent from *Watchmen*: compare the *RATATATATAT* that fills a panel in *Rorschach* issue 3 with the *BRAKKA BRAKKA BRAK* that dominates an early firefight in *Dark Knight Returns*.[61]

King was already known for his 2015 series *The Omega Men*, which paid explicit homage to *Watchmen* through its nine-panel grid – '*Omega Men* is like almost the direct one-to-one rip off of *Watchmen*', King admitted[62] – and the pages of *Rorschach* are also carefully structured, but here the grid arrangement switches dramatically throughout: a two-page splash at the start of issue

1 narrows to twelve panels towards the middle of the chapter and splits into fifteen on the final page. Issue 2 opens with another full-page illustration establishing location, then moves directly to eleven panels, then four. Though the use of colour to distinguish between present day and flashback creates alternating patterns across the page very much like *Watchmen*'s scenes set near the Rum Runner neon sign – cold, warm, cold, warm – or the flashbacks to Blake's murder, which shift from naturalistic tones to glaring crimson – they also recall the bravura sequence in *Pax Americana* where Morrison, Quitely and Fairbairn use colour to convey three time periods in the same location across a single double spread.[63]

If King's detective, opening drawers and digging through clues in issue 2, resembles Rorschach investigating Blake's apartment in *Watchmen* chapter 1, he could equally be The Question, who parodied Rorschach in *Pax Americana* and predated him in the 1968 Steve Ditko incarnation. King recognizes this intertextual relationship and complicates it even further by making his prime suspect a fictional comic-book creator called William Meyerson, who wrote and drew a faceless, trenchcoated vigilante called The Citizen: yet another analogue of The Question, which positions Meyerson as a fictional version of Steve Ditko himself.

The layers of intertextuality become denser, and the connections between *Rorschach* and the rest of the *Watchmen* matrix even more complex, when King introduces Frank Miller as a character who, in this universe, wrote pirate comics including the gritty 'Seaman' reboot, *The Dark Fife*. A background image confirms that this is a nautical variant of *The Dark Knight*.[64] *Watchmen* played this game to an extent within its own alternate universe, referring of course to actors like Redford and, briefly, real-life comics creator Joe Orlando, but writing Miller into the story is a move that radically stretches the boundaries of Moore's worldbuilding.[65] We must assume that Miller always existed here and was present throughout *Watchmen*'s history since his birth in 1957, just as Brian Azzarello's *Before Watchmen* asks us to accept that Travis Bickle met Rorschach in 1970s New York, with the implication that Bickle was, logically,

PREQUELS, SEQUELS, SUPPLEMENTS AND REMIXES

part of the *Watchmen* universe during the 1950s and 1960s.[66] (Presumably, in this universe, Bickle never became a vigilante because Rorschach was already doing the job for him.) I'll return to this key concept of retconning later in this chapter.

The superheroes from *Watchmen* reappear in King's story but, by contrast with Miller, only in brief flashback and cameo; even Rorschach is an enigmatic, absent presence. When we revisit scenes such as Dr Manhattan on Mars, Fornés redraws Gibbons's art respectfully, but guest covers to the first issue offer wilder creative takes. Jae Lee, who illustrated the idiosyncratic *Before Watchmen: Ozymandias*, presents a bizarre portrait of Rorschach working out in front of a mirror, and Brian Bolland renders Rorschach in the iconic and instantly recognizable style of his own collaboration with Moore, *The Killing Joke*.[67] Other elements of the original are incorporated within the diegesis – a smiley face, a Gunga Diner T-shirt, a painting of Alexander the Great, even the full-body Rorschach suit that Gibbons only ever drew in preliminary art[68] – but as in the HBO *Watchmen*, decades have passed, and times have changed. Indeed, there are hints that this story takes place in the same sequel universe as the TV series: the years since Ozymandias's fake alien attack on New York City have seen the rise of vigilante groups and a paranoia about the 'squids' – a term never used in the original *Watchmen* but common in Lindelof's version – and the first issue includes a passing reference to the Rorschach masks remaining popular 'even after Oklahoma'.[69]

This, then, was *Watchmen* in 2020: a dense web of references featuring tributes not just to Moore but also to his fellow titan of 1980s comics Frank Miller, fundamentally informed by 1970s cinema, incorporating Lindelof's TV show of 2019 and of course not bearing the name of the original author: the credits page states only that *Watchmen* was co-created by Dave Gibbons.

All these sequels, prequels, spin-offs and remixes follow the same underlying dynamic: familiarity and difference, fidelity and novelty. And this dynamic is common to all such supplementary texts. As well as the 'sameness' that reassures readers they are re-entering a fictional world, a follow-on story must explore a new aspect of that world whether temporally or geographically, shifting focus to a different time or place, character or perspective. Geraldine Brooks sets *March* 'far away, where the fighting was';[70] Updike and Stoppard relegate Hamlet to a marginal role in their revisiting of the Shakespeare play. Longbourn offers the neglected perspective of the Bennett sisters' servants. These are all allographic, according to Parey's categories, and return to a text that the original author closed centuries ago, but autographic examples by writers expanding their own ongoing franchise follow a similar pattern: E. L. James's *Grey* (2015) and Stephenie Meyer's *Midnight Sun* (2020) provide the male protagonists' point of view of the *Fifty Shades* and *Twilight* narratives, while Suzanne Collins's *The Ballad of Songbirds and Snakes* (2020) explores the history of *The Hunger Games* with a focus on the series' villain, Coriolanus Snow. All these fictions are based around questions that the original does not resolve. What was Jane Fairfax doing during *Emma*? What did Edward Cullen really think of Bella? Why did Elphaba become wicked? Where did Alice go after Wonderland? How did the Hunger Games begin?

Remember that Ray Winninger was transparent about this process. 'I mine the comics and scripts for background details and pitch stories fleshing them out. What sparked off the police riots in the 1970s? What is Dr Manhattan doing in that government laboratory? What is the connection between the second generation of masked heroes and five-term president Richard Nixon?' All of the *Watchmen* stories discussed here follow that approach, asking similar questions. What if Dr Manhattan met Superman (*Doomsday Clock*)? What if Travis Bickle met Rorschach (*Before Watchmen*)?[71] How did Ozymandias's alien hoax change society in the early 1990s (*Doomsday Clock*) and the late 2010s (*Rorschach*, HBO's *Watchmen*)? What new world did Dr Manhattan create after his departure from Earth (*Doomsday Clock*, HBO's *Watchmen*)? What was Laurie's life like in the 1960s, before the Crimebusters meeting (*Before Watchmen*), and how did she develop in the twenty-first century (HBO's *Watchmen*)? What are the backstories of supervillains like Moloch (*Before Watchmen*), Captain Carnage (*Rorschach*) and Jimmy the Gimmick

PREQUELS, SEQUELS, SUPPLEMENTS AND REMIXES

(*The End is Nigh*)? How did the existence of costumed crimefighters affect Nixon's election (*The Watchmen Sourcebook*) and Watergate (*The End is Nigh*)? Who was Hooded Justice, the most mysterious member of the Minutemen (*Before Watchmen*, HBO's *Watchmen*)?

Each story extrapolates from Moore and Gibbons's text, filling in the gaps of the existing framework and allowing it to branch out further, with the intention that each annex and extension to the original building will fit naturally and convincingly. *Watchmen* then becomes a much larger text – a sprawling estate, rather than a stately home – with many more rooms for readers to explore. That is the intention. As we've already seen, it is not always the result. One problem is that Moore's writing abilities during the mid-1980s were peerless. The spin-off projects are often beautifully illustrated, but even talented professional writers struggle to produce material that comes close to Moore's standards: we witnessed earlier their failures even to reproduce Rorschach's narrative voice with the same startling force. As Moore observed, with characteristic provocation: 'When Dave Gibbons phoned me up, he assured me that these prequels and sequels would be handled by "the industry's top-flight talents". Now, I don't think that the contemporary industry actually has a "top-flight" of talent. I don't think it's even got a middle-flight or a bottom-flight of talent.'[72] We don't have to agree with his every word here to acknowledge that at his peak, Moore was in a league of his own.

Beyond this is another problem. The extensions to *Watchmen* are not consistently planned and maintained. Most obviously, Snyder's version replaces the 'squid' with an energy weapon: in that respect, *Watchmen* (2009) is out of step with every other spin-off and cannot possibly be reconciled with the three sequels *Doomsday Clock*, *Rorschach* or HBO's *Watchmen*, all of which refer to the alien creature, or of course with the original text. However, as we saw, *The End Is Nigh* draws on the film's costume designs and reuses its voice talents, implying that the video game creates a 'past' for the movie characters, and its story, a conspiracy in which Woodward and Bernstein are murdered by Comedian, is developed from a panel in *Watchmen*: it therefore branches out from and bridges both texts.[73]

Sometimes the extrapolations from Moore's original take entirely different directions from each other. Cooke's *Before Watchmen: Minutemen* explores the history of Hooded Justice, confirming the hint in *Watchmen* that he was in a secret gay relationship with Nelson Gardner but inventing a further subplot where Comedian attempts to frame Hooded Justice for child murders and sets him up to be killed, in turn, by Nite Owl. Lindelof's *Watchmen* also leans into the gay relationship with Gardner but reveals, by contrast, that Hooded Justice was Will Reeves, a Black hero who escaped the Tulsa massacre as a boy and disguised himself as a white man, surviving until the events of the present day.[74]

There are many other examples, as these multiple stories intersect, clash and conflict in various ways. In *Doomsday Clock*, Rorschach's journal was widely published and exposed Veidt's scheme as a hoax. In HBO's *Watchmen*, the journal is cherished only by a group of racist vigilantes. Geoff Johns confirms that Seymour, who discovered Rorschach's journal, was killed shortly after its publication,[75] while in Damon Lindelof's TV universe, the former newspaper assistant becomes a successful academic of postmodern theory.[76] In *Doomsday Clock*, Reggie Long, the son of Rorschach's psychiatrist in *Watchmen*, has become a second Rorschach. In *Rorschach*, several individuals believe they have inherited his spirit, including a circus strongman, comic-book writer Wil Meyerson and, ultimately, the detective himself; Reggie Long is never mentioned. There are paradoxical overlaps, too. Despite the apparently irreconcilable differences between Snyder's film and the comic books, *Before Watchmen* lifts a detail from the film that is absent from the original: in Cooke's *Minutemen* story, a glimpse of Silhouette's murder, with 'LESBIAN WHORES' painted on her bedroom wall, is derived from the movie's opening sequence, not from Moore and Gibbons's *Watchmen*.[77]

The contradictions go deep, from broad plot points to incidental details. Snyder's *Watchmen*, picking up on a throwaway line in the original, shows

PREQUELS, SEQUELS, SUPPLEMENTS AND REMIXES

the Comedian assassinating JFK. *Before Watchmen* has Comedian hearing the news of the assassination while he is across the country, following a false lead on Moloch.[78] *Before Watchmen* rewrites Nite Owl's relationship with Twilight Lady as a graphically nude, crudely drawn romance rather than a one-sided, sick fixation as *Watchmen* implies; in *The End Is Nigh*, the two fight viciously hand to hand in 1977, with little indication of any previous emotional attachment. *Before Watchmen*, which was expanded beyond its original scope, even manages to contradict itself: a late addition to the series, *Moloch*, undermines the plotline in *Ozymandias* by having minor characters alive when they should be dead.[79]

And each new addition changes what was already built. When Geoff Johns decides to introduce the Mime and the Marionette, two new villains based, appropriately, on Steve Ditko's Charlton Comics characters Punch and Jewelee, he writes them into the history, rather than just the future, of *Watchmen*. They have not just appeared – Marionette indicates that she's met the original Rorschach before – so they must have always been in the background but for some reason were never mentioned alongside the other old enemies like Jimmy the Gimmick and the King of Skin. Tom King's additions, comic-book creators Wil Meyerson and Frank Miller, must also have always been there, though they were never mentioned in *Watchmen*'s extensive discussion of pirate comics. If we accept *Before Watchmen* as canon, we must also accept that fictional characters like Travis Bickle can co-exist in this universe alongside Walter Kovacs and John F. Kennedy. And when Lindelof reveals that Hooded Justice is Black, he alters the world of *Watchmen* not just in his own series, set in 2019, but also in Moore's 1939, when the Minutemen formed. The skin we saw beneath his cowl in *Watchmen* chapter 2 was, we are now invited to realize, pale make-up, and his comments about staying out of politics were just for show.[80] 'Part of Will Reeves's camouflage in terms of hiding his true identity required making statements like that in the presence of the other Minutemen so as to throw off the scent of who he truly was', Lindelof explained.[81]

This narrative shift, the retcon or retroactive continuity, is clearly explained by Geoff Klock with reference to Miller's *Dark Knight*.

> When Batman takes a rifle shot to the chest, which any reader assumes would kill him instantly, it reveals metal shielding. Batman says, 'Why do you think I wear a target on my chest – can't armor my head', and with that one line a thirty-year mystery dissolves as every reader runs mentally through previous stories, understanding that plate as having always been there. This example of Miller's realism is paradigmatic of his revisionary strategy.[82]

With *The Dark Knight Returns*, Klock writes, 'the reader is forced to confront what has been going on for years between the panels'. Other readings, he continues, 'appear to have "fallen away" from the strongest version that is retroactively constituted as always already true'.[83]

Lindelof playfully foregrounds this narrative device in the penultimate episode of his own series. Dr Manhattan, who has returned from exile on Mars and disguised himself in a new body, is questioned by his wife, Angela Abar. Simultaneously, due to Manhattan's experience of time, he is holding a conversation ten years ago with Angela's grandfather, Will Reeves. Attempting to clear up a series-long mystery, Angela directs Manhattan to interrogate her grandfather in the past. How did he know that her boss, police chief Judd Crawford, was a member of a racist organization and that he had a Klan robe in his closet?

Back in time, but at the same time, Manhattan dutifully repeats the question. Will Reeves is baffled. 'Who's Judd Crawford?' Returning to Angela, Manhattan reports in puzzlement that Reeves didn't know the name. 'But he does now.' Angela has just provided her grandfather with the information that will set him on an arc to investigate and ultimately murder Crawford. Her question in the present day didn't solve the mystery: it created it, seeding the plot by rewriting the past.

The actual texts of previous stories cannot physically change of course, but new information can nevertheless radically transform our understanding and encourage us to revisit the original from a different perspective: if it is

PREQUELS, SEQUELS, SUPPLEMENTS AND REMIXES

persuasive enough, the new interpretive frame may even prevent us from seeing it in any other way. Mireia Aragay and Gemma López remark that *Bridget Jones*, as a modern reworking of Jane Austen, casts 'a fresh light' on *Pride and Prejudice* when the viewer/reader returns to the original: 'inevitably, the inauspicious beginning of Elizabeth's and Darcy's relationship at the Meryton ball is coloured by the comically disastrous first meeting between Bridget and Mark Darcy at Bridget's parents' New Year's turkey curry buffet.'[84] Similarly, to borrow Aragay and López's terms, *Watchmen* spin-offs will 'infect/inflect' the original. A reader who encounters (or returns to) Moore and Gibbons's *Watchmen* after watching the HBO series could insist that Hooded Justice was always white, but it would be a conscious act of resistance, a decision to reject Lindelof's interpretation.

And changes of this kind, though not all as major as Lindelof's Hooded Justice twist, are manifold. They all alter *Watchmen's* history like a time-travelling butterfly effect that sends ripples through the past. *The End Is Nigh* fleshes out Jimmy The Gimmick, a 1970s villain briefly mentioned by Rorschach in *Watchmen*: now Jimmy The Gimmick has always looked and acted this way. *Before Watchmen: Minutemen* features The Liquidator, who we learn killed Silhouette, and introduces the idea that this universe has comic-book analogues to Batman and Robin called Bluecoat and Scout: The Liquidator, Bluecoat and Scout have, at a stroke, always existed in this universe. In Snyder's film, Batman comics were published in the 1940s: they plaster the wall of a cinema when Nite Owl makes an early appearance. In Lindelof's series, Superman debuted in 1938 but *Batman* was a 1970s Vietnamese video parodying Nite Owl.[85] *Rorschach* adds various pirate titles and spin-off movies – Seaman, Pontius Pirate – to *Watchmen's* cultural past. *Before Watchmen: Ozymandias* crowds the 1950s with colourful villains never mentioned in the original: Wheeler-Dealer, Low-Jack, Three Dollar Bill. *Doomsday Clock* tells us that, some time before 1985, Rorschach dropped Marionette down an elevator, as *Watchmen* tell us he did with Captain Carnage.[86] Through the very different art styles of Brian Rizzo and Adam Hughes, *Before Watchmen* depicts Edgar 'Moloch'

Jacobi – a normal human being in the original – as a deformed, goblin-like creature who has always been shunned for his looks and Janey Slater – again, a perfectly normal woman in the original – as a 'cheesecake' pin-up.

It transpires from *Before Watchmen: Silk Spectre* that Laurie has already killed a criminal (a Frank Sinatra figure called the Chairman) before her appearance as a naive near-innocent at the first Crimebusters meeting in 1966. In *Doomsday Clock*, Gunga Diner is still extant despite being replaced by Burgers'n'Borscht at the end of *Watchmen*.[87] Brian Azzarello's prequel has Rorschach type his journal entries, implying that everything we saw in *Watchmen* was a handwritten draft.[88] Each of these stories seems to take place in a subtly different world and carries its own distinct history.

The result, when we try to combine them, is not a sprawling estate, an expanded world of *Watchmen*, a rich theme park for fan exploration, but an impossible geography, a space crowded with contradiction. If this was a house, it would have three new wings built in the same place but in different styles, somehow co-existing at angles to each other. It would be a house with rooms that vanish or change when the doors are closed – a mansion with an occasional basement, an extension that flickers in and out of view and a roof that alternates between spires and domes depending on the angle and the time of day. Navigating them, we have to choose what we accept and reject, like a citizen of China Miéville's 2009 science-fiction novel *The City and the City*, opting to see one set of streets while 'unseeing' the other.

The closest equivalent in superhero comics is perhaps Arkham Asylum as depicted in Morrison's *Animal Man*: an optical illusion of a building, a series of architectural spectres. A gothic spire hovers hazily above; a modern ziggurat of the same building protrudes uncertainly, fading out at the margins. But Arkham Asylum, at that point in Morrison's story, is caught at a moment of crisis, shifting between realities, between multiple universes.[89]

This is what we now encounter when we engage with *Watchmen*: not a straightforward expanded universe but a series of multiple fictional worlds, running alongside each other and sharing the same name. The *Watchmen*

PREQUELS, SEQUELS, SUPPLEMENTS AND REMIXES 183

wiki now has separate drop-down menus for 'Comic', 'Film' and 'HBO Series', with a different incarnation of Ozymandias listed under each. Its 'Chronology' page is broken down into five sections – Original, Snyder, DC, HBO and DC Black Label – detailing different versions of the same decade as though they were variants of the same brand (Classic, Cherry, Diet). A typical article from December 2019, as *Doomsday Clock* and *Watchmen* reached their conclusions, referred to 'the various *Watchmen* universes'.[90] Another, from March 2022, has to specify '*Doomsday Clock*'s *Watchmen* universe' rather than simply 'the *Watchmen* universe'.[91] Compiling a timeline of the HBO series and the original 1986 *Watchmen*, a writer from *Den of Geek* adds the disclaimer: 'I don't consider DC's *Before Watchmen* prequels canon (and apparently neither does this show)'.[92] *ScreenRant* was obliged to add a similarly complex explanation: 'Lindelof's *Watchmen* picks up the story of the graphic novel (not the movie) thirty years later and treats the events of Moore and Gibbons' story as canon. (The series is also unrelated to DC Comics' *Watchmen* sequel *Doomsday Clock*.)'[93] In January 2021, the *DC Database* had to correct and revise its categories:

> We've been treating *Rorschach* by Tom King as though it's set in the universe of the *Watchmen* comics (*Watchmen, Before Watchmen, Doomsday Clock*). But there are a few key details that prove this incorrect, and that it is, in fact, set in canon with HBO's *Watchmen* universe (*Watchmen*, HBO's *Watchmen*, Peteypedia). So here's . . . that.[94]

Fans, during summer 2019 when *Doomsday Clock* and HBO's *Watchmen* were both active and unfinished – before *Rorschach* had added an extra layer of complexity – found their own personal ways to navigate those universes. I asked Reddit's *Watchmen* forum how they negotiated the inconsistencies. While they agreed about the continuing status of the 'original', they approached the spin-off texts with varying degrees of flexibility.

I don't think 'true' is the right way to describe the tension between HBO *Watchmen* and stuff like *Doomsday Clock*. HBO *Watchmen* is the canon that I'm most interested in, but that doesn't mean that I think of other interpretations of the *Watchmen* characters as false – just different, because the authors had different ideas that they wanted to communicate. I think I would challenge the idea that a story has one 'truth' – instead, I think a lot of storytelling uses characters as archetypes. It seems like human nature to use archetypes in stories, even if they aren't positioned as explicitly so today like they were in the past (thinking of things like Greek mythology and Commedia dell'arte). We understand stories not as something that happens to one individual with only one lived history, but as the types of things that might happen to a character that takes this particular form. Characters like Sherlock Holmes, James Bond, Jim Kirk, etc. have contradictory histories across a myriad of reimagining and reinterpretations, but we understand them more as archetypes than as real people, so it isn't hard for our brains to juggle and reconcile multiple branching situations across different imagined universes.[95]

Watchmen is fundamentally a singular graphic novel/twelve-issue run of comics that sought to comment on comic tropes and use comic conventions to tell a story in a way that wouldn't just be 'a movie without movement'. It's Alan Moore and Dave Gibbons, and finishes how they meant it to finish.

Everything else is deuterocanon.[96]

The only 'true' *Watchmen* for me is the original. I view the HBO show as a proper continuation of the *Watchmen* story in a new medium. Instead of the comic story within the comic story, we have the silent films and *American Hero Story* clips. And because questions of race and reckoning with American racial violence dominate much of our political discourse, that dominates the show. It is fantastic. I see no need to reconcile it with the source material or any other *Watchmen* film or comic book. It is just another interpretation of what happened next. Moore will probably never approve of it for his own reasons, but I do, because it resonates with the original thematically even if it departs from it in medium.[97]

PREQUELS, SEQUELS, SUPPLEMENTS AND REMIXES   185

Only the original novel is canon to the show. It only really makes a difference in understanding the show; you have to know what's canon and what's not. It's their relation to each other that matters, not some authoritative view of what's 'canon'. And with *Watchmen* and comics in general I think basically everyone gets that. Like it really doesn't matter what's part of the 'main timeline' and what's a separate one. They're all just fictional stories anyway.[98]

I'm going to stick with authorial intent here. Of all the spin-offs, prequels, and sequels, the only ones that had any input or engagement from Alan Moore were the Mayfair Games modules and sourcebook for the DC Heroes RPG, so they're the only ones I consider accurate representations of the *Watchmen* universe. (I know Dave Gibbons was a co-creator who has lent degrees of approval to various projects, but I still consider Moore the primary author.)

That puts all the *Before Watchmen* titles, *Doomsday Clock* et al, and the show on effectively equal footing in terms of legitimacy, which doesn't seem quite right given the diverging levels of quality and rank exploitation. Since DC Comics is probably akin to the Vatican here in authority to determine canon, *Before Watchmen* probably prevails.[99]

As the reference to the Vatican and Deuterocanon suggest, these fans of '*Watchmen*' – whatever that meant in Summer 2019 – see the debates between the different story verses as comparable in some ways to religious exegesis. One explained the parallel in detail:

There's 'official' religious canon too, but people tell the stories they like, and retell them. You almost certainly know some non-canonical Judaeo-Christian myths. for instance, the *Paradise Lost* version of the war in Heaven and fall of Satan is way more popular than its Biblical basis. And you probably know it through several indirect sources – TV, movies, maybe even church – rather than reading *Paradise Lost*. that version has reinformed, retconned if you will, the older forms of the myth in the minds of millions of modern believers.[100]

But fans also made sense of these inconsistencies through reference to more popular mythology: Kirk, Bond, Holmes and comic-book heroes. As cultural studies scholars have pointed out for many years, folk characters – and commercial properties who have acquired mythic qualities over time, like Batman – have long been multiple, paradoxical and contradictory, existing in many forms at once.[101]

These contradictions are not unique to contemporary popular culture. Inevitably, the sequels to Austen would clash with and undermine each other if Janeites attempted to combine them into the same universe; the problem is solved within that fan community by treating them as unrelated, secondary interpretations, some more successful than others, that spring from the same canonical, and infinitely superior, core text.[102] There is no attempt to try to make sense of them as a collective fictional space, any more than Carrollians argue about which unofficial spin-off from *Alice in Wonderland* is 'true' – whether Alice went *Behind the Moon* next or *Through the Needle's Eye*[103] – there is only one original, and the others are inferior, fascinating exercises at best.

In these cases from classic literature, the hierarchy is clear. The situation is far more complex in recent popular franchise narratives, which have less sense of sole authorship, ownership and long-established canon. *Terminator: Dark Fate* (2019) continues directly from *Terminator 2* (1991), ignoring three feature films released in between and celebrating the return of original director James Cameron. The *Fantastic Beasts* prequel film series, with which author J. K. Rowling is actively involved, contradicts (or creatively reframes and retcons) the *Harry Potter* films. *Star Wars* TV series like *Kenobi* (2022) struggle to fix continuity issues between the original trilogy (1977–83), the prequels (1999–2005) – all directed by George Lucas – and other episodes inserted in the middle, such as *Rogue One* (2016). All these new *Star Wars* texts cancel out the narratives previously provided by comics and books before Disney's take over in 2015, which relegated them to 'legends' – just as *Blade Runner 2049* (2017) and the short movies that accompanied it undermine the previous sequels by K. W. Jeter (1995–2000). The TV series

PREQUELS, SEQUELS, SUPPLEMENTS AND REMIXES

Game of Thrones began as an adaptation of George R. R. Martin's *Song of Ice and Fire* novels but overtook them and had to invent its own stories; the same was true of the TV series *The Man in the High Castle* (Amazon Prime) and *The Handmaid's Tale* (MGM) which went far beyond the original novels by Phillip K. Dick and Margaret Atwood. The TV shows *Hannibal* and *Bates Motel* take place before the events of Demme's *Silence of the Lambs* (1991) and Hitchcock's *Psycho* (1960) but play fast and loose with chronology; *Hannibal* holds an ambiguous, impossible, before-but-also-after position in relation to the existing novels and films, while *Bates Motel* – despite providing the backstory to a 1960 movie – takes place in the present day.[104] *Doctor Sleep*, the movie from 2019, was both an adaptation of Stephen King's (2013) novel and a sequel to Stanley Kubrick's 1980 film *The Shining*, which was quite different from King's novel *The Shining* (1977).

Some of these examples are simply treated as messy continuity, where truths depend, as Kenobi in *Star Wars* puts it, on 'a certain point of view'. Others draw on the comic-book term 'continuity' to separate incompatible timelines.[105] But a few, tellingly, employ the science-fiction trope of the multiverse to make sense of their separate narrative spheres and storyworlds. 'Bryan Fuller's *Hannibal* TV show in some ways serves as an addition to the Lecter movie continuity, and is in other ways an alternate universe.'[106] *Doctor Sleep* 'exists very much in the same cinematic universe that Kubrick established in his adaptation of *The Shining*'.[107] *Star Trek*, too, currently operates both a 'Prime Universe' and a 'Kelvin Timeline' to separate the main adventures from the trilogy that began with J. J. Abrams' *Star Trek* in 2009.[108]

Popular discussion of *Watchmen*, as we saw, regularly uses alternate-earth terminology to make sense of the multiple plotlines. That journalists are so quick to label these contradictory narratives as separate 'universes' (one fan above referred, similarly, to the concepts of a *Watchmen* 'main timeline' and a 'separate one') is no doubt partly because *Watchmen* itself plays so explicitly with these ideas through Dr Manhattan. At the end of Moore's *Watchmen*, Manhattan – who can see every moment of his own life simultaneously – declares his intention to make a new world; *Before Watchmen* and *Doomsday Clock* have him actively interfering in events to create, rather than just observe, branching timelines.[109]

This device, in turn, has an established history in the superhero genre. Comic books began to rationalize internal contradictions into multiple universes as long ago as September 1961, when Gardner Fox and Carmine Infantino's story 'Flash of Two Worlds!' in *Flash* issue 123 explained the existence of two different characters with the same name by placing one on the newly created 'Earth-Two', designating that as the home of DC's original superheroes, and allowing them to visit each other in times of crisis. The first major 'Crisis' of 1986 was an attempt to streamline and make sense of a crowded continuity; *Doomsday Clock* is a more (but not the most) recent example. Comic-book fans accept that Batman's origin can be regularly rebooted and that different interpretations of the character exist within the current DC multiverse – Frank Miller's Batman currently occupies Earth-31, for instance.

The 'many-worlds interpretation' of quantum mechanics – that every possible outcome occurs in a different possible universe – was proposed in 1957 by Hugh Everett[110] and quickly migrated to popular literature – novels as well as comics. Michael Moorcock's first 'Elric' story, launching his multiverse saga, was published in 1961, the same year as 'Flash of Two Worlds'. Bryan Talbot's parallel-worlds comic-book adventure *Luther Arkwright*, originally from 1978, is heavily inspired by Moorcock, as are Grant Morrison's 'Gideon Stargrave' stories, which began in the same year. Stephen King has, over several decades, evolved a multiverse that connects all his work, centred on the Dark Tower series (the first episode, *The Gunslinger*, was published in 1982).[111] Phillip Pullman's *His Dark Materials* series, originating with *Northern Lights* in 1995 and continuing with *The Book of Dust* series (2017 onwards), is set across many worlds. Comics, as we saw, have been exploring the idea extensively since the 1960s.

But what was a relatively niche trope is now becoming part of mainstream culture and discourse, as popular stories increasingly evoke and explore the

PREQUELS, SEQUELS, SUPPLEMENTS AND REMIXES

idea of multiple earths. Although the film adaptation of Pullman's *Northern Lights*, *The Golden Compass* flopped in 2009, it was successfully remade as the BBC/HBO TV series *His Dark Materials* in 2019. King's *The Dark Tower* reached cinemas in 2017 without much impact, but *Spider-Man: Into the Spider-Verse*, a riotous explosion of styles and Spidey variants across different parallels, was a surprise hit in 2018. In 2019, DC Comics' television characters from multiple universes met in a 'Crisis' storyline, the same year that *Spider-Man: Far from Home* tentatively introduced the idea of alternate earths to the Marvel Cinematic Universe. The TV series *WandaVision* and *Loki* confirmed the existence of a Marvel multiverse during 2021, and *Spider-Man: No Way Home* pushed the concept further in December of the same year. In spring 2022, two of the biggest movies were *Doctor Strange in the Multiverse of Madness* and its unlikely competitor *Everything Everywhere All at Once*: a horror-superhero blockbuster within a vast franchise and a one-off comedy drama about a Chinese-American laundromat owner, united by their setting across multiple worlds.

One reason for this recent mainstreaming of the multiverse concept is that it helps to resolve a problem caused by the splitting of franchise properties between multiple producers and media platforms, prompted in turn by the increase of sequels and spin-offs,[112] and the rise to dominance of the superhero genre, which lends its 'multiverse' metaphor to TV and film texts as a tried and tested model of untangling crowded, contradictory timelines.[113] For instance, in 2015, there were two entirely different cinematic versions of the character Quicksilver on-screen, in Marvel's *Age of Ultron* and the *X-Men* films owned by Fox. Todd Phillips's movie *Joker* (2019) centred on a completely different character to the villain in David Ayer's *Suicide Squad* (2016), who appeared again in *Zack Snyder's Justice League* (2021) – but not in the alternative *Justice League* cut of 2017 – an entirely different version of the Joker, again, cameoed in Matt Reeves's *The Batman* and an entirely different Batman cameoed in the TV show *Gotham* (2019).[114] In *The Batman*, Jeffrey Wright played Commissioner Gordon. In *Justice League*, J. K. Simmons played Gordon. At the same time, Simmons was also playing J. Jonah Jameson, Spider-Man's antagonist within the completely separate Marvel series. How are viewers supposed to make sense of this? The answer is simple and significant. One of them, Simmons-Jameson, lives in the Marvel Cinematic Universe, and the other, Simmons-Gordon, in the DC Extended Universe: exactly the same explanation that clarified the existence of two superheroes called *The Flash*, in 1961.

TV and cinema are increasingly borrowing from the narrative methods of comic books, making sense of contradictions through the motif of separate universes that cross over in crisis. The 'Crisis on Infinite Earths' storyline within DC's television 'Arrowverse' (which originated with the show *Arrow* in 2012) finally connected to DC's cinematic universe in 2020, as Ezra Miller's Flash from the movies met Grant Gustin's Flash from television. Notably, one consequence was an opening up of new commercial possibilities, as characters from TV no longer had to be legally cleared to appear in DC's movies.

The MCU multiverse, tested through a fake-out storyline in *Spider-Man: Far from Home*, then enabled the three Spider-Men from three different franchises (owned by two different production companies) to work together in *Spider-Man: No Way Home*. As a consequence, Sony's Spider-Man villains like Venom can now appear in the MCU, rather than operating in a separate corporate sphere. The discrepancy between Fox and Marvel versions of Quicksilver was explored, if not explained, in *WandaVision* by casting Evan Peters, from the Fox franchise, as a temporary replacement. Previous Batmen can now be incorporated within DC films, through the same device of alternate timelines and many worlds: Michael Keaton, from the 1989–92 movies, is due to appear alongside Ben Affleck in the forthcoming *The Flash* and *Batgirl*.[115] No wonder some *Star Wars* fans are now suggesting that an alternate universe could reinstate their favourite stories and give them the validation of having 'really happened' in a different version of the chronology.[116]

It will, inevitably, only happen if it can make more money for Disney. These multiple worlds are driven by commercial imperatives. A crisis is

PREQUELS, SEQUELS, SUPPLEMENTS AND REMIXES

inherently capitalist: it keeps things running smoothly, satisfies fans, provides an accessible jumping-on point and enables multiple extant versions of the same property.[117]

This commercial driver is one reason for the increase in many-world stories, which in turn, as the trope becomes more common, enables independent, idiosyncratic play with the ideas outside of franchise properties, in surprise hits like *Everything Everywhere All at* Once.

Another reason is more fundamental and relates to an underlying cultural moment and mood. The multiverse, I will argue, articulates a specific cultural crisis of meaning.

Note that the trend I identify earlier is clustered around the second half of the 2010s, from 2016 onwards. In 2016, the Oxford Dictionary declared 'post-truth' its word of the year, noting that while the term was not new – it first appeared in 1992, with reference to the Persian Gulf War, and the 2003 invasion of Iraq provides further examples of the tendency – its use spiked during the Brexit referendum and the American election, increasing 2000 per cent from the previous year.[118] After this point it appeared regularly in newspaper headlines without a need for explanation, qualifying as 'a mainstay in political commentary'.[119] Associated primarily with then president Donald Trump, who deliberately erased details of his own history, invented facts and labelled all criticism of himself as 'fake news', the concept of post-truth did not pass out of popular discourse with Trump's reluctant departure from the White House.

Dorian Lynskey's study of *Nineteen Eighty-Four*'s changing meanings during the Trump era catalogues this breakdown, this splitting and fragmentation. Quotations attributed to Orwell, warning about the power of the media, were successfully circulated by a Russian troll farm – fake Facebook profiles, with fake photographs and biographies – during the 2016 election campaign. Orwell had never voiced these warnings; the term 'the media' did not enter common usage until after his death. (We could speculate that the quotations were from an alternate Orwell who had lived beyond 1950.)

'What the Russians exploited,' said Barack Obama, 'is we are operating in completely different information universes.'[120]

America's epistemological crisis was Trump's golden opportunity. He could only win the 2016 election because a significant number of Americans were effectively living in a parallel reality. [. . .] It is truly Orwellian that the phrase 'fake news' has been turned on its head by Trump and his fellow authoritarians to describe real news that is not to their liking, while flagrant lies become 'alternative facts' . . . Trump creates his own reality and measures his power by the number of people who subscribe to it.[121]

'What you're seeing and what you're reading is not what's happening', Trump declared in July 2018.[122] His lawyer Rudy Giuliani 'accidentally provided a crude motto for Versionland USA when he snapped at an interviewer, "Truth isn't truth!"'[123] And as Lynskey warns, things will only get worse. Deepfake technology has created a 'paranoid labyrinth in which, according to the viewer's bias, fake images will pass as real while real ones are dismissed as fake'. In the *Star Wars* and Marvel cinematic universes, Mark Hamill and Samuel L. Jackson can now play far younger versions of themselves; more seriously, in March 2022 deepfakes of Vladimir Putin appearing to declare peace with Ukraine, and Volodymr Zelensky appearing to surrender to Russia, circulated convincingly on social media. In the same month, Russia's foreign minister declared that the nation 'did not attack Ukraine', and commentators claimed that Will Smith's on-camera assault of Chris Rock at the Oscars had been faked.[124]

While social media commentators and fact checkers wrestled with the paradoxes of parallel truth universes, debating whether 'disinformation' could still be 'authentic',[125] so popular stories recognized, reflected and articulated the increasingly uneasy relationship between fact and fiction. In February 2022, Netflix's *The Tinder Swindler* explored the true lies of a conman with false online identities; the same theme was central to the fictional BBC/ Amazon series *Chloe*, in the same month, and, also in February, *Inventing*

PREQUELS, SEQUELS, SUPPLEMENTS AND REMIXES

Anna, inspired by the long cons of Anna Sorokin/Anna Delvey. These shows, according to one journalist, have 'taken over social media and our collective psyches'[126] – an exaggeration, perhaps, but a revealing indication that these narratives tapped into a broader social condition.

Inventing Anna itself sat between documentary and drama – its main character, Vivian Kent, is imaginary, based on journalist Jessica Pressler – but by 2022, this limbo had become a crowded space. The recent semi-biopic *Aline* (2021) had been marketed as 'a fiction freely inspired by the life of Céline Dion', a claim instantly dismissed as 'disingenuous; this is Dion's life story'.[127] It starred Valérie Lemercier as both 'Aline Dieu' and, through uncanny, unearthly CGI superimposition of adult features onto a young actor, her child self. The mood of uncertainty was also captured by Channel 4's comedy drama *The Curse* (February 2022), which opened each week with the message 'Some of this might have happened', and ITV's *The Thief, His Wife and the Canoe* (March 2022), with the slogan 'An unbelievably true story'.

The joke 'we live in the darkest timeline', originally a throwaway idea from TV comedy *Community* in 2011, gained traction in 2016 with Trump's election and has become a common meme to explain the current state of the world.[128] The 'Mandela Effect' – a belief that minor changes and false memories point to alternate universes – has also grown from a playful suggestion on a 2009 website to a widely recognized phenomenon in 2022, again with an increase of interest in 2016.[129] Finally, a fascination with *Nineteen Eighty-Four* spiked in the same year, and Orwell quotations, real and fake, are now prevalent on social media.[130]

Is this the logical consequence of the postmodernism whose peak coincided with the release of *Watchmen*? The fragmentation of society that Jameson remarked had 'begun' by 1988, with 'each group coming to speak a curious private language of its own, each profession developing its private code or idiolect, and finally each individual coming to be a kind of linguistic island, separated from everyone else'.[131] Is this the end state of the emptying process that Jean Baudrillard warned of in 1988, when 'the real is no longer what it was' and simulation does not simply replace truth but conceals the absence of any underlying truth?[132] Is this the decentred existence his fellow postmodern theorist Jean-Francois Lyotard described, which has allowed 'the totality of life to be independent specialties . . . this splintering of culture' that follows the breakdown of legitimating narratives of explanation?[133]

We are, perhaps, as yet too close to our present moment to label the change. But something is going on. Something is disintegrating. We are witnessing a crisis of language, narrative, meaning, truth and interpretation.

If America under Trump became Versionland, perhaps we now live in the age of Multiversity.

Journalist Jesse Singal uses another geographical term to describe the contemporary fragmentation of beliefs into multiple smaller states, separate and in constant conflict, reading same words and images in diametrically opposed ways. Discussing responses to the trial of Kenosha, Wisconsin shooter Kyle Rittenhouse in November 2021, he worried about 'what feels like endlessly accelerating Balkanization. We seem headed toward a point where every major news story generates at least two distinct versions of reality that are summarily adopted as true by many partisans.'[134] We are in Bizarro World, or Looking-Glass Land, where everything is reversed: we are there, or perhaps they are, our enemies on the other side of the argument and the other side of the mirror.

Singal continues to see this balkanization (or 'tribalization', as he also calls it)[135] in contemporary debates about transgender rights, an issue that has particularly attracted Orwell quotations[136] and multiverse metaphors. We now live in in a cultural universe where, for instance, 'Ellen Page' never existed, where Caitlyn Jenner won the 1976 men's decathlon event, where the Wachowski sisters directed *The Matrix* in 1999 and any reference to Grant Morrison's life and career must be rewritten with 'they' as the writer's pronoun: a culture of sweeping and overwhelmingly successful retcons.[137] Or at least, some of us occupy that universe, while some refuse it, and insist on another, which to them is equally real, true, authentic and obvious.

Singal was one of many struck by the exchange, on 12 July 2022, between Professor Khiara Bridges and Republican senator Josh Hawley during a debate on abortion rights. The substance of their disagreement was, essentially, the definition of 'woman' within a context of transgender identity. The broader issue, and Singal's concern, was how different viewers read each participant as conclusively humiliating the other, based on their own previously and firmly established views. 'We're fucked', he concluded, seeing one group believing the professor was 'schooled by Hawley'[138] and another certain that 'Hawley got destroyed'.[139] Not only was the definition of 'woman' now up for debate, but there seemed no agreement about the meaning of other common words. 'Did the definition of "humiliate" change?' asked one Reddit commentator.[140] These radically different interpretations, Singal despaired, existed only within their own 'bubble':[141] multiple worlds of interpretation have shrunk down into tiny, sealed, self-sufficient spheres. The clip, gender-critical academic Helen Joyce suggested, 'is a Rorschach test for American's political alignment'.[142]

Watchmen is now part of a multiverse of separate, contradictory, incompatible, clashing and sometimes overlapping storylines – but perhaps we all are. Perhaps Alan Moore's 1986 comic-book series, shaped by and in its way, shaping the surrounding culture, has evolved into the kind of cross-platform, multimedia franchise that suits this age of dislocation and fragmentation. But what does *Watchmen* mean at this cultural moment, in the summer of 2022?

Conclusion
The end of the beginning

It is 23 January 2020. The Doomsday Clock 'lurches to 100 seconds to midnight – closest to catastrophe yet'.[1]

It is 14 July 2020. The British government makes mask wearing mandatory in public.[2]

It is 24 February 2022. The United States threatens severe consequences as Russian tanks roll into Ukraine.[3]

Where is *Watchmen* now, in our own twenty-first-century timeline that in some ways strangely echoes Alan Moore's New York, 1985? At the time of writing, in July 2022, there are no official *Watchmen* spin-offs, sequels, prequels or remixes currently active.[4] Zach Snyder's 2009 movie is enjoying an unforeseen spike in popularity on streaming services,[5] while *Peacemaker*, the original Charlton Comics character who became The Comedian, is the surprise hit TV show of 2022:[6] a dark comedy, rather than a hard-hitting action series. 'Peacemaker ... what a joke', declared the dying Rick Flag at the end of *The Suicide Squad* (2021), precisely matching Jeffrey Dean Morgan's wryly bitter delivery of the line 'It's all a joke' at the start of Snyder's film.

As we've seen, *Watchmen* has inspired homages, parodies and pastiches since its first publication. *Watchcats* paid homage to the smiley-face front cover image in 1987. In 1997, the cover of *Stormwatch* issue 44 – a doll lying in a bloody gutter, with the title turned vertically down the side of the page – offered another tribute. In June 2011, issue 13 of the *Simpsons Super Spectacular* comic presented *Splotchmen,* starring Dr New Haven and Pastry Face: the solemn title of chapter 1 is 'TASTE YOUR WARE', attributed to the Simple Simon rhyme. In 2012, artist Brendan Tobin offered 'Reign of the Rorschachs', a parodic crossover between *Watchmen* and the 'Death of Superman' DC storyline.[7] In 2018, Dave Gibbons drew a cover for *Venom* comic based explicitly on his opening image for *Watchmen* issue 1, with a badge lying in fast-flowing blood.[8]

But those references have always been relatively clear. *Pax Americana* and *Peter Cannon: Thunderbolt* wear their influence on their sleeve; to a reader unfamiliar with *Watchmen,* they would barely make sense. More recently, the links between source material and tribute (whether celebratory, satirical or a combination of the two) have been strained to the point that it is hard to tell whether any reference is intended. The first teased image of Michael Keaton's Batsuit for the forthcoming *Flash* movie, in June 2021, was a close-up of the insignia with a bloodstain on the left-hand side. As *Den of Geek* noted, it 'evokes the classic image from Alan Moore and Dave Gibbons' seminal 1986 comic-book *Watchmen,* a work that has been a north star for the DCEU since its inception. But what does *Watchmen* have to do with *The Flash* movie?' After paragraphs of guesswork, the author concludes, 'It's still too early to say. The blood could just be a detail added to the picture to get fans talking and speculating.'[9]

These ambiguous references are becoming a theme. The children's show *Hey Duggee,* season 3, episode 34 (March 2021), has the main character winning a 'Comic Badge': on the wall behind him is a Pop Art canvas mimicking Gibbons's iconic cover, labelled *Watchdog.* Is this an Easter Egg for elderly parents, an in-joke by the artist? Would four-year-olds encountering *Watchmen* now recognize it from *Hey Duggee*? Duran Duran's video for 'More Joy!' (2021) includes figures with TVs for heads, their screens black and white blotches, labelled 'Rorschach Clowns'. Is this a *Watchmen* reference? If so, what does it mean? In July 2022, YouTube videos mocking Amber Heard's performance in her trial against Johnny Depp are uploaded by 'That Umbrella Guy', depicted as an anonymous figure with female cleavage, an umbrella for a face and what is obviously Rorschach's

CONCLUSION

costume. What point, if any, is this Depp superfan, real name Matthew Lewis, trying to make through the subversion of Moore and Gibbons's trenchcoated vigilante? *Newsweek* refers to his avatar as a 'hooded cartoon character';[10] is the reference to Rorschach lost on the media and Lewis's thousands of viewers?

In June 2021, fast-food chain Wendy's tweeted an image of their mascot with a blue face over a Mars landscape, with the words 'I am tired of lunch. These clowns. I am tired of people caught in the freezers of their beef', the link to Dr Manhattan was knowing, if enigmatic. (The target seemed to be McDonald's.) Some readers, inevitably, entirely missed the reference: 'I have no idea what this means but I absolutely love it.'[11]

Wendy's replied, with deliberate lazy lowercase: 'it just means i wanted to post a funny picture and make fun of frozen beef.'[12] If there was a point, the corporate account denied it, matching the current vibe for shrugging, throwaway indifference. It's just a joke; it's just a meme.

Dr Manhattan on Mars has indeed become a meme, officially titled 'I Am Tired Of Earth. These People',[13] which, significantly, mashes up an image from the comic with a line of dialogue from Snyder's movie (the comic monologue is 'I am tired of this world; these people' and takes place while Manhattan is still at Gila Flats, rather than on Mars).[14] The image now circulates, with a new, amateurishly hand-lettered panel, in various forms, featuring characters as diverse as Michel Foucault, Bernie Sanders, Mark Zuckerberg, SpongeBob SquarePants and Bobby from *King of the Hill*. Its relationship to the original panel in Watchmen, which does not bear that caption and is not even from the same chapter as the line 'I am tired of this world', has drifted until the connection has stretched or perhaps snapped. An image of Will Smith's blue Genie from *Aladdin* (2019) with the words 'I am tired of Earth. These people'[15] has floated so far from *Watchmen*, losing its art, its words and its context, that it seems to operate independently as a meme, rather than a quotation from a 1986 source.

In 1999, I argued that Batman was evolving into something more than a corporate property, and had the potential to become a figure more like

Dracula, Robin Hood and Holmes, separated from ownership and authorship, and circulating freely within popular (even 'folk') culture.[16] If there had been no more official Batman comics, films, games and animated series from the end of the twentieth century onwards, would Batman have continued as a character in some fan-generated form until 2022? I believe he would. And if there were no more official *Watchmen* sequels, spin-offs, prequels, remixes and adaptations, I believe the Dr Manhattan meme would continue to change and evolve, perhaps increasingly losing touch with its original source, and becoming 'blue naked man', but retaining a place in online visual discourse. Perhaps Rorschach – or 'hooded cartoon character' – would continue too, in some variant form: 'Dr Manhattan Kills Rorschach' is already a meme in its own right, tellingly reduced from a complex parody in 2015 – an 'early iteration' – to an exploitable template in 2018 to a two-panel gag with the punchline 'VIBE CHECK' in 2019. 'On May 27th, 2021, another shaving down of the meme came from the subreddit /r/memes in a post by Redditor u/fanboyx27, earning 43,000 upvotes in four months and taking the panel count down to one.'[17]

This panel has no character names and contains no dialogue from *Watchmen*. Rorschach appears as a disintegrated outline and Manhattan in obscure profile. The words 'Friend coming out as gay' have been pasted over Rorschach. 'That's pretty gay, NGL' emits from Manhattan's outstretched hand. No doubt incomprehensible to a generation of readers – 'NGL' is, or was at the time of writing, the abbreviation for 'Not gonna lie' – its meaning is deliberately non-committal. Is it homophobic or a satire of homophobia? Is it an attempt to play on the changing meanings of the word 'gay'? Does it have any relevance at all to panel 4, page 24 of *Watchmen* chapter 12 by Alan Moore, Dave Gibbons and John Higgins, with a cover date of October 1987? Perhaps not, any more than a contemporary cartoon about genetically modified 'Frankenstein food', featuring the movie monster, would be directly related to the young scientist Victor Frankenstein from the 1818 Mary Shelley novel subtitled *The Modern Prometheus*. That is how characters become cultural icons; they lose something, they gain something, they change, they

CONCLUSION   201

are both reduced and expanded, stripped down and modified; they may fade but do not die; they are reborn and take new forms, as convenient vehicles for changing contemporary meanings.

We may have reached the end of *Watchmen*'s first stage, as a commercial media property, and the start of its second life as something different. Scholars in 2086 will have to judge what this comic book, once one of *Time* magazine's 100 best novels, means – if anything – to readers on its centenary in 2086, when Moore and Morrison, Dave Gibbons, Kieron Gillen, John Higgins, Geoff Johns and I are gone. For now all we can do is watch and wait.

NOTES

Introduction

1 The contribution of John Higgins as colourist is often overlooked. However, for convenience, I will tend to refer to Moore and Gibbons as creators and, where appropriate, Moore alone as the writer. The original comic book maxiseries was published between 1986 and 1987 and collected as a 'graphic novel' in 1987. While the term 'graphic novel' is subject to debate (see Annalisa Di Liddo, *Alan Moore: Comics as Performance, Fiction as Scalpel* (Jackson: University Press of Mississippi, 2009), 15–21), I use it here, again for convenience, to describe the 'trade paperback' edition. References to *Watchmen* are in the form of chapter, page, and use the 1987 DC Comics edition.

2 There have been many more subtle echoes of the smiley face throughout the twelve chapters; this literally in-your-face repetition clearly has heavy significance.

3 See Sara J. Van Ness, *Watchmen As Literature* (Jefferson: McFarland & Co, 2010), 68–72, for further discussion of the final page's implications.

4 See Timothy Callaghan, 'Revisiting Alan Moore's Official *Watchmen* Prequel', *Comic Book Resources* (10 September 2008, accessed 2 June 2021), https://www.cbr.com/revisiting-alan-moores-official-watchmen-prequel; see also the *Fantasy Advertiser* roundtable discussion with Alan Moore and Dave Gibbons (March 1988), reproduced by John Coulthart, *Feuilleton* (24 June 2006, accessed 2 June 2021), http://www.johncoulthart.com/feuilleton/2006/06/24/watchmen/.

5 See Van Ness, *Watchmen As Literature*, 171–2, and also Jack Shepherd, '*Watchmen* at 10', *The Independent* (23 February 2019, accessed 2 June 2021), https://www.independent.co.uk/arts-entertainment/films/features/watchmen-10-anniversary-zack-snyder-terry-gilliam-darren-aronofsky-paul-greengrass-a8792791.html; see also '*Watchmen*: Unused Sam Hamm Script', *Watchmen Wiki* (1988, accessed 2 June 2021), https://watchmen.fandom.com/wiki/Watchmen_(unused_Sam_Hamm_script).

6 See Shepherd, '*Watchmen* at 10'.

7 Vanessa Gabriel, 'Before *Watchmen*: Watching the Controversy', *CNN.com* (6 June 2012, accessed 2 June 2021), https://edition.cnn.com/2012/06/06/living/before-watchmen-watching-the-controversy/index.html

8 Mikhail Bakhtin, 'Discourse in the Novel', in Michael Holquist (ed.), *The Dialogic Imagination: Four Essays by M. M. Bakhtin* (Austin: University of Texas Press, 1981), 272.

204 NOTES

9 Ibid., 276.

10 Mikhail Bakhtin, 'From Notes Made in 1970-1', in Caryl Emerson and Michael Holquist (eds), *Speech Genres & Other Late Essays* (Austin: University of Texas Press, 1986), 146.

11 Di Liddo, *Alan Moore*, 55–61; Julia Kristeva, 'Word, Dialogue and Novel', in Toril Moi (ed.), *The Kristeva Reader* (Oxford: Blackwell, 1986), 37.

12 Gilles Deleuze and Felix Guattari, *A Thousand Plateaus* (London: Continuum, 2011), 124.

13 See for instance Eric Francisco, '*Falcon and Winter Soldier* Just Copied *Watchmen*'s Best and Most Brutal Idea', *Inverse.com* (10 April 2021, accessed 8 June 2021), https://www.inverse.com/entertainment/falcon-winter-soldier-watchmen-superheroes -supremacy; and Tia Alphonse, '*Watchmen* Walked So That *Lovecraft Country* Could Run', *Flow Journal* (3 November 2020, accessed 8 June 2021), https://www.flowjournal .org/2020/11/watchmen-lovecraft-country-black-sci-fi/.

Chapter 1

1 Di Liddo, *Alan Moore*, 55.

2 We can follow the historical thread of this approach from Swiss linguist Ferdinand de Saussure (1910s) through Russian theorist Mikhail Bakhtin, who was writing in the 1940s but whose work was only published, and translated, decades later, to French philosophers Julia Kristeva and Roland Barthes in the 1960s. For a detailed guide, see Graham Allen, *Intertextuality* (London: Taylor & Francis, 2000).

3 Roland Barthes (trans. Steven Heath), 'From Work to Text', in *Image Music Text* (London: Fontana, 1977), 159.

4 Ibid.

5 Ibid., 160.

6 Di Liddo, *Alan Moore*, 55.

7 A slight misquotation: Dylan's lyric runs '*the* superhuman crew *come out* and round up everyone / *That* knows more than they do'. The John Cale quotation is also inaccurate: the original runs 'A stronger world . . . a strong though loving world'.

8 Alan Moore, Dave Gibbons and Neil Gaiman, 'A Portal To Another Dimension', *The Comics Journal* 116 (July 1987), reprinted at *TCJ.com* (6 June 2012, accessed 17 June 2021).

9 Alan Moore, Dave Gibbons and John Higgins, *Watchmen* (New York: DC Comics, 1987), chapter 12, 3.

10 Ibid., 28.

NOTES

11 Ibid., chapter 5, 7.

12 Ibid., chapter 1, 10.

13 See Alan Moore, Dave Gibbons and John Higgins, *Absolute Watchmen* (New York: DC Comics, 2005), n.p. Moore also compares Meltdowns to the British sweet 'Treets', which was discontinued in 1988.

14 Julian Darius, '58 Varieties: *Watchmen* and Revisionism', in Richard Bensam (ed.), *Minutes to Midnight: Twelve Essays on Watchmen* (Illinois: Sequart, 2012), n.p. The bean can is barely visible at the bottom of Moore and Gibbons, *Watchmen*, chapter 1, 10.

15 The editorial cartoon is also by 'Walt Feinberg': see *Watchmen*, chapter 10, 24. One website jokily but convincingly proposes that Rorschach's psyche profile is based on *The Goodies* book from the 1970s: see Janeanpatience, 'The Alan Moore Plagiarism Scandal', *Suggested For Mature Readers* (1 May 2013, accessed 21 June 2021), https://suggestedformaturereaders.wordpress.com/2013/05/01/the-alan-moore-plagiarism-scandal/.

16 In the supplements to chapters 1, 11 and 5, respectively.

17 Alan Moore, Dave Gibbons and John Higgins, *Watchmen* (New York: DC Comics, 1987), chapter 8, 27.

18 The '1940's balloons are virtually the same as those in the Tijuana Bible, an artefact of the past that bridges the gap from Silk Spectre's flashback to the present day: ibid., chapter 2, 8.

19 See Di Liddo, *Alan Moore*, 62.

20 Moore and Gibbons, *Watchmen*, chapter 3, 2.

21 Ibid., chapter 5, 21–2.

22 Ibid., chapter 5, 9.

23 Ibid., chapter 12, 27.

24 See for instance ibid., chapter 3, 2, 'He's a survivor', and chapter 3, 3, the close-up of the figurehead's face.

25 Later editions of the comic, with more advanced colouring techniques, add Ben Day dots to the pirate images and captions.

26 Di Liddo, *Alan Moore*, 59.

27 Moore, Gibbons and Higgins, *Watchmen*, chapter 2, 17.

28 See ibid., chapter 11, 18.

29 The team name was first proposed in a reader's letter to *Captain Atom* in 1967: see Matthew Perpetua, 'This Detail In *Watchmen* Was Directly Inspired By A Fan Letter from 1967', *BuzzFeed.com* (3 October 2017, accessed 8 June 2021), https://www.buzzfeed.com/perpetua/watchmen-crimebusters-letter.

30 The comic-book characters are still referred to as 'the Watchmen'; see Ariana Brockington, 'Who Exactly Are The *Watchmen*?' *Refinery29.com* (20 October 2019, accessed 8 June 2021), https://www.refinery29.com/en-us/2019/10/8576241/who-are-the-original-watchmen-hbo-series; https://www.refinery29.com/en-us/2019/10/8576241/who-are-the-original-watchmen-hbo-series.

31 Moore, Gibbons and Higgins, *Watchmen*, chapter 1, 18: the newspaper on Veidt's desk mentions the 'Nuclear Doomsday Clock'.

32 Lance Parkin, *Magic Words: The Extraordinary Life of Alan Moore* (London: Arum Press, 2013), 191.

33 More specifically to *Watchmen*, Ted Kord was also a student of the first Blue Beetle, Dan Garrett.

34 Although Ozymandias also shares some of Superman's traits, such as the remote Fortress of Solitude, which he patrols with his alien pet. See Di Liddo, *Alan Moore*, 56. He has a perspective in common with the vigilante from Moore's *V for Vendetta* who, naked in a blaze of napalm, looks at other humans 'as if I were an insect . . . as if I were something mounted on a slide'. Alan Moore and David Lloyd, *V For Vendetta* (New York: DC Comics, 1990), 83. As we'll see, Rorschach's silent infiltrations of his targets' homes owe something to V, too.

35 In the comics themselves, they were briefly known as the Sentinels of Justice, a team that included all the main *Watchmen* heroes except Peter Cannon/Thunderbolt. See Alan Kistler, 'Before They Were *Watchmen*', *MTV.com* (4 March 2009, accessed 8 June 2021), http://www.mtv.com/news/2593711/before-they-were-watchmen-the-charlton-comics-characters-who-became-dr-manhattan-ozymandias/.

36 Paul Duncan, 'Interview: Dave Gibbons on *Watchmen*', *Wordsmith* (13 October 2009, accessed 8 June 2021), http://wordsmith-uk.blogspot.com/2009/10/interview-dave-gibbons-on-watchmen.html. For an early sketch of 'Silk', see Dave Gibbons, Chip Kidd and Mike Essl, *Watching the Watchmen* (London: Titan Books 2008), 44.

37 Jon B. Cooke, 'Toasting Absent Heroes', *Comic Book Artist* 9 (August 2000, accessed 8 June 2021), https://www.twomorrows.com/comicbookartist/articles/09moore.html.

38 Brian Cronin, 'Comic Book Urban Legends Revealed #124', *ComicBookResources .com* (11 October 2007, accessed 8 June 2021), https://www.cbr.com/comic-book-urban-legends-revealed-124/.

39 Andrew Hoberek, *Considering Watchmen: Poetics, Property, Politics* (New Brunswick: Rutgers, 2014), 60.

40 The *Watchmen* characters were always 'clones of clones', argues Matthew Wolf-Meyer: see Matthew Wolf-Meyer, 'The World Ozymandias Made: Utopias in the Superhero Comic, Subculture, and the Conservation of Difference', *Journal of Popular Culture* 36, no. 3 (March 2003), 507.

NOTES

41 Moloch the Mystic is, in turn, the comic strip character Mandrake the Magician, originally from 1934; see also his parallel incarnation, Nocturno the Necromancer, from Moore's *In Pictopia* (1986).

42 See Gibbons, Kidd and Essl, *Watching the Watchmen*, 36–7.

43 Anonymous, '*Watchmen* Secrets Revealed', *WatchmenComicMovie* (3 November 2008, accessed 8 April 2022), http://www.watchmencomicmovie.com/110308 -watchmen-movie-dave-gibbons.php. Manhattan, particularly in his relationship with Laurie, is also reminiscent of the uncanny, godlike Miracleman.

44 Gibbons, Kidd and Essl, *Watching the Watchmen*, 45.

45 Moore, Gibbons and Higgins, *Absolute Watchmen*, n.p.

46 Gibbons, Kidd and Essl, *Watching the Watchmen*, 45.

47 Moore, Gibbons and Higgins, *Absolute Watchmen*, n.p.

48 Cooke, 'Toasting Absent Heroes', n.p. The *Before Watchmen* prequel series makes this connection literal, placing Liddy and the Comedian in a scene together.

49 Gibbons, Kidd and Essl, *Watching the Watchmen*, 53.

50 Ibid., 46.

51 See Parkin, *Magic Words*, 198. Son of Sam is, in turn, namechecked by *Watchmen*'s newspaper editor Hector Godfrey when he hears the first page of Rorschach's journal.

52 Moore, Gibbons and Higgins, *Absolute Watchmen*, n.p.

53 Cooke, 'Toasting Absent Heroes', n.p.

54 Di Liddo, *Alan Moore*, 55.

55 Moore, Gibbons and Higgins, *Absolute Watchmen*, n.p.

56 'Archie' makes it into *Watchmen* as the name of Nite Owl's ship (officially Archimedes), while Rorschach is raised at the Charlton Home for Problem Children.

57 See Parkin, *Magic Words*, 192.

58 See Jeremy Larance, 'Alan Moore's *Miracleman*: Harbinger of the Modern Age of Comics', *Works and Days* 32, no. 1–2 (2015), 124.

59 Parkin, *Magic Words*, 190.

60 Gary Spencer Millidge, *Alan Moore Storyteller* (New York: Universe Publishing, 2011), 128. It is important to remember that Gibbons and Moore's innovation was not the storytelling device of the nine-panel grid itself but the consistent use of it throughout. Grant Morrison attributes it to Steve Ditko: see Grant Morrison, *Supergods: Our World in the Age of the Superhero* (London: Jonathan Cape 2011), 196.

NOTES

61 Ibid.

62 Ibid.

63 Vincent Eno and El Csawza, Alan Moore interview, originally published in Strange Things Are Happening, vol. 1, no. 2 (May/June 1988), reproduced by John Coulthart, *Feuilleton* (20 February 2006, accessed 2 June 2021), www.johncoulthart .com/feuilleton/2006/02/20/alan-moore-interview-1988/.

64 Christian W. Schneider, '"Nothing Ever Ends": Facing the Apocalypse in *Watchmen*', in Matthew J. A. Green (ed.), *Alan Moore and the Gothic Tradition* (Manchester: Manchester University Press, 2013), 94.

65 Iain Thomson, 'Deconstructing the Hero', in Jeff McLaughlin (ed.), *Comics as Philosophy* (Jackson: University of Mississippi Press, 2005) (range = 100–29).

66 Walter Hudsick. 'Reassembling the Components in the Correct Sequence: Why You Shouldn't Read *Watchmen* First', in Bensam (ed.), *Minutes to Midnight*, n.p.

67 Chad Nevett, 'The Smartest Man in the Morgue: *Watchmen* and "Twelve Notes on the Mystery Story"', in Bensam (ed.), *Minutes to Midnight*, n.p.

68 Robert Arp, 'Hooded Justice and Captain Metropolis: The Ambiguously Gay Duo', in Mark D. White (ed.), *Watchmen and Philosophy* (Hoboken: John Wiley & Sons, 2009), 186. (range = 185–96).

69 Ibid., 190.

70 Kate Willaert, 'Did Watchmen Steal from The Outer Limits, or From Jack Kirby?' *Comicsbeat.com* (8 October 2015, accessed 22 June 2021), https://www.comicsbeat .com/did-watchmen-steal-from-the-outer-limits-or-from-jack-kirby/.

71 James Gifford, 'Occulted Watchmen', *Nitrosyncretic.com* (2003, accessed 9 June 2021), http://www.nitrosyncretic.com/pdfs/occulted_watchmen_2003.pdf.

72 Mugrimm, 'We Need to Acknowledge That Rorschach is Racist', *Reddit.com* (June 2020, accessed 9 June 2021), https://www.reddit.com/r/Watchmen/comments/ doey0w/we_need_to_acknowledge_that_rorschach_is_racist/.

73 KoomGER, 'Dr Manhattan Created the Smurfs before the DC Universe', *Reddit.c om* (June 2017, accessed 10 June 2021), https://www.reddit.com/r/FanTheories/ comments/57ac2e/watchmendc_dr_manhattan_created_the_smurfs_before/.

74 Curdl3dm1lk, 'Cherry', *An Archive of Our Own* (22 August 2020, accessed 17 June 2021), https://archiveofourown.org/works/25978024.

75 quietprofanlity, 'Hard as Silk', *An Archive of Our Own* (12 April 2017, accessed 22 June 2021), https://archiveofourown.org/works/10602822/chapters/23442450.

76 Anon, '*Watchmen*'s Hot Gay Romances (You Never Knew About)', *Queerty.com* (7 April 2009, accessed 17 June 2021), https://www.queerty.com/watchmens-hot-gay -romances-you-never-knew-about-20090407/3.

77 See 'Rule 63 Comedian', *Omega-Level.net* (7 April 2014, accessed 2 July 2021), https://www.omega-level.net/2014/04/07/cosplay-rule-63-comedian/.

NOTES

78 See 'Parodies: *Watchmen*', *Doujinshi.org* (7 January 2017, accessed 2 July 2017), https://www.doujinshi.org/browse/parody/3595/WATCHMEN/.

79 Tom Smith, 'Rorschach Love', *TomSmithBandcamp.com* (20 May 2009, accessed 2 July 2021), https://tomsmith.bandcamp.com/track/rorschach-love.

80 Christopher Sharrett, 'Alan Moore', *David Kraft's Comics Interview* 65 (1988), reprinted *Alan Moore: Conversations*, ed. Eric L. Berlatsky (Jackson: University Press of Mississippi, 2012), 87–8.

81 The video interview, conducted by LeJorne Pindling of Street Law productions in 2008, is no longer available, but this transcribed quotation appears on multiple websites. See for instance Rosie Knight, 'Women Watch The *Watchmen*', *Shelfdust.com* (10 May 2019, accessed 10 June 2021), https://shelfdust.com/2019/05/10/rosie-knight-on-watchmen-2/.

82 Richard Bensam, 'Obsolete Models A Specialty: An Introduction', in Bensam (ed.), *Minutes to Midnight*, n.p.

83 Barthes, 'The Death of the Author', in *Image Music Text*, 146.

84 Jackson Ayres, *Alan Moore: A Critical Guide* (London: Bloomsbury, 2021), 2.

85 Ibid.

86 Barthes, 'Death of the Author', 148.

87 Ibid., 145–7.

88 Alan Moore, 'Behind the Painted Smile', in Moore and Lloyd, *V For Vendetta*, 270.

89 Ibid.

90 Ayres, *Alan Moore*, 164.

91 Di Liddo, *Alan Moore*, 86.

92 Alan Moore, Rick Veitch and Rob Liefield, 'New Jack City', in *Supreme: The Return* 6 (Canada: Awesome Entertainment, March 2000).

93 Fredric Jameson, 'Postmodernism and Consumer Society', in Peter Brooker (ed.), *Modernism/Postmodernism* (Essex.: Longman, 1992), 169.

94 Moore recycles his own ideas, too, on both a broad and more trivial level; aside from the big concepts of shared fictional space throughout his work, there are echoes like a man called Rorschach in the *Future Shock* 'Sunburn', the Prometheus cab company in *Watchmen,* long before *Promethea,* and the Exit Gardens for legal suicide in *Halo Jones*, prefiguring the Lethal Chambers in *Providence* some thirty-one years later.

95 Geoff Klock, *How to Read Superhero Comics and Why* (London: Continuum, 2002), 63.

96 Ibid., 64.

97 Moore and Gibbons, *Watchmen*, chapter 7, 8.

98 Alan Moore, Stephen Bissette and John Totleben, *Swamp Thing* 24 (New York: DC Comics, May 1984), 1.

99 Gardner Fox, Mike Sekowsky and Bernard Sachs, *Justice League of America* 21 (August 1963), reprinted in *The Greatest Team-Up Stories Ever Told* (New York: DC Comics 1990), 90.

100 Gardner Fox, Carmine Infantino and Joe Giella, 'Flash of Two Worlds', *The Flash* 123 (September 1961), reprinted in *The Greatest Team-Up Stories*, 72.

101 Originally Marvelman and renamed for copyright reasons.

102 Alan Moore and John Totleben, *Miracleman Book Three: Olympus* (Kent: Panini Publishers, 2015), 61–3.

103 Parkin, *Magic Words*, 166.

104 Alan Moore, Gary Leach and Alan Davis, *Miracleman Book One: A Dream of Flying* (New York: Marvel Comics, 2014), 15. Pádraig Ó Méalóid suggests that this introduction, with its Nietzsche quotation, was 'put there by the editorial people at Eclipse, perhaps with input from Dez Skinn, to try to give the American audience a taste of what went before', and that Moore, who was not responsible for it himself, asked for the material to be excised. See Pádraig Ó Méalóid, 'Alan Moore and *Superfolks* Part 2: The Case for the Defence', *Comicbeat.com* (11 November 2012, accessed 23 July 2021), https://www.comicsbeat.com/alan-moore-and-superfolks -part-2-the-case-for-the-defence/.

105 Moore and Gibbons, *Watchmen*, chapter 6, 28.

106 Note that the image of an innocent smiley face with a violent rip in the forehead was used by Moore (drawn by Alan Davis) in the *Captain Britain* episode 'Arrivals', *The Daredevils* 8 (August 1983), reprinted in *Captain Britain* (New York: Marvel Comics, 2009), n.p.

107 Moore and Gibbons, *Watchmen*, chapter 11, 27.

108 Moore and Totleben, *Miracleman Book Three*, 84.

109 Alan Moore, Rick Veitch and John Totleben, *Swamp Thing* 37 (New York: DC Comics, June 1985), 21.

110 This climax may be inspired by Miller's *Ronin* (1983), which 'culminates in a New York City devastated by an explosion that takes up four, full, fold-out pages'. See Greg S. McCue with Clive Bloom, *Dark Knights: The New Comics in Context* (London: Pluto Press 1993), 69.

111 Alan Moore, Steve Bissette and John Totleben, *Swamp Thing* 43 (New York: DC Comics, March 1986), 1; Alan Moore and Alan Davis, 'Waiting For The End Of The World', *The Daredevils* 9 (September 1983), reprinted in *Captain Britain* (New York: Marvel Comics, 2009), n.p. We also see a brief hallucination of similar butchery in *V For Vendetta*: see Moore and Lloyd, *V For Vendetta*, 211.

112 Ozymandias kills 'half New York', but the total is given as three million dead; Johnny Bates leaves 'half of London simply gone' with a total of forty thousand dead.

NOTES

113 Tim Callaghan, 'The Great Alan Moore Reread: *Marvelman/Miracleman*, Part Four' (21 November 2011, accessed 20 June 2021), https://www.tor.com/2011/11/21/the-great-alan-moore-reread-marvelman-miracleman-part-4/.

114 Moore and Totleben, *Miracleman Book Three*, 88–9.

115 Ibid., 90.

116 Ibid., 252–3.

117 Sharrett, 'Alan Moore', 92.

118 Ayres, *Alan Moore,* 182.

119 Alan Moore and Alan Davis, 'But They Never Really Die', in *Daredevils* 11 (November 1983), reprinted in *Captain Britain* (New York: Marvel Comics, 2009), n.p.

120 Alan Moore and Ian Gibson, 'Armies of the Night', reprinted in *The Ballad of Halo Jones Volume 3* (Oxford: Rebellion, 2018).

121 Ayres, *Alan Moore*, 186.

122 Alan Moore, Steve Bissette and John Totleben, *Swamp Thing* 22 (New York: DC Comics 1984), 9. See for instance Douglas Wolk, 'Please Sir, I Want Some Moore', *Slate.com* (17 December 2003, accessed 15 June 2021), https://slate.com/culture/2003/12/how-alan-moore-transformed-american-comics.html. Moore was aware that this line, 'that I personally quite liked', attracted mockery: see *Alan Moore's Guide to Writing Comics* (Illinois: Avatar, 2010), 39.

123 Alan Moore and Jim Baikie, 'Skizz', in *2000AD* 308 (London: Fleetway, 19 March 1983).

124 Alan Moore and Mike White, 'Going Native', in *2000AD* 318 (London: Fleetway, 28 May 1983).

125 Alan Moore, Steve Bissette and John Totleben, *Saga of the Swamp Thing Book One* (New York: DC Comics, 1987), 13.

126 Ibid., 35.

127 Alan Moore and Dave Gibbons, 'For The Man Who Has Everything', in *Superman Annual* 11 (New York: DC Comics, 1985), 32.

128 Alan Moore and Kevin O'Neill, 'Tygers', in *Tales of The Green Lantern Corps Annual* 2 (New York: DC Comics, 1986).

129 Moore and Totleben, *Miracleman Book Three*, 17.

130 Alan Moore, Rick Veitch and Al Williamson, *Superman and Swamp Thing: The Jungle Line* (New York: DC Comics, September 1985), 16.

131 Moore and Gibbons, *Watchmen*, chapter 1, 15.

132 Ibid., chapter 9, 28.

133 Parkin, *Magic Words*, 184.

134 Ayres, *Alan Moore*, 184.

135 Moore and Gibbons, *Watchmen*, chapter 2, 27–8.

136 Ibid., chapter 1, 12.

137 Parkin, *Magic Words*, 198.

138 Moore and Gibbons, *Watchmen*, chapter 1, 1.

139 Ibid., 19.

140 Ibid., chapter 10, 16.

141 Ibid., chapter 1, 22. Note that Rorschach's tough-guy demeanour is not just a front: he seems barely shaken by the teleportation, whereas Laurie, who has experienced it many times, vomits on each occasion. When Jon transports a crowd from outside the White House in 1977, two of them suffer heart attacks: ibid., chapter 4, 22.

142 Ibid., 17.

143 Ibid., chapter 5, 24.

144 Parkin points out that the description 'Though he is capable of a very black sense of humour, we can never be sure if he thinks his remarks are funny' applies equally to Rorschach as to Judge Dredd. Parkin, *Magic Words*, 189.

145 Moore and Gibbons, *Watchmen*, chapter 12, 21.

146 Alan Moore and Jim Baikie, *The Complete Skizz* (Oxford: Rebellion, 2017), n.p.

147 Di Liddo, *Alan Moore*, 54. The comic in question is *Swamp Thing* 32, 'Pog' (New York: DC Comics, January 1985).

148 Alan Moore, Steve Bissette and John Totleben, 'A Time of Running', in *Swamp Thing* 26 (New York: DC Comics, July 1984), 23.

149 Moore and Lloyd, *V For Vendetta*, 219.

150 Ibid., 99.

151 Ibid., 196.

152 Ibid., 223.

153 Ibid., 59.

154 Quoted in Parkin, *Magic Words*, 190.

155 Moore and Gibbons, *Watchmen*, chapter 5, 12–17.

156 Alan Moore and Ian Gibson, 'Grawks Bearing Gifts', in *2000AD* 203 (London: Fleetway, 14 March 1981) reprinted in *The Complete Alan Moore Future Shocks* (Oxford: Rebellion, 2013), n.p.

157 Alan Moore and John Higgins, 'Salad Days', in *2000AD* 247 (London: Fleetway, 16 January 1982), reprinted ibid.

NOTES

213

158   Alan Moore and Jesus Redondo, 'Sunburn', in *2000AD* 282 (London: Fleetway, 18 September 1982), reprinted ibid.

159   Alan Moore and Paul Neary, 'An American Werewolf in Space', in *2000AD* 252 (London: Fleetway, 20 February 1982), reprinted ibid.

160   Alan Moore and Mike White, 'The Reversible Man', in *2000AD* 308 (London: Fleetway, 19 March 1983), reprinted ibid.

161   Alan Moore and Mike White, 'Eureka!', in *2000AD* 325 (London: Fleetway, 16 July 1983), reprinted ibid.

162   Alan Moore and Kevin O'Neill, 'Brief Lives', in *The Omega Men* 26 (New York: DC Comics, May 1985). Moore's *ABC Warriors* story, 'Red Planet Blues', is also remarkably similar in its imagery and tone. See Alan Moore, Steve Dillon and John Higgins, 'Red Planet Blues', in *2000AD Annual 1985* (London: Fleetway, August 1984), n.p. Higgins's art on this story prompted Gibbons and Moore to invite him to colour *Watchmen*. See tweet from Dave Gibbons (24 October 2016, accessed 12 April 2022), https://twitter.com/davegibbons90/status/790537404344041473.

163   Parkin, *Magic Words*, 204.

164   Alan Moore and Alan Davis, 'D.R. and Quinch Get Drafted', Part 4, *2000AD* 358 (London: Fleetway, 3 March 1984), reprinted in *The Complete D.R. & Quinch* (Oxford: Rebellion, 2013), n.p.

165   Moore and Gibbons, *Watchmen*, chapter 1, 2–3.

166   Van Ness, *Watchmen as Literature*, 87–8. In fact, Blake's head is hitting the glass front of a framed pin-up in this image, not the window.

167   Moore and Gibbons, *Watchmen*, chapter 3, 13.

168   Klock, *How To Read Superhero Comics*, 67.

169   Moore and Lloyd, *V For Vendetta*, 82.

170   Ibid., 109–10.

171   The previous chapter, 'The Veil', also experiments with the *Watchmen* counterpoint technique – Rose Almond's narration comments on Evey's situation – but the effect here is less sustained. See ibid., 102–3.

172   Alan Moore and Jim Baikie, 'Father's Day', in *Vigilante* 17 (New York: DC Comics, May 1985), 3–4.

173   Moore and Gibbons, *Watchmen*, chapter 5, 6–7.

174   Alan Moore and Jim Baikie, 'Father's Day', 10.

175   Moore and Gibbons, 'For the Man Who Has Everything', 9.

176   Alan Moore, Rick Veitch, Alfredo Alcala and John Totleben, 'Earth to Earth', in *Swamp Thing* 55 (New York: DC Comics, December 1986), 1.

NOTES

177 Van Ness, *Watchmen as Literature*, 88–9.

178 Moore and Gibbons, *Watchmen*, chapter 2, 9.

179 Moore, Veitch, Alcala and Totleben, 'Earth to Earth', 5.

180 Moore and Gibbons, *Watchmen*, chapter 5, 7–8; see also Van Ness *Watchmen as Literature*, 90.

181 Parkin, *Magic Words*, 210. Moore claims he was writing it during *Watchmen*, 'or just after'. See George Khoury et al., *The Extraordinary Works of Alan Moore* (Raleigh: TwoMorrows Publishing, 2003), 122. However, Elizabeth Sandifer makes a convincing case that Moore has confused the dates and that *The Killing Joke* was indeed written in 1985: see Elizabeth Sandifer, 'Chapter Six: Hello From The Cracks (The Abyss Gazes Also)', *EruditorumPress.com* (3 June 2020, accessed 19 August 2021), https://www.eruditorumpress.com/blog/last-war-in-albion-book-two-chapter-six-hello-from-the-cracks-the-abyss-gazes-also.

182 Alan Moore, Brian Bolland and John Higgins, *Batman: The Killing Joke* (New York: DC Comics, 1988), n.p.

183 Ibid.

184 There is a similar sequence in the *V* chapter 'Vectors', where the parallel lines of a motorway are echoed by a railway track, but this episode was written after *Watchmen* and published in March 1989, so it can be considered a late example. See Moore and Lloyd, *V For Vendetta*, 224.

185 Moore, *Guide to Writing Comics*, 36.

186 Paul Gravett, *Graphic Novels: Stories to Change Your Life* (London: Aurum, 2005), 82.

187 Elizabeth Sandifer, 'Chapter One: A Machine That Kills (At Midnight All The Agents)', *EruditorumPress.com* (18 May 2020, accessed 17 June 2021), https://www.eruditorumpress.com/blog/last-war-in-albion-book-two-chapter-one-a-machine-that-kills-at-midnight-all-the-agents.

188 Moore, *Guide to Writing Comics*, 18.

189 Moore explains his use of silent 'beats' in the same guide: ibid., 19.

190 Ibid., 3.

191 Moore and Gibbons, *Fantasy Advertiser* roundtable discussion, *Feuilleton*.

192 Compare for instance V appearing at night in Delia's bedroom with Rorschach waking Moloch: Moore and Lloyd, *V For Vendetta* 70; and Moore and Gibbons, *Watchmen*, chapter 5, 1–3.

193 Moore and Gibbons, *Watchmen*, chapter 1, 16.

194 Ibid., chapter 11, 16.

195 Ibid., chapter 1, 1.

NOTES

215

196 Moore, Veitch, Alcala and Totleben, 'Earth to Earth', 18–21.

197 Alan Moore and Dave Gibbons, 'Mogo Doesn't Socialize', *Green Lantern* 188 (New York: DC Comics, May 1985), 6.

198 Alan Moore and Ian Gibson, 'The Ballad of Halo Jones', reprinted in *The Ballad of Halo Jones Volume 1* (Oxford: Rebellion, 2018). See also Moore, *Guide to Writing Comics*, 17.

199 Alan Moore and John Totleben, 'The Garden of Earthly Delights', *Swamp Thing* 53 (New York: DC Comics, October 1986), 32.

200 Alan Moore and Chuck Austen, *Miracleman Book 2: The Red King Syndrome* (Kent: Panini Publishers, 2014), 59–65.

201 Alan Moore and Klaus Janson, 'Night Olympics Part Two', in *Detective Comics* 550 (New York: DC Comics, May 1985), 5.

202 Moore and Baikie, 'Father's Day', 9.

203 Alan Moore and Alan Davis, 'D.R. and Quinch Go Straight', in *2000AD* 350 (January 1984), reprinted in *The Complete D.R. & Quinch* (Oxford: Rebellion, 2013), n.p.

204 Alan Moore and Alan Davis, 'Thicker Than Water', in *Daredevils* 3 (March 1983), reprinted in *Captain Britain* (New York: Marvel Comics, 2009), n.p.

205 Moore and Lloyd, *V For Vendetta*, 54.

206 Ibid., 48.

207 Ibid., 77.

208 Kieron Gillen refers to this fixed-camera technique as a 'steady' in his own work, but I have not encountered this term elsewhere. See Kieron Gillen, 'Writer Notes: *The Wicked +the Divine* 34', *KieronGillen.Tumblr.com* (27 March 2018, accessed 13 August 2021), *KieronGillen.Tumblr.com*, https://kierongillen.tumblr.com/post/172305230757/writer-notes-the-wicked-the-divine-34.

209 See for instance Archie Goodwin, Johnny Craig and Sam Grainger, 'Alone Against A.I.M.!', *The Invincible Iron Man* 25 (New York: Marvel Comics May 1970), 3, 9; Stan Lee, Jack Kirby and Joe Sinnott, 'The Long Journey Home!', *Fantastic Four* 100 (New York: Marvel Comics, July 1970), 6; and Roy Thomas and Herb Trimpe, 'If I Kill You . . . I Die!', *The Incredible Hulk* 130 (New York: Marvel Comics, August 1970), 2.

210 Millidge, *Alan Moore: Storyteller*, 128.

211 Tasha Robinson, 'Alan Moore', *AVClub.com* (25 June 2003, accessed 23 June 2021), https://www.avclub.com/alan-moore-1798208283.

212 Moore, *Guide to Writing Comics*, 44.

213 'At least for the time being, I'm going to steer away from superhero work', he told *Comics Interview* in April 1987. 'I think I'd love to play the field a little more.' See Parkin, *Magic Words*, 238. See also Berlatsky, *Conversations,* 12: 'After his first

departure from DC, for instance, Moore . . . declared his intentions to abandon superhero and other genre fiction altogether.'

214 In a neat example of intertextuality, Girl One's costume in the early 2000s *Top Ten* is explicitly based on 'Rohrschach' [*sic*], according to artist Gene Ha, but also on 1890s comic strip icon The Yellow Kid. Alan Moore, Gene Ha and Zander Cannon, *Top Ten Book Two* (California: America's Best Comics, 2002), n.p.

215 Moore, *Guide to Writing Comics*, 38.

216 Moore and Gibbons, *Fantasy Advertiser* roundtable discussion, *Feuilleton*.

217 See Jess Nevins, 'Annotations to *League of Extraordinary Gentlemen* Volume III Chapter 2' (accessed 22 June 2021), http://jessnevins.com/annotations /1969annotations.html.

218 Alan Moore and Jacen Burroughs, *Providence* Chapter XII (Illinois: Avatar Press, April 17), n.p.

219 Alan Moore and Jacen Burroughs, *Neonomicon* (Illinois: Avatar Press, 2010), n.p. The end of this issue also features a crane shot, reminiscent of the final pages in *Watchmen*, chapters 1 and 9.

220 There is, however, a *Watchmen*-like segue in *Top Ten*, as a police officer remarks over a fallen body, 'maybe it's a game', and we cut to her colleague across town playing a handheld console: 'I'm dead again! This game is a gyp!' Moore, Ha and Cannon, *Top Ten Book Two*, n.p.

221 Alan Moore and Jacen Burroughs, *The Courtyard* (Illinois: Avatar Press, 2003), n.p. Note that the comic is based on a prose story by Moore, written in 1994.

222 Alan Moore and Kevin O'Neill, *The League of Extraordinary Gentlemen: Century: 1969* (Georgia: Top Shelf Productions, 2011), n.p.

223 See Alex Link, 'Psychogeography's Legacy in *From Hell* and *Watchmen*', *European Comic Art*, 9, no. 2 (Autumn 2016).

224 Moore and O'Neill, *Century: 1969*, n.p.

225 Cooke, 'Toasting Absent Heroes', n.p.

226 We could also trace a line directly from the closing scene of Moore's other key Superman tale, 'Whatever Happened to the Man of Tomorrow?', where Lois and a Clark live happily but secretly together as Mr and Mrs Jordan Elliot, and the final appearance of Dan and Laurie – or Sam and Sandra Hollis – in *Watchmen*. See Alan Moore and Curt Swan, 'Whatever Happened to the Man of Tomorrow?', *Action Comics* 583 (New York: DC Comics, September 1986).

227 Moore and Gibbons, 'For the Man Who Has Everything', 2.

228 Moore and Gibbons, *Watchmen*, chapter 12, 11.

229 Moore, *Guide to Writing Comics*, 8.

NOTES

230 See Pádraig Ó Méalóid, 'Last Alan Moore Interview?' *Slovobooks. Wordpress.com* (9 January 2014, accessed 24 June 2021), https://slovobooks.wordpress.com/2014/01/09/last-alan-moore-interview/.

231 Sam Thielman, 'Goodbye, Alan Moore: The King of Comics Bows Out', *The Guardian* (18 July 2019, accessed 24 June 2021), https://www.theguardian.com/books/2019/jul/18/goodbye-alan-moore-the-king-of-comics-bows-out.

232 See Parkin, *Magic Words*, 209. Gibbons told *Arkensword* magazine that DC had floated *Rorschach's Journal* and *The Comedian's War Diary* (Parkin, *Magic Words*, 223) and suggested to *Fantasy Advertiser* that they also proposed a possible Nite Owl/Rorschach title. Moore comments, 'we might do a Minutemen book. There would be no sequel.' Moore and Gibbons, *Fantasy Advertiser* roundtable discussion, *Feuilleton.*

Chapter 2

1 Ayres, *Alan Moore*, 77.

2 David Hughes, *The Greatest Sci-Fi Movies Never Made* (London: Titan Books, 2008), 148. Discussed in Van Ness, *Watchmen as Literature*, 13.

3 Quoted in Millidge, *Alan Moore: Storyteller*, 133.

4 Quoted in Julia Round, *Gothic in Comics and Graphic Novels* (North Carolina: McFarland & Company, 2014), 48.

5 Van Ness, *Watchmen as Literature*, 14.

6 Millidge, *Alan Moore: Storyteller*, 132.

7 Quoted in Milledge, *Alan Moore: Storyteller*, 132–3.

8 Quoted in Van Ness, *Watchmen as Literature*, 14.

9 Wired Staff, 'Artist Dave Gibbons' Gut Feelings on the *Watchmen* Movie', *Wired* (23 February 2009, accessed 13 April 2022), https://www.wired.com/2009/02/ff-gibbons-qa/.

10 Gerard Jones and Will Jacobs, *The Comic Book Heroes* (California: Prima Publishing, 1987), 313.

11 Ibid., 314.

12 Ibid., 319.

13 Ibid.

14 Ibid., 319–20.

15 Ibid., 319.

16 Ibid., 323.

218 NOTES

17 Ibid., 322.

18 Ibid., 323.

19 Ibid, 323–4.

20 Ibid., 313.

21 Ibid., 324.

22 Ibid., 323.

23 Elizabeth Sandifer, 'Chapter Twelve: In The End (A Stronger Loving World)', *EruditoriumPress.com* (3 August 2020, accessed 12 August 2021), https://www .eruditorumpress.com/blog/last-war-in-albion-book-two-chapter-twelve-in-the-end -a-stronger-loving-world.

24 Elizabeth Sandifer, 'Chapter Ten: Where The Moon and the Earth Were Joined (Two Riders Were Approaching)', *EruditoriumPress.com* (6 July 2020, accessed 12 August 2021), https://www.eruditorumpress.com/blog/category/last-war-in-albion/page/3.

25 Joe Queenan, 'Drawing on the Dark Side', *New York Times Magazine* Section 6, 32 (30 April 1989, accessed 5 July 2021), https://www.nytimes.com/1989/04/30/ magazine/drawing-on-the-dark-side.html.

26 Jackson Ayres, 'When Were Superheroes Grim and Gritty?' *LA Review of Books* (20 February 2016, accessed 12 July 2021), https://lareviewofbooks.org/article/when -were-superheroes-grim-and-gritty/.

27 Ibid. See also William Proctor, 'The Dark Age: Superheroes in the 1980s', in Sebastian Domsch, Dan Hassler-Forest and Dirk Vanderbeke (eds), *Handbook of Comics and Graphic Narratives* (Berlin: De Gruyter, 2021), 351.

28 Klock, *How To Read Superhero Comics*, 12.

29 Harold Bloom, *The Anxiety of Influence*: *A Theory of Poetry* (Oxford: Oxford University, Press, 1997), xiii.

30 See Klock, *How To Read Superhero Comics*, 13; see also Harold Bloom, *A Map of Misreading* (Oxford: Oxford University Press, 1975), 3–4.

31 Ibid., 13.

32 Parkin, *Magic Words*, 207.

33 Glenn Hauman, 'Neil Gaiman's *Watchmen* Parody: Watchdogs', *ComicMix.com* (10 March 2009, accessed 2 July 2021), https://www.comicmix.com/2009/03/10/neil -gaimans-watchmen-parody-watchdogs/.

34 Will Eisner used the term for his *A Contract with God* (1978): see Van Ness, *Watchmen as Literature*, 5.

35 'In the late 1980s it appeared as if everyone in the television and print news media was asking the question'; Van Ness, *Watchmen as Literature*.

NOTES

219

36   Parkin notes that in 2010, DC management credited the marketing department and the trade paperback format, rather than the content itself, with *Watchmen*'s success; Moore was seen as simply 'part of the original process'; Parkin, *Magic Words*, 231–2.

37   See for instance Paul Gravett, 'Graphic Novels: Can You Hear The Trucks?' *PaulGravett.com* (31 December 2006, accessed 25 July 2022), http://paulgravett.com /articles/article/graphic_novels2.

38   See also Parkin, *Magic Words,* 207.

39   Queenan, 'Drawing on the Dark Side'.

40   Kurt Amacker, 'Interview With Alan Moore', *Seraphemera.org* (2006, accessed 23 July 2021), http://www.seraphemera.org/seraphemera_books/AlanMoore_Page1 .html.

41   See Marv Wolfman, George Pérez and Jerry Ordway, *Crisis on Infinite Earths* 5 (New York: DC Comics, July 1985), 24–5, and Moore and Gibbons, *Watchmen*, chapter 11, 28.

42   See Klock, *How To Read Superhero Comics*, 19–21.

43   See for instance Len Wein, Paris Cullins and Bruce D. Patterson, *Blue Beetle* 2 (New York: DC Comics, July 1986), interior front cover.

44   We could see this as an example of the 'selective tradition' discussed by Raymond Williams in relation to literature: see Raymond Williams, *The Long Revolution* (Middlesex: Pelican Books, 1965), 67.

45   Alan Moore, Mike Collins and Mark Farmer, *The Daredevils* 8 (August 1983), available online at *Comics_Scans* (accessed 7 April 2022), https://comics-scans .livejournal.com/114153.html.

46   *Green Lantern* 76, from April 1970, challenged its hero for ignoring 'the black skins' while helping diverse alien groups; *Green Lantern/Green Arrow* 85 (August– September 1981) featured the sidekick Speedy as a 'junkie'. We should remember too that Marvel's anti-hero The Punisher, one of the inspirations for Comedian's cynical brutality, debuted in 1974.

47   Khoury et al. *The Extraordinary Works of Alan Moore*, 110.

48   Moore and Gibbons, *Fantasy Advertiser* roundtable discussion, *Feuilleton*.

49   See Hoberek, *Considering Watchmen*, 63.

50   Klock, *How to Read Superhero Comics,* 65.

51   Khoury, *The Extraordinary Works of Alan Moore*, 120.

52   Peter Cannon followed in September 1992.

53   Joe Gill and Pat Boyette, 'Introducing: The Peacemaker', in *Fightin 5* 40 (Connecticut: Charlton Comics, November 1966), 1.

54   Paul Kupperberg, Tod Smith and Pablo Marcos, *Peacemaker* 3 (New York: DC Comics, March 1988), 23.

220 NOTES

55 Ibid., 22.

56 Moore and Gibbons, *Watchmen*, chapter 2, 16.

57 Paul Kupperberg, 'He Loves Peace So Much He's Willing To Kill For It . . .' *Kuppsmalibulist. com* (29 May 2020, accessed 1 August 2021), https://kupps .malibulist.com/2011/05/29/he-loves-peace-so-much-hes-willing-to-kill-for-it-and -hes-downloadable-too/.

58 Paul Kupperberg, Tod Smith and Pablo Marcos, *Peacemaker* 1 (New York: DC Comics, January 1988), 25.

59 I will discuss *Saturday Morning Watchmen* in Chapter 3.

60 Cary Bates and Pat Broderick, *Captain Atom* 1 (New York: DC Comics, March 1987), 39.

61 Ibid.

62 Ibid., 6.

63 Moore and Gibbons, *Watchmen*, chapter 4, 9.

64 Cary Bates, Pat Broderick and Bob Smith, *Captain Atom* 6 (New York: DC Comics, August 1987), 7.

65 Bates and Broderick, *Captain Atom* 1, 7.

66 Ibid., 12.

67 Ibid., 14.

68 Cary Bates and Patrick Broderick, *Captain Atom 2* (New York: DC Comics, April 1987), 19.

69 Len Wein, Don Heck and Danny Bulanadi, *Blue Beetle* 24 (New York: DC Comics, May 1988), 23.

70 Len Wein, Paris Cullins and Bruce D. Patterson, *Blue Beetle* 10 (New York: DC Comics, March 1987), 6.

71 Moore and Gibbons, *Watchmen*, chapter 7, 22.

72 While there are glancing similarities to *Watchmen* 7 in *Blue Beetle* 1 – Nite Owl and Blue Beetle both fly their gimmick ships towards a city fire, and both scenes involve a gag about Smokey the Bear – any influence would, logically, have to be the other way around, as the *Blue Beetle* issue was published in June 1986 and *Watchmen* 7 in March 1987. As Moore and Gibbons found, sometimes a similarity proves simply to be synchronicity.

73 Stan Lee and John Romita, 'Spider-Man No More!' in *The Amazing Spider-Man* 50 (New York: Marvel Comics, July 1967), 15–16.

74 The 'watchman' here is a night watchman, rather than a superhero; and it must simply be coincidence, too, that Blue Beetle's issue 1 opponent Firefist clings so possessively to his mask, crying 'No – not my face –!!' (Rorschach, at the end of chapter 5, screams 'No! My face! Give it back!')

75 Moore and Gibbons, *Watchmen*, chapter 11, 16–17.

76 Len Wein, Paris Cullins and Bruce D. Patterson, *Blue Beetle* 1 (New York: DC Comics, June 1986), 4.

77 Lee and Romita, 'Spider-Man No More!', 2–3.

78 *Justice League America* 54 from September 1991 also used Blue Beetle in a pastiche of the 'Spider-Man No More!' image.

79 Perhaps in a further coincidence, a 1968 *Question,* scripted and drawn by Ditko, features a painting of boots walking past a gutter, with a soup can and cigarette butt in the foreground. See Steve Ditko, 'The Question', in D. C. Glanzman and Steve Ditko, *The Blue Beetle* 5 (Connecticut: Charlton Comics, November 1968), 1.

80 Stan Lee and Steve Ditko, *The Amazing Spider-Man* 33 (New York: Marvel Comics, February 1966), 3.

81 Wein, Cullins and Patterson, *Blue Beetle* 2, 3.

82 Moore and Gibbons, *Watchmen*, chapter 2, 20; chapter 2, 27.

83 D.C. Glanzman and Steve Ditko, *Blue Beetle* 1 (June 1967), 4.

84 Wein, Cullins and Patterson, *Blue Beetle* 1, 5.

85 Ibid., 1.

86 Dan Dreiberg, fittingly, wears Nostalgia cologne.

87 Blue Beetle did appear in the *Crisis* but remarks on that occasion, 'And here I thought I'd be forgotten after all this time', confirming the sense of previous absence. Marv Wolfman, George Pérez and Dick Giordano, *Crisis on Infinite Earths* 1 (New York: DC Comics, April 1985), 18.

88 Moore and Gibbons, *Watchmen,* chapter 7, 28.

89 The 1985 Eclipse reprint of the first Alan Moore *Miracleman* stories is even titled 'Rebirth'.

90 Dennis O'Neil, Denys Cowan and Rick Magyar, *The Question* 1 (New York: DC Comics, February 1987), 1.

91 Quoted in Matt Brady, 'Revisiting the Question', *Gamesradar.com* (29 July 2020, accessed 14 July 2021), https://www.gamesradar.com/uk/revisiting-the-question-by -denny-oneil-and-denys-cowan/.

92 He and his Charlton teammates (Peacemaker, Nightshade, Captain Atom, Judomaster) had a brief cameo in *Crisis* but, unlike Blue Beetle, did not play a significant role. See Marv Wolfman, George Pérez and Jerry Ordway, *Crisis on Infinite Earths* 6 (New York: DC Comics, September 1985), 15.

222   NOTES

93 Len Wein, Paris Cullins and Bruce D. Patterson, *Blue Beetle* 5 (New York: DC Comics, October 1986), 20.

94 Moore and Gibbons, *Watchmen*, chapter 8, 17.

95 Len Wein, Paris Cullins and Del Barrag, *Blue Beetle* 7 (New York: DC Comics, December 1986), 22.

96 O'Neil, Cowan and Magyar, *The Question* 1, 1.

97 Denny O'Neil, Neal Adams and Dick Giordano, 'A Vow from the Grave!', in *Detective Comics* 4010 (New York: DC Comics, April 1971), 1–2.

98 Dennis O'Neil, Denys Cowan and Rick Magyar, *The Question* 17 (New York: DC Comics, May 1988), 11.

99 Ibid., 27.

100 All in J. M. DeMatteis and Mark Badger, *Martian Manhunter* 2 (New York: DC Comics, June 1988).

101 Advertisement for *Power of the Atom* in J. M. DeMatteis and Mark Badger, *Martian Manhunter* 3 (New York: DC Comics, July 1988), n.p.

102 Jeanette Kahn, 'Publishorial', in J. M. DeMatteis and Mark Badger, *Martian Manhunter* 4 (New York: DC Comics, August 1988), n.p.

103 Andrew Helfer and José Luis Garcia Lopez, *Deadman* 1 (New York: DC Comics, March 1986), 2. The theme of rebirth in a vague, mystical 'East' is common in the comics of this period. It overlaps to an extent with *Watchmen* (Ozymandias's origin) but can probably be sourced to a broader 1980s Orientalism.

104 Paul Kupperberg, Rick Hoberg and Anne Starr, *Power Girl* 1 (New York: DC Comics, June 1988), 4.

105 Doug Moench, Dave Hoover and Robert Campanella, *The Wanderers* 1 (New York: DC Comics, June 1988), 10–11.

106 John Byrne and Dick Giordano, *Man of Steel* 1 (New York: DC Comics, July 1986), 3.

107 Howard Chaykin, *The Shadow: Blood and Judgement* 1 (New York: DC Comics, May 1986), n.p.

108 Howard Chaykin, *The Shadow: Blood and Judgement* 4 (New York: DC Comics, August 1986), n.p.

109 George Pérez, 'The Wonder of It All', in Greg Potter, George Pérez and Bruce Patterson, *Wonder Woman 1* (New York: DC Comics, February 1987), n.p.

110 Mike Baron, Jackson Guice and Larry Mahlstedt, *Flash* 1 (New York: DC Comics, June 1987), 11.

111 Ibid., 18.

NOTES

112 Ibid., 7.

113 Ibid., 18.

114 Miller with Janson and Varley, *Batman: The Dark Knight Returns* Book One, 40–3.

115 Howard Chaykin, *Blackhawk: Blood and Iron* 1 (New York: DC Comics, March 1988), 7–9.

116 Ibid., 5.

117 Mindy Newell, J. J. Birch and Michael Bair, *Catwoman* 4 (New York: DC Comics, May 1989), 1.

118 J. M. DeMatteis and Mark Badger, *Martian Manhunter* 2 (New York: DC Comics, June 1988), 4.

119 J. M. DeMatteis and Mark Badger, *Martian Manhunter* 4 (New York: DC Comics, August 1988), 3.

120 J. M. DeMatteis and Mark Badger, *Martian Manhunter* 3 (New York: DC Comics, July 1988), 7.

121 DeMatteis and Badger, *Martian Manhunter* 4, 21.

122 Mike Grell, *Green Arrow: The Longbow Hunters* 1 (New York: DC Comics, August 1987), 22.

123 While perhaps inspired by recent work like Miller's *Dark Knight Returns*, which featured Selina Kyle beaten and bound, note that this sexualized depiction of victimized women was far from new within the genre; Black Canary herself was tied to a chair wearing underwear in Michael Fleischer, Dick Giordano and Terry Austin, *The Brave and the Bold* 166 (New York: DC Comics, September 1980), 15.

124 Ibid., 28.

125 Ibid., 13–14.

126 Ibid., 42.

127 Moore and Gibbons, *Watchmen*, chapter 1, 14.

128 Moore and Gibbons, *Watchmen*, chapter 7, 20.

129 Ibid., 28.

130 Mike Grell, *Green Arrow: The Longbow Hunters* 2 (New York: DC Comics, September 1987), 19.

131 Moore and Gibbons, *Watchmen*, chapter 5, 19.

132 Grell, *Longbow Hunters* 2, 16.

133 Grell, *Longbow Hunters* 1, 2–4.

134 Alan Moore and Klaus Janson, 'Night Olympics', *Detective Comics* 549 (New York: DC Comics, April 1985), 1.

NOTES

135 Alan Moore and Klaus Janson, 'Night Olympics Part Two', *Detective Comics* 550 (New York: DC Comics, May 1985), 7. In the second paragraph, which closes the story, Moore again cannot resist a pun; Dinah Lance's middle name is Laurel.

136 Grell, *Longbow Hunters* 1, 40.

137 Frank Miller with Klaus Janson and Lynn Varley, *Batman: The Dark Knight Returns* Book Three (London: Titan Books, 1986), 6.

138 Grell, *Longbow Hunters* 1, 34.

139 Frank Miller with Klaus Janson and Lynn Varley, *Batman: The Dark Knight Returns* Book One (London: Titan Books, 1986), 36.

140 Ibid., 26–7.

141 Ibid., 7.

142 Ibid., 13.

143 Roy and Dan Thomas and Tom Mandrake, *Shazam! The New Beginning* 1 (New York: DC Comics, April 1987), 8.

144 Even this storyline – in particular the 'Reign of the Supermen!' arc that followed in 1993 – could in fact be seen as a repudiation and rejection of 'dark' twists on the main character.

145 See for instance Greg Carpenter, *The British Invasion! Alan Moore, Neil Gaiman, Grant Morrison, and the Invention of the Modern Comic Book Writer* (Illinois: Sequart, 2016). See also Proctor, 'The Dark Age: Superheroes in the 1980s', 355. Milligan's previous *Skreemer*, a tale of gangsters across generations published by DC in 1989, was also indebted in some ways to *Watchmen*, in addition to *The Long Good Friday* and *Finnegans Wake*: its running theme 'finn and begin egan', from the Irish drinking song that inspired Joyce, echoes *Watchmen*'s 'nothing ever ends'.

146 Khoury, *The Extraordinary Works of Alan Moore*, 120.

147 In a personal interview with academic Julia Round, 'Berger describes Vertigo's beginnings in relation to two key texts: DC's *House of Mystery* and Alan Moore's run on *Saga of the Swamp Thing* . . .'. See Round, *Gothic in Comics and Graphic Novels*, 45.

148 Jamie Delano and John Ridgway, *John Constantine: Hellblazer* 1 (New York: DC Comics, January 1988), 4.

149 Smith's earlier story for *2000AD*, *Tyranny Rex*, had hidden a smiley face in its mise en scène: see John Smith and Steve Dillon, *Tyranny Rex*, *2000AD* 567 (London: Fleetway, 26 March 1988), 3.

150 John Smith, Jim Baikie, Duncan Fegredo and Sean Phillips, *The Complete New Statesmen* (London: Fleetway, 1990), 47.

151 Ibid., 33.

NOTES

225

152 Ibid., 50.

153 Paradoxically, Smith's introduction to the collected edition does not mention *Watchmen*'s influence or Moore at all. However, in a later interview he admitted that *New Statesmen* had 'tried too hard to be grim and adult and *Watchmen* instead of going for all-out fun and weirdness'. See Grant Goggans, 'John Smith Interview' (n.d., accessed 12 April 2022), http://homepage.eircom.net/~okku/scifi/jsmith.htm.

154 Janeanpatience, 'A Big, Gaudy Picturebook', *SuggestedForMatureReaders.com* (1 October 2012, accessed 19 July 2021), https://suggestedformaturereaders.wordpress .com/2012/10/01/a-big-gaudy-picturebook/.

155 See Elizabeth Sandifer, *The Last War in Albion* at *EruditorumPress.com*, https://www .eruditorumpress.com/last-war-in-albion.

Chapter 3

1 See for instance Alex Larman, 'Has *Watchmen* Solved the Case of the Unfilmable Novel?' *The Guardian* (5 March 2009, accessed 11 April 2022), https://www .theguardian.com/books/booksblog/2009/mar/05/watchmen-unfilmable-novels; see also Aaron Taylor, 'The Continuing Adventures of the "Inherently Unfilmable" Book: Zack Snyder's *Watchmen*', *Cinema Journal* 56, no. 2 (Winter 2017), 125–31, and Mike Goodridge, 'Filming the Unfilmable of *Watchmen*', *ScreenDaily.com* (6 March 2009, accessed 13 April 2022), https://www.avclub.com/alan-moore-1798208192https:// www.screendaily.com/zack-snyder-filming-the-unfilmable-of-watchmen/4043527 .article. Moore himself opined, 'Personally, I tend to think it's unfilmable', in a 2001 interview: see Tasha Robinson, 'Alan Moore', *AVClub* (24 October 2001, accessed 13 April 2022), https://www.avclub.com/alan-moore-1798208192.

2 Willow Green, 'Python Won't Bite for *Watchmen*', *Empire Online* (13 November 2000, accessed 11 April 2022), https://www.empireonline.com/movies/news/python-wont -bite-watchmen/.

3 Jack Shepherd, '*Watchmen* at 10: The Fascinating Story of How The "Unfilmable" Comic Book Series Finally Made It to the Big Screen', *The Independent* (23 February 2019, accessed 11 April 2022), https://www.independent.co.uk/arts-entertainment/ films/features/watchmen-10-anniversary-zack-snyder-terry-gilliam-darren-aronofsky -paul-greengrass-a8792791.html.

4 Anon, '*Watchmen* Screenwriter David Hayter Reveals Huge Differences in First Draft of Superhero Movie', *NME.com* (15 July 2020, accessed 11 April 2022), https://www .nme.com/news/film/watchmen-screenwriter-david-hayter-reveals-huge-differences -in-first-draft-of-superhero-movie-2708479.

5 See also Parkin, *Magic Words*, 302–4 and 330–1.

6   See also Duncan McLean, 'HBO's *Watchmen* and Generic Revision in a Genre of Adaptation', *Journal of Popular Film and Television* 49, no. 4 (Winter 2021), 202 [page range 196–209]: 'Snyder's film . . . came relatively early in the establishment of the superhero film as a distinct screen genre.'

7   *X-Men: The Last Stand* (2006) gained a *Rotten Tomatoes* rating of 57 per cent, and the series returned with *X-Men: First Class* in 2010. *Spider-Man* 3 (2007) gained 63 per cent, and the series was rebooted with *The Amazing Spider-Man* in 2012.

8   Ayres, *Alan Moore*, 195. Parkin suggests that *Unbreakable* (2000) was also influenced by *Watchmen*; see Parkin, *Magic Words,* 330.

9   They converged, in the finale, at the fictional Kirby Plaza, named after legendary Marvel creator Jack Kirby: Tim Sale, known for his work on *Spider-Man*, *Daredevil* and *Batman* comics, provided the show's in-universe illustrations.

10 Stephen Lynch, '*Heroes* Pulls Rug From Under *Watchmen*', *New York Post* (24 April 2007, accessed 11 April 2022), https://nypost.com/2007/04/24/heroes-pulls-rug-from -under-watchmen/.

11 Jim Collins, 'Batman: The Movie, Narrative: The Hyperconscious', in Roberta Pearson, William Uricchio and Will Brooker (eds), *Many More Lives of the Batman* (London: BFI Palgrave, 2015), 160.

12 Ibid. See also 'The Superhero With A Thousand Faces: Visual Narratives on Film and Paper', in Andrew Horton and Stuart T. McDougal, *Play It Again, Sam: Retakes on Remakes* (Berkeley: University of California Press, 1998), 279–95.

13 Moore, Gibbons and Higgins, *Watchmen*, chapter 1, 3.

14 Ibid., 1.

15 Drew Morton, '"Watched Any Good Books Lately?" The Formal Failure of the *Watchmen* Motion Comic', *Cinema Journal* 56, no. 2 (Winter 2017), [range 132–7], 136.

16 For more on this influential term, see Jay David Bolter and Richard Grusin, *Remediation: Understanding New Media* (Cambridge, MA: MIT Press, 2000).

17 Michael Moran, 'Dave Gibbons Talks About the *Watchmen* DVD, and Staying Out of the Water', *Times Online* (21 July 2009, accessed 12 April 2022), archived at http:// timesonline.typepad.com/blockbuster_buzz/2009/07/dave-gibbons-talks-about-the -watchmen-dvd-and-staying-out-of-the-water.html.

18 Hilary Lewis, '*Watchmen* Flops', *Business Insider* (8 March 2009, accessed 12 April 2022), https://www.businessinsider.com/watchmen-flops-opening-weekend-2009-3?r =US&IR=T.

19 These reviews are no longer available on their original platforms but are archived at *Rotten Tomatoes* (accessed 13 April 2022), https://www.rottentomatoes.com/m/ watchmen/reviews?type=top_critics.

NOTES

20 Geoff Boucher, 'Go Hollywood? Never', *Los Angeles Times* (19 September 2008, accessed 13 April 2022), https://www.latimes.com/archives/la-xpm-2008-sep-19-et-hero19-story.html.

21 Jake Wilson, '*Watchmen*', *The Age* (6 March 2009, accessed 13 April 2022), https://www.theage.com.au/entertainment/movies/watchmen-20090306-ge7pvg.html.

22 Robert Stam, 'Introduction: The Practice and Theory of Adaptation', in Stam and Alessandra Raengo, *Literature and Film: A Guide to the Theory and Practice of Film Adaptation* (Oxford: Blackwell, 2005), 3.

23 Deborah Cartmell and Imelda Whelehan, 'Adaptations: Theories, Interpretations and New Dilemmas', in Cartmell and Whelehan (eds), *Screen Adaptation: Impure Cinema* (London: Palgrave Macmillan, 2010), 20–1.

24 Wired Staff, 'Artist Dave Gibbons' Gut Feelings on the *Watchmen* Movie'.

25 Ibid.

26 Paul Owen, '*Watchmen* is Too Faithful to Alan Moore's Book', *The Guardian* (22 July 2009, accessed 13 April 2022), https://www.theguardian.com/film/filmblog/2009/jul/22/watchmen-book-film-alan-moore.

27 James Parker, 'The Sorcery of Alan Moore', *The Atlantic* (May 2009, accessed 13 April 2022), https://www.theatlantic.com/magazine/archive/2009/05/the-sorcery-of-alan-moore/307371/.

28 Tom Breihan, 'The *Watchmen* Movie Shows You Can Be Faithful to a Comic and Still Miss Its Whole Damn Point', *AV Club* (16 November 2018, accessed 13 April 2022), https://www.avclub.com/the-watchmen-movie-proves-you-can-be-faithful-to-a-comi-1830312684.

29 Darren Mooney, 'Zack Snyder's *Watchmen* Shows the Limits of Faithful Adaptations', *The Escapist* (25 October 2019, accessed 14 April 2022), https://www.escapistmagazine.com/zack-snyder-watchmen-shows-the-limits-of-faithful-adaptations/.

30 Will Leitch, 'This Week in Genre History: *Watchmen* Was Perhaps Too Faithful to the "Unfilmable" Comic' (3 March 2021, accessed 13 April 2022), https://www.syfy.com/syfy-wire/watchmen-movie-anniversary-zack-snyder-comic-graphic-novel. See also Duncan McLean from the same year: 'when the 2009 film was released, it was noted for the hyper-fidelity of its approach. From the opening scene, in which the Comedian is murdered by a mysterious assailant, it was apparent that this adaptation was to be slavishly faithful to the graphic novel.' McLean, 'HBO's *Watchmen* and Generic Revision in a Genre of Adaptation', 203.

31 Mooney, 'Zack Snyder's *Watchmen*'.

32 Leitch, '*Watchmen* Was Perhaps Too Faithful'.

33 Dave Itzkoff, 'How Zack Snyder (Just Barely) Got *Watchmen* to the Screen', *New York Times* (30 January 2009, accessed 13 April 2022), https://artsbeat.blogs.nytimes.com/2009/01/30/how-zack-snyder-just-barely-got-watchmen-to-the-screen/.

34 See Anon, 'The Squid Is Out', *WatchmenComicMovie.com* (10 November 2008, accessed 13 April 2022), http://www.watchmencomicmovie.com/111008-watchmen-movie-zack-snyder-ending-changed.php.

35 Kaleem Aftab, '*Watchmen* Film Adaptation May Be Faithful to a Fault', *The National* (5 March 2009, accessed 13 April 2022), https://www.thenationalnews.com/arts/watchmen-film-adaptation-may-be-faithful-to-a-fault-1.588671.

36 Stam, 'Introduction', 17.

37 Ibid.

38 Ibid., 18.

39 Moore and Gibbons, *Watchmen*, chapter 2, 22–3.

40 'Alan Moore Reads *Watchmen* as Rorschach', *YouTube* (25 September 2007, accessed 14 April 2022), https://www.youtube.com/watch?v=1FS60iN0g2I.

41 See André Bazin, 'The Ontology of the Photographic Image', in *What is Cinema? Volume 1* (Berkeley: University of California Press, 1967), 9–16.

42 Although he omits the red flashing neon, Snyder is careful to include purple and yellow light that references John Higgins's colour scheme.

43 Roland Barthes, *Camera Lucida* (London: Vintage, 2000), 25.

44 Ibid.

45 Ibid., 28.

46 Ibid., 30.

47 Ibid., 27.

48 This event actually took place before the JFK assassination.

49 See Annette Michelson, ed. and Kevin O'Brien, trans. *Kino-Eye: The Writings of Dziga Vertov* (Berkeley: University of California Press, 1984), 17–18.

50 Matt Yockey makes similar observations in his chapter 'Infinite Crisis: Intertextuality and *Watchmen*', in James Kendrick (ed.), *A Companion to the Action Film* (Hoboken: Wiley & Sons, 2019), 360–1.

51 Steve Weintraub, 'Zack Snyder Interview: *Watchmen*', *Collider* (10 August 2008, accessed 15 April 2022), https://collider.com/zack-snyder-interview-watchmen/.

52 Mike Ryan, 'Zack Snyder Strikes Back', *HuffPost* (3 March 2014, accessed 15 April 2022), https://www.huffingtonpost.co.uk/entry/zack-snyder-batman-superman_n_4886277.

53 Originally in *Crave Online*, no longer available; quoted by 'Adrian' at *Leonard Cohen Forum* (10 March 2009, accessed 15 April 2022), https://www.leonardcohenforum.com/viewtopic.php?t=13901.

NOTES

54 David Ehrlich, 'Zack Snyder Movies From Worst to Best', *IndieWire* (15 November 2017, accessed 15 April 2022), https://www.indiewire.com/2017/11/zack-snyder-movies-ranked-justice-league-batman-superman-1201897518/.

55 Paul Ridd, 'Where to Begin With Zack Snyder', *BFI.com* (22 March 2021, accessed 15 April 2022), https://www.bfi.org.uk/features/where-begin-with-zack-snyder.

56 Both, by coincidence, refer directly to the Pale Horse from the Book of Revelation: *Dawn of the Dead* in its opening voice-over, *Watchmen* in the name of the punk band at its climax.

57 Bakhtin, 'Discourse in the Novel', 272.

58 I thank my students in the 'Film and Adaptation' MA module at Kingston University, 2022, for their discussion and insights: Anika Braunschmidt, Summer Gamble, Bhavika Koli, Lidiia Lositskaia, Nattamon Nantanasarid, Shafkat Rahman, Nahiyan Rashid and Alan Watt.

Chapter 4

1 Brian Hiatt, 'Exclusive: Comic-Book Superstar Grant Morrison Channelled John Lennon. Hear the Song They Wrote', *Rolling Stone* (14 June 2022, accessed 13 July 2022) https://www.rollingstone.com/music/music-features/grant-morrison-ezra-miller-john-lennon-superman-1367662/.

2 See for instance Elizabeth Sandifer, 'Chapter One: A Machine That Kills (At Midnight All the Agents)', *EruditorumPress.com* (18 May 2020, accessed 21 July 2021), https://www.eruditorumpress.com/blog/last-war-in-albion-book-two-chapter-one-a-machine-that-kills-at-midnight-all-the-agents.

3 See Anon, 'Comics Written By Alan Moore Then By Grant Morrison', *TractorForklift.wordpress.com* (26 March 2019, accessed 23 July 2021), https://tractorforklift.wordpress.com/2019/03/26/comics-written-by-alan-moore-then-by-grant-morrison/.

4 Quoted in *Grant Morrison: Talking With Gods* (2010) [Film] Dir. Patrick Meaney, USA: Sequart Organisation.

5 See Ó Méalóid, 'Last Alan Moore Interview?'

6 Morrison, *Supergods*, 213.

7 Grant Morrison and Steve Yeowell, *Zenith Phase I* (London: Rebellion, 2014), n.p.

8 Ibid.

9 Phase One is called 'Tygers'; note that *Miracleman* episode 4 refers to Kid Marvelman repeatedly as a 'tiger'; see Moore, Leach and Davis, *Miracleman Book One*, 35.

10 He introduced a character with Cthulhuian tentacles at his mouth even earlier in *Zoids*: see Grant Morrison and Ron Smith, 'Deserts', in *Spider-Man and Zoids* 30 (London: Marvel Comics, 27 September 1986), 4.

230 NOTES

11 The Sheeda in Morrison's *Seven Soldiers* (2005–6) are the exception, as they seem closer to Faerie tradition than Lovecraft.

12 Grant Morrison, Steve Yeowell et al. *The Invisibles*, volume 3, 2 (New York: DC Comics, May 2000), 14; and Alan Moore and Jacen Burroughs, *Providence* Chapter X (Illinois: Avatar Press, July 2016), n.p. Morrison had these pages of *The Invisibles* redrawn for the trade paperback so that they reflected his ideas accurately.

13 In *Captain Britain*, Archie is renamed 'Andy'. We also see Miracleman, 'Tom Rosetta' (a version of Tim Kelly, from the *Knockout/Valiant* strip 'Kelly's Eye') and 'Tusker', an analogue of General Jumbo from *Beano*, who also appears in *Zenith*. Archie appeared again in Leah Moore and John Reppion's *Albion* (2005), plotted by Alan Moore, with other heroes from British comics who had featured in *Zenith* such as Steel Claw and Tri-Man.

14 Grant Morrison and Steve Yeowell, *Zenith Phase IV* (London: Rebellion, 2015), n.p.

15 See for instance Grant Morrison and Colin MacNeil, 'Fruitcake and Veg', in *2000AD* 508-509 (London: Fleetway, 7–14 February 1987); and Grant Morrison and Colin MacNeil, 'Fair Exchange', in *2000AD* 514 (London: Fleetway, 21 March 1987), and compare with Alan Moore and Alan Davis, 'D.R. and Quinch Have Fun On Earth', in *2000AD* 317 (London: Fleetway, 21 May 1983). See also Elizabeth Sandifer, 'Dead Kings Walking Around (The Last War in Albion Part 104: Grant Morrison's Future Shocks)', *EruditoriumPress.com* (10 July 2015, accessed 1 August 2021), https://www.eruditorumpress.com/blog/dead-kings-walking-underground-the-last-war-in -albion-part-104-grant-morrisons-future-shocks.

16 Morrison's first work for *Zoids* incorporates Moore's characteristic mid-1980s technique of the same phrases bookmarking the start and finish of a story like an epic refrain ('Once upon a time, there was a planet called Roquindel'). See Morrison and Smith, 'Deserts', 3, and Grant Morrison and Geoff Senior, 'Deserts Part Two', in *Spider-Man and Zoids* 31 (London: Marvel Comics, 4 October 1986), 6. One of his last episodes lifts the parallel fantasy world/fever dream device from 'For The Man Who Has Everything'; see Grant Morrison and Steve Yeowell, 'Out of the Blue', in *Zoids* 48 (London: Marvel Comics, 31 January 1987), 6. His final, unpublished work for *Zoids*, which would have appeared on 12 March 1987, includes the line 'tastes like a battery does when you put your tongue to one of the terminals'; compare 'it's like licking a flashlight battery' in Moore and Gibbons, *Watchmen*, chapter 3, 5. See Rich Johnston, 'The First 6 Pages of Grant Morrison and Steve Yeowell's *Zoids*', *Bleedingcool.com* (17 May 2020, accessed 2 August 2021), https://bleedingcool.com/comics/6-pages-grant-morrison-steve-yeowell-zoids/.

17 See Grant Morrison and Joe Quesada, 'The October Incident: 1966', in *Miracleman Annual* 1 (New York: Marvel Comics, 2014), n.p.

18 Quoted in David Bishop, *Thrill-Power Overload: Thirty Years of 2000AD* (Oxford: Rebellion Developments, 2007), 120.

19 Grant Morrison, Chas Truog and Doug Hazlewood, *Animal Man* 1 (New York: DC Comics, September 1988), 1.

NOTES

20 Ibid., 20–1.

21 Grant Morrison, Chas Truog and Doug Hazlewood, *Animal Man* 2 (New York: DC Comics, October 1988), 22.

22 Moore and Austen, *Miracleman Book 2: The Red King Syndrome*, 59–65.

23 Ibid., 24. Of course, this could be the work of penciller Chas Truog and inker Doug Hazlewood, but Morrison was, and is, also a very competent artist, and his scripts of the time are detailed (though not quite on the Alan Moore level), so we can imagine he wanted significant input into the visual content of his first, career-making series for DC.

24 Grant Morrison, Chas Truog and Doug Hazlewood, *Animal Man* 19 (New York: DC Comics, January 1990), n.p.

25 Moore and Gibbons, *Watchmen*, chapter 8, 8.

26 See the cover of *Watchmen*, chapter 5, for instance.

27 Grant Morrison, Chas Truog and Doug Hazlewood, *Animal Man* 7 (New York: DC Comics, January 1989), 21.

28 Grant Morrison, Chas Truog and Mark McKenna, *Animal Man* 10 (New York: DC Comics, April 1989), 22.

29 Note also that Buddy Baker's wife Ellen was an illustrator whose income supported them both; Mike Moran's wife Liz, in *Miracleman*, was also an illustrator and the main breadwinner.

30 See Anon, 'Grant Morrison Writes Spoofs About Alan Moore (And Says Nice Things)', *TractorForklift.Wordpress.com* (23 March 2019, accessed 22 July 2021), https://tractorforklift.wordpress.com/2019/03/23/grant-morrison-writes-spoofs -about-alan-moore-and-says-nice-things/.

31 Moore and Gibbons, *Watchmen*, chapter 2, 6. Note also that Morrison's original script for *The Invisibles* 1 includes the line 'Look on my works ye mighty and despair' [*sic*]. See 'The Invisibles 1', *ComicsExperience.com* (no date, accessed 13 August 2021), https://www.comicsexperience.com/wp-content/uploads/2017/01/Invisibles _1.txt.

32 See also Moore's Jack Kirby tribute in *Supreme* 6 of June 2000.

33 Laura Sneddon, 'The Strange Case of Grant Morrison and Alan Moore As Told By Grant Morrison', *Comicsbeat.com* (24 November 2012, accessed 23 July 2021), https://www.comicsbeat.com/the-strange-case-of-grant-morrison-and-alan-moore -as-told-by-grant-morrison/.

34 Alan Moore, Joe Bennett and Norm Rapmund, *Supreme* 41 (California: Image Comics, August 1996), n.p.; Grant Morrison, Chas Truog and Mark Farmer, *Animal Man* 25 (New York: DC Comics, July 1990), n.p.

NOTES

35 Joshua Riviera, 'Frank Quitely, Grant Morrison Discuss *Multiversity: Pax Americana*', *Entertainment Weekly* (17 November 2014, accessed 23 July 2021), https://ew.com/article/2014/11/17/morrison-quitely-multiversity-pax-americana/.

36 Confusingly, a version of the silver-costumed Captain Atom from the 1987 revamp – real name Nathaniel Adam – still exists within mainstream DC continuity.

37 This linguistic fluidity may remind us of Derrida on *différance*, in keeping with *Pax Americana's* play with apparent oppositions. See Jacques Derrida, 'Différance', in *Margins of Philosophy* (Sussex: Harvester Press), 11. Morrison has often seemed to engage with Derridean ideas, although he claims to dislike academic theory. 'they had little interest in postmodern philosophers like Jacques Derrida and Michel Foucault, complaining, "I hate postmodern theory because it's just gibberish! The jargon is so dense."' Elizabeth Sandifer, 'The Most Escapist of Fantasies', *EruditorumPress.com* (10 May 2021, accessed 25 July 2022), https://www.eruditorumpress.com/blog/the-most-escapist-of-fantasies-book-three-part-7-continuity-postmodernism.

38 His first appearance was in Grant Morrison, Mike Dringenberg and Doug Hazlewood, *Doom Patrol* 42 (New York: DC Comics, March 1991), 12. In this story, he is said to have 'vanished in '58'.

39 In another comic-book complication, the 'Earth-2' on which this story is set later became 'Earth-3'.

40 Grant Morrison and Frank Quitely, *We3* 2 (New York: DC Comics, December 2004), n.p.

41 Charles Pulliam-Moore, 'Grant Morrison Opens Up About Feuding With Alan Moore And Why He Still Doesn't Like *Watchmen*', *Gizmodo.com* (11 December 2018, accessed 23 July 2021), https://gizmodo.com/exclusive-grant-morrison-opens-up-about-feuding-with-a-1831011198.

42 Matt D. Wilson, 'That Mad Rush: Digging Deep Into *The Multiversity* With Grant Morrison', *ComicsAlliance.com* (28 January 2015, accessed 1 August 2021), https://comicsalliance.com/multiversity-interview-grant-morrison/.

43 Others are featured even more obscurely; we see the jester's hat of Charlton character Punch, which will become more relevant in a later chapter.

44 See Dave Kaler, Steve Ditko and Rocco Mastroserio, *Captain Atom* 82 (Connecticut: Charlton Comics, September 1966), 5.

45 Grant Morrison, Frank Quitely and Nathan Fairbairn, *Multiversity: Pax Americana* 1 (New York: DC Comics, January 2015).

46 'Black and White World', like 'The Comedians', which Moore uses as the title for *Watchmen's* second chapter, is also asong by Elvis Costello.

47 Josie Campbell, 'MorrisonCon: Morrison and Artists Talk *Batman Inc*, *Happy!* and *Multiversity*', *CBR.com* (30 September 2012, accessed 1 August 2021), https://www.cbr.com/morrisoncon-morrison-and-artists-talk-batman-inc-happy-multiversity/.

NOTES

233

48 Cyriaque Lamar, 'Grant Morrison Talks *Pax Americana*, His "Updated" *Watchmen*', *Gizmodo.com* (18 October 2010, accessed 1 August 2021), https://gizmodo.com/grant-morrison-talks-pax-americana-his-updated-watch-5641665.

49 Grant Morrison and Dave McKean, *Batman: Arkham Asylum* (New York: DC Comics, 1989), n.p.

50 See for instance Peter Suderman, 'The Comic Book Moment That Gave Us the Era of the Superhero Movie', *Vox.com* (16 May 2016, accessed 27 July 2021), https://www.vox.com/2016/5/16/11661702/widescreen-comics-superhero-movies-civil-war-authority.

51 Frank Miller with Klaus Janson and Lynn Varley, *Batman: The Dark Knight Returns Book Two* (London: Titan Books, 1986), 28.

52 Marc Singer, '*Pax Americana*', *Notthebeastmaster.typepad.com* (24 November 2014, accessed 1 August 2021), https://notthebeastmaster.typepad.com/weblog/2014/11/pax-americana.html.

53 Morrison, Quitely and Fairbairn, *Multiversity*, *Pax Americana*, n.p.

54 https://comicsalliance.com/multiversity-interview-grant-morrison/.

55 See for example Sergio Pereira, 'Why Doesn't Batman Use His Money To Help Gotham?' *Fortress of Solitude* (25 September 2020, accessed 28 July 2021), https://www.fortressofsolitude.co.za/why-doesnt-batman-use-his-money-to-help-gotham/.

56 Beetle suggests 'The Sentinels' for the team name, referring to the short-lived superhero squad published in 1983, between the closure of Charlton and the buy-up of the characters by DC.

57 Fredric Jameson, *Postmodernism: Or, The Cultural Logic of Late Capitalism* (London: Verso, 1991), 17.

58 Moore and Gibbons, *Watchmen*, chapter 2, 9.

59 Ibid., chapter 4, 10.

60 Matt D. Wilson, 'That Mad Rush: Digging Deep into *The Multiversity* With Grant Morrison', *Comicsalliance.com* (28 January 2015, accessed 1 August 2021), https://comicsalliance.com/multiversity-interview-grant-morrison/.

61 Moore and Gibbons, *Watchmen*, chapter 12, 11.

62 Ibid., 18.

63 Gregory L. Reece, 'It's Hard to Love The Pieces: *The Multiversity: Pax Americana* 1', *Popmatters.com* (25 November 2015, accessed 1 August 2021), https://www.popmatters.com/188458-the-multiversity-pax-americana-1-2495582820.html.

64 Bloom, *The Anxiety of Influence*, xii.

65 Ibid., 5.

66 Klock, *How To Read Superhero Comics*, 68.

67 Bloom, *The Anxiety of Influence*, 14.

234 NOTES

68 Klock, *How To Read Superhero Comics*, 65.

69 Ibid., 69–71.

70 Ibid., 72.

71 Ibid., 75.

72 Illogical Volume, 'PaxMan: An Experiment in Assisted Re-Viewing', *Mindlessones.com* (10 December 2014, accessed 1 August 2021), http://mindlessones.com/2014/12/10/paxman-an-experiment-in-assisted-re-viewing/.

73 Klock, *How to Read Superhero Comics*, 68.

74 Bloom, *The Anxiety of Influence*, 16.

75 gizmodo see below.

76 Elizabeth Sandifer, 'She Saw Places That Aren't Even There Anymore! The Last War in Albion Book 2 Part 12: *Pax Americana*', *EruditorumPress.com* (2 October 2015, accessed 1 August 2021), https://www.eruditorumpress.com/blog/she-saw-places-that-arent-even-there-any-more-the-last-war-in-albion-book-two-part-12-pax-americana.

77 Morrison, *Supergods*, 204.

78 Lamar, 'Grant Morrison Talks *Pax Americana*'.

79 Dave Whittaker, 'The Character Remain Unaware of My Scrutiny, But Their Thoughts Are Transparent: *The Multiversity: Pax Americana 1*', *Sequart.org* (1 December 2014, accessed 1 August 2021), http://sequart.org/magazine/52644/the-multiversity-pax-americana-1/.

80 Morrison, *Supergods*, 204.

81 Laura Sneddon, 'Grant Morrison: Why I'm Stepping Away from Superheroes', *NewStatesman.com* (15 September 2012, accessed 1 August 2021), https://www.newstatesman.com/blogs/voices/2012/09/grant-morrison-gay-batman-superheroes-wonder-woman.

82 Timothy Callaghan, 'Exploring Morrison & Quitely's *Watchmen*-esque *Pax Americana*', *ComicBookResources.com* (21 November 2014, accessed 1 August 2021), https://www.cbr.com/exploring-morrison-quitelys-watchmen-esque-pax-americana/.

83 Pat Boyette, *The Peacemaker* 1 (Connecticut: Charlton Comics, March 1967), cover. As we saw, the line was used in a less concise form on Peacemaker's first appearance, *Fightin' Five* issue 40 (November 1966).

84 Joshua Rivera, 'Frank Quitely, Grant Morrison Discuss *Multiversity: Pax Americana*', *EntertainmentWeekly.com* (17 November 2014, accessed 1 August 2021), https://ew.com/article/2014/11/17/morrison-quitely-multiversity-pax-americana/.

85 Grant Morrison, Doug Mahnke and Christian Alamy, *Final Crisis: Superman Beyond* 2 (New York: DC Comics, March 2009), n.p.

NOTES

235

86   Rivera, 'Frank Quitely, Grant Morrison Discuss *Multiversity: Pax Americana*'. This is the only comment of Morrison's from the *Pax Americana* period that could possibly be conceived as referring obliquely to the 2009 *Watchmen* movie: his issue is entirely with Alan Moore, and as such it would make sense that Snyder's film, produced without Moore's involvement or blessing, was irrelevant to him.

87   As a minor but interesting addition to this intertextual network, note that episode 6 of Alan Moore's *Halo Jones* Book One is called, with a deliberate pun, 'Fleurs Du Mall'.

88   Bloom, *The Anxiety of Influence*, 139.

89   Andrew Hickey, 'In Which We Burn', *Mindlessones.com* (10 May 2015, accessed 1 August 2021), https://mindlessones.com/2015/05/10/in-which-we-burn/.

90   Morrison, *Supergods*, 204.

91   Bloom, *The Anxiety of Influence*, 152.

92   Ó Méalóid, 'Last Alan Moore Interview?'

93   See Grant Morrison, Frank Quitely and Nathan Fairbairn, *Multiversity: Pax Americana Director's Cut* (New York: DC Comics, June 2015), n.p.

94   Anon, 'Alan Moore Describes the Persistence of Grant Morrison . . .', *TractorForklift.wordpress.com* (8 April 2019, accessed 1 August 2021), https://tractorforklift.wordpress.com/2019/04/08/alan-moore-describes-the-persistence-of-grant-morrison-and-morrison-shuts-up-for-four-years-2014/.

95   Millidge, *Alan Moore: Storyteller*, 123.

96   Grant Morrison and Liam Sharp, *The Green Lantern: Intergalactic Lawman* 1 (New York: DC Comics, November 2018).

97   See Laura Sneddon, 'The Strange Case of Alan Moore and Grant Morrison, As Told By Grant Morrison', *ComicsBeat.com* (24 November 2012, accessed 23 July 2021), https://www.comicsbeat.com/the-strange-case-of-grant-morrison-and-alan-moore-as-told-by-grant-morrison/.

98   Tomfoolery Ltd, *Kieron Gillen Talks Watchmen* (3 March 2015, accessed 12 August 2021), https://www.youtube.com/watch?v=J0I4BSiRxO0.

99   Eliot Borenstein, 'Form's Fallow Function', *The Watchmen Watch, EliotBorenstein.net* (9 October 2019, accessed 12 August 2021) https://www.eliotborenstein.net/thewatchmenwatch/forms-fallow-function-peter-cannon-thunderbolt.

100   Tomfoolery Ltd, *Kieron Gillen Talks Watchmen*.

101   Wolfman, Perez and Ordway, *Crisis on Infinite Earths* 6, 14. As Borenstein points out, George Pérez fails to recognize the character and draws him as a 'speedster', as fast as The Flash: see Borenstein, 'Form's Fallow Function'.

102   Borenstein, 'Form's Fallow Function'.

NOTES

103 Kelly Kanayama, 'Kieron Gillen – The Scary Thing About *WicDiv* Is, It Worked' (10 July 2018, accessed 12 August 2021), https://www.comicsbeat.com/nycc-18-interview-kieron-gillen-the-scary-thing-about-wicdiv-is-it-worked/.

104 Kieron Gillen, 'Writer Notes: *The Wicked + the Divine* 37', *KieronGillen.Tumblr.com* (25 July 2018, accessed 12 August 2021), https://kierongillen.tumblr.com/post/176265398102/writer-notes-the-wicked-the-divine-37.

105 See '*The Wicked + the Divine* 34: "Mothering Invention" Part 1', *Scans-Daily.Dreamwidth.org* (24 November 2018, accessed 13 August 2021), https://scans-daily.dreamwidth.org/8071699.html?thread=198531859&style=light.

106 Gillen, 'Writer Notes: *The Wicked +the Divine* 34'.

107 Kieron Gillen, Jamie McKelvie and Matthew Wilson, *The Wicked + the Divine* 22 (Oregon: Image, August 2016), n.p.

108 Kieron Gillen, Jamie McKelvie and Matthew Wilson, *The Wicked + the Divine* 38 (Oregon: Image, August 2018), n.p. Issue 34 had planted the image with a definition of friendship as 'a raft made of broken people staying afloat'. See Kieron Gillen, Jamie McKelvie and Matthew Wilson, *The Wicked + the Divine* 34 (Oregon: Image, March 2018), n.p.

109 Kieron Gillen, 'Writer Notes: *The Wicked +the Divine* 38', *KieronGillen.Tumblr.com* (10 September 2018, accessed 12 August 2021), *KieronGillen.Tumblr.com*, https://kierongillen.tumblr.com/post/177938176427/writer-notes-the-wicked-the-divine-38/amp.

110 Kieron Gillen, 'Writer Notes: *The Wicked + the Divine* 26', *KieronGillen.Tumblr.com* (10 February 2017, accessed 12 August 2021), *KieronGillen.Tumblr.com,* https://kierongillen.tumblr.com/post/157066230267/writer-notes-the-wicked-the-divine-26.

111 He also wears a 'YOLO' T-shirt, with an infinity symbol as the second 'O': the intertextuality never ends.

112 Kieron Gillen and Stephanie Hans, *DIE* 1 (Oregon: Image, December 2018), n.p.

113 See Kieron Gillen, *KieronGillen.Tumblr.com* (31 May 2016, accessed 12 August 2021), https://kierongillen.tumblr.com/post/145205508627/not-reading-anything-that-has-the-watchmen/amp.

114 See Kieron Gillen, *KieronGillen.Tumblr.com* (31 October 2015, accessed 12 August 2021), https://kierongillen.tumblr.com/post/132288976707/so-you-may-or-may-not-know-alan-moore-in-his.

115 Rich Johnson, 'Kieron Gillen's Writer's Commentary on *Peter Cannon: Thunderbolt 3*', *BleedingCool.com* (29 March 2019, accessed 12 August 2021), https://bleedingcool.com/comics/kieron-gillen-writers-commentary-peter-cannon-thunderbolt-3-mark-millar/.

116 Ibid. Issue 3's line 'what does this stand for?', referring to the cog insignia on the bad guy's forehead, references a notorious scene from Millar's *The Ultimates*, where

NOTES

237

Captain America rages 'Surrender? . . . You think this letter on my head stands for France?' See Mark Millar, Bryan Hitch and Paul Neary, *The Ultimates* 12 (New York: Marvel Comics, November 2003), n.p.

117 Note that Gillen describes the initial violence as 'like something out of a Wile E. Coyote cartoon', which links it back not to Millar but to Morrison's *Animal Man 5*. See Johnson, 'Kieron Gillen's Writer's Commentary on *Peter Cannon: Thunderbolt 3*'.

118 Of course, Campbell is now best known for his work with Moore on *From Hell*, which gives this tribute to his work a further resonance.

119 Rich Johnson, 'Kieron Gillen's Writer's Commentary on *Peter Cannon: Thunderbolt 1*', *BleedingCool.com* (31 January 2019, accessed 12 August 2021), https://bleedingcool.com/comics/kieron-gillens-writers-commentary-on-peter-cannon-thunderbolt-1/.

120 *Crisis* is one such influence: Gillen referred to Issue 2 as 'Crisis on Infinite *Watchmen*'. See Rich Johnson, 'Kieron Gillen's Writer's Commentary on *Peter Cannon: Thunderbolt 2*', *BleedingCool.com* (4 March 2019, accessed 12 August 2021), https://bleedingcool.com/comics/kieron-gillen-writer-commentary-peter-cannon-thunderbolt-2/.

121 Ibid.

122 Ibid.

123 See for instance Kieron Gillen, Jamie McKelvie and Mike Norton, *Young Avengers* 2 (New York: Marvel Comics, April 2013), n.p.

124 Pete Morisi, *Peter Cannon . . . Thunderbolt!* 1 (Connecticut: Charlton Comics, January 1966), 8.

125 Johnson, 'Kieron Gillen's Writer's Commentary on *Peter Cannon: Thunderbolt 3*'.

126 Jim Starlin, George Pérez, Josef Rubinstein et al. *The Infinity Gauntlet* 4 (New York: Marvel Comics, October 1991).

127 Botswana Beast, 'A Hall Of Mirrors II: The Prismatic Age', *Mindlessones.com* (3 August 2008, accessed 12 August 2021), https://mindlessones.com/2008/08/03/a-hall-of-mirrors-ii-prismatic-age/. The author's name, 'Botswana Beast', is a reference to 'B'wana Beast', a character who plays a key role in Morrison's *Animal Man*. This 'age', itself inevitably a simplification, is often associated with Grant Morrison's work on Batman. See also Will Brooker, *Hunting the Dark Knight: Twenty-First Century Batman* (London: I.B. Tauris, 2012).

128 Matt D. Wilson, 'What "Age" Of Comics Is This?' *ComicsAlliance.com* (21 August 2012, accessed 12 August 2021), https://comicsalliance.com/thought-bubble-4-age-comics-silver-age-golden-age-prismatic-age/.

129 Chris Sims, 'Kieron Gillen Talks 'Young Avengers,' Pop Music And Why Subtlety Is Overrated', *ComicsAlliance.com* (17 October 2013, accessed 12 August 2021), https://comicsalliance.com/kieron-gillen-young-avengers-pop-music-interivew-nycc-2013.

130 The most extreme brutality in *Peter Cannon* 3, though – the villain tearing a hero's head from his shoulders – while supposedly a tribute to Millar, is also reminiscent of the killings in *Zenith,* and through it the work of Alan Moore: the image strongly recalls John Totleben's blurry horrors in *Swamp Thing* and the no-holds-barred combat of *Miracleman's* 'Nemesis' issue.

131 Johnson, 'Kieron Gillen's Writer's Commentary on *Peter Cannon: Thunderbolt 1'*.

132 Alan Moore, Donald Simpson et al., *In Pictopia*, 3. Reproduced in Khoury, *The Extraordinary Works of Alan Moore.*

133 Eddie Campbell, *Alec: The Years Have Pants* (Georgia: Top Shelf Publishers, 2009), 9. This early strip is in fact dated 1981, pre-*Watchmen*, though it was republished in 1990.

134 Millidge, *Alan Moore: Storyteller*, 125.

135 Johnson, 'Kieron Gillen's Writer's Commentary on *Peter Cannon: Thunderbolt 2'*.

136 Ibid.

137 Moore and Gibbons, *Watchmen*, chapter 11, 18.

138 Johnson, 'Kieron Gillen's Writer's Commentary on *Peter Cannon: Thunderbolt 3'*.

139 A probably unintentional call back to Moore's *In Pictopia*, where the buildings are constructed from comic panels.

140 The layers of intertextuality become more complex when we consider that Morrison's unusually indie, semi-autobiographical *St Swithin's Day*, drawn by Paul Grist (1989), was shaped by and appeared alongside Eddie Campbell's work of the time, and that *St Swithin's Day* in turn seems a clear influence on Gillen and McKelvie's *Phonogram*.

141 Eddie and Dr K from *Peter Cannon* also recall a Campbell illustration of himself and Moore arm wrestling, for the article 'Out On The Perimeter', in *Escape Magazine* 5 (1984). See Khoury, *The Extraordinary Works of Alan Moore*, 120.

142 Khoury, *The Extraordinary Works of Alan Moore*, 120.

Chapter 5

1 Jameson, *Postmodernism*, 17.

2 Ibid.

3 Alan Moore, Mike Collins and Alan Farmer, 'Grit! Featuring Dourdevil', *The Daredevils* 8 (August 1983), 14.

4 Ibid.

5 See Jameson, 'Postmodernism and Consumer Society', in E. Ann Kaplan (ed.), *Postmodernism and Its Discontents* (London and New York: Verso, 1988), 13–29.

NOTES

6 Desmond Devlin, Glen Fabry and Melvin Coznowski, 'Botchmen', *Mad Magazine* 499 (March 2009), 5–14.

7 Ibid., 6.

8 Ibid., 12.

9 Ibid.

10 Colourist Melvin Coznowski seems to be a *Mad Magazine* in-joke, as an alternate name for mascot Alfred E. Neumann.

11 Devlin, Fabry and Coznowski, 'Botchmen', 8.

12 Where there are changes to the visual environment, they compound the sense that this is a different but equally valid version of *Watchmen*: Funnyman has portraits of Laurel and Hardy and the Marx Brothers on his wall rather than the Comedian's presidents and pin-ups, which seems a feasible alternative rather than a joke.

13 See also Rich Johnson and Simon Rohrmüller's *Watchmensch*, which combines a recreation of *Watchmen*'s key scenes and artistic style with a meta-commentary about the comic industry's treatment of creators like Alan Moore. Tellingly, this satire also includes a joke about Dr Manhattan 'shrinking' in the cold of the Antarctic. Rich Johnson and Simon Rohrmüller, *Watchmensch* (BrainScan Studios, 2009), 16.

14 Devlin, Fabry and Coznowski, 'Botchmen', 14.

15 Lubomír Doležel, *Heterocosmica: Fiction and Possible Worlds* (Baltimore: Johns Hopkins University Press, 1998), 217.

16 Armelle Parey, 'Introduction', to Parey (ed.), *Prequels, Coquels and Sequels in Contemporary Anglophone Fiction* (London: Routledge, 2019), 3.

17 Carol Shields, quoted in ibid.

18 Phillip Pullman, quoted in ibid., 4.

19 *Before Watchmen: Dr Manhattan* 4: 'Changes in Perspective', in Cooke et al., *Before Watchmen Omnibus* (Burbank: DC Comics, 2018), 916–19.

20 It may certainly change our perspective of the original, as HBO's *Watchmen* does with *Watchmen*, *Wild Sargasso Sea* does with *Jane Eyre,* and J. M. Coetzee's *Foe* does with Defoe's *Robinson Crusoe.*

21 P. D. James, quoted in Isabelle Roblin, '*Death Comes To Pemberley* (2011), a Sequel with Many Twists', in Parey (ed.), *Prequels, Coquels and Sequels*, 165.

22 Ray Winninger, 'Introduction', in *Watchmen Companion* (California: DC Comics, 2019), 6.

23 Dan Greenberg, 'Who Watches the Watchmen?', in *Watchmen Companion*, 23–4.

24 Moore and Gibbons, *Watchmen*, chapter 2, 10. Captain Metropolis's letter to Sally, reproduced at the end of chapter 9, further conveys his prissy, self-important style.

NOTES

25 Greenberg, 'Who Watches the Watchmen?', 21.

26 Winninger, 'The Watchmen Sourcebook', in *Watchmen Companion*, 125.

27 Ibid., 115.

28 Ibid., 129.

29 It is credited to Len Wein.

30 Quoted in Andy Khouri, 'Alan Moore and *Before Watchmen* Creators Comment on the Ethics of *Watchmen* Prequel', *Comics Alliance* (1 February 2012, accessed 5 July 2022), https://comicsalliance.com/alan-moore-dave-gibbons-before-watchmen -creators-quotes-ethics-prequel/. DC offered him the rights to *Watchmen* in 2010 in exchange for expanding the series, but he turned them down.

31 Cooke and Conner, for instance, base images of the teenage Silk Spectre in combat on Gibbons's depiction of the character's mother being sexually assaulted by Comedian. See Moore and Gibbons, *Watchmen*, chapter 2, 6–7, and Darwyn Cooke and Amanda Conner, *Before Watchmen: Silk Spectre* 3: 'No Illusion', in *Before Watchmen Omnibus*, 378–89.

32 See for instance Darwyn Cooke and Amanda Conner, *Before Watchmen: Silk Spectre* 2: 'Getting Into the World', in *Before Watchmen Omnibus*, 177, and J. Michael Straczynski and Andy Kubert, *Before Watchmen: Nite Owl* 2: 'Some Things Are Just Inevitable', in *Before Watchmen Omnibus*, 230–1.

33 *Minutemen* 1 has the block capitals title and no end quotation; *Silk Spectre* 1 has the title at the end above the quotation, with a motif of a cartoon flower losing its petals replacing the clock countdown. *Ozymandias* takes all its titles ('I Met A Traveller . . .', 'The Hand That Mocked Them . . .') from a single poem, Shelley's 'Ozymandias', while providing Horace Smith's full verse at the end. Many of the other stories decide not to engage with this *Watchmen* convention at all.

34 See for instance Cooke and Conner, *Before Watchmen: Silk Spectre* 1: 'Mean Goodbye', in *Before Watchmen Omnibus*, 43; Cooke, *Before Watchmen: Minutemen* 2: 'Golden Years', in *Before Watchmen Omnibus*, 163; Straczynski and Kubert, *Before Watchmen: Nite Owl* 3: 'Thanks For Coming', in *Before Watchmen Omnibus*, 432.

35 See for instance J. Michael Straczynski and Adam Hughes, *Dr Manhattan* 2: 'One-Fifteen PM', in *Before Watchmen Omnibus*, 516–17.

36 Darwyn Cooke, *Minutemen* 1: 'The Moment of Truth', in *Before Watchmen Omnibus*, 10–11.

37 Although ironically, Cooke returns to the match cut storytelling again, transitioning from a bullet to a capital O to a circular sign and a fried egg yolk at the start of his chapter 3 and concluding his story with a similar device that moves through other circular shapes (including the Owlship) and ends on Hollis Mason's face. Perhaps the initial gambit is a clever strategy, a false authorial humility that sets the bar lower while aiming to comfortably clear it. See Darwyn Cooke, *Before Watchmen: Minutemen* 3: 'Child's Play', in *Before Watchmen Omnibus*, 147, and

NOTES

Cooke, *Before Watchmen: Minutemen* 6: 'The Last Minute', in *Before Watchmen Omnibus*, 820.

38   Prox Centuri, 'Pyrotechnics: Alan Moore on Anarchy, Psychedelics, and the Art of Storytelling', *InsideTheRift.net* (8 January 2018, accessed 6 July 2022), https://www.insidetherift.net/art/2018/1/4/pyrotechnics-alan-moore-on-anarchy-psychedelics-and-the-art-of-storytelling.

39   Compare the almost identical panels of Ozymandias in Geoff Johns and Gary Frank, *Doomsday Clock* Part One (Burbank: DC Comics, 2019), 26, with Moore and Gibbons, *Watchmen*, chapter 12, 27.

40   Johns and Frank, *Doomsday Clock*, 17.

41   Moore and Gibbons, *Watchmen*, chapter 10, 15.

42   Johns and Frank, *Doomsday Clock*, 1.

43   There is an interesting precedent here: Len Wein's *Before Watchmen: Ozymandias* ends with the same poem, describing the verse as 'written in competition with' Shelley's original. As Chad Nevitt says, it seems 'a not-so-subtle suggestion that this entire thing is a distant second to Watchmen' but not intended as such by the author. See Brian Cronin, 'Before *Watchmen*: The Plotting For Ozymandias' Famous Plan Ends With A Whimper', *CBR.com* (14 July 2020, accessed 13 July 2022), https://www.cbr.com/before-watchmen-ozymandias-plot-ends-with-whimper/.

44   Dr Manhattan's presence had been implicit within the DC Universe since 'The Button' (i.e. Comedian's badge) storyline that began in April 2017. Following *Doomsday Clock* he was incorporated into the *Death Metal* event, taking the bizarre hybrid form of 'Batmanhattan', an electric blue Dark Knight. See Scott Snyder and Greg Capullo, *Dark Knights: Death Metal* 2 (Burbank: DC Comics, September 2020). Nite Owl joined the Justice League soon after *Doomsday Clock* too, albeit for an isolated cross over event. See Scott Snyder and James Tynion IV with Bruno Redondo and Howard Porter, *Justice League* 34 (Burbank: DC Comics, December 2019), n.p.

45   Nick Venable, 'How *Lost* Was Inspired by *Watchmen*, According to Damon Lindelof', *Cinemablend.com* (4 September 2019, accessed 14 July 2022), https://www.cinemablend.com/television/2479098/how-lost-was-inspired-by-watchmen-according-to-damon-lindelof.

46   Noah Dominguez, 'Watchmen Artist Dave Gibbons Draws HBO Series' Sister Night', *CBR.com* (17 October 2019, accessed 6 July 2022). Sister Night is, in turn, based on Brother Night, the original name for Hooded Justice: see Moore, Gibbons and Higgins, *Absolute Watchmen*, n.p.

47   Sydney Bucksbaum, 'Damon Lindelof to *Watchmen* Creator Alan Moore: F – You, I'm Doing It Anyway', *Entertainment Weekly* (24 July 2019, accessed 6 July 2022), https://ew.com/tv/2019/07/24/damon-lindelof-watchmen-hbo-series-alan-moore-tca-2019/.

48   The titles are excerpted from longer quotations; here, 'It's Summer and We're Running Out of Ice' is a line from *Oklahoma!* Two of the later titles are taken directly from *Watchmen*, in what seems an act of homage.

NOTES

49   Lindelof also picks up on Snyder's idea that Andy Warhol would have painted the Crimebusters – an idea absent from the original *Watchmen*. However, the 2019 paintings are quite different from the ones we see briefly in the 2009 movie.

50   The squid itself finally appears in episode 5 of the series.

51   This is only true of the 2008 recoloured version. Lindelof's *Watchmen* also mentions a Spielberg film called *Pale Horse*, shot in black and white with occasional red details, which parallels both *Schindler's List* and the 'Red Hood' flashback scenes in *The Killing Joke*.

52   See David Bordwell, 'Who Will Match The Watchmen?' *Observations on Film Art* (12 April 2020, accessed 13 July 2022), http://www.davidbordwell.net/blog/2020/04 /12/who-will-match-the-watchmen/.

53   Eggs become crucial to Angela's story; breaking eggs also feature in close-up on the opening pages of Morrison and Quitely's *Flex Mentallo*, in a sequence that includes Rorschach-analogue The Fact. See Grant Morrison and Frank Quitely, *Flex Mentallo: Man of Muscle Mystery, The Deluxe Edition* (Burbank: DC Comics, 2012), 1–2.

54   An attack on the Statue of Liberty opens the Sam Hamm screenplay of *Watchmen* and also features in Darwyn Cooke's *Minutemen*: Lindelof could be nodding to either, or both. See Sam Hamm, *Watchmen*, http://www.watchmencomicmovie .com/downloads/watchmen-script-hamm-1989.pdf and Cooke, *Before Watchmen: Minutemen* 5: 'The Demon Core', in *Before Watchmen Omnibus*, 672.

55   Moore and Gibbons, *Watchmen*, chapter 1, 4.

56   Ibid., 14. Perhaps by coincidence, an early shot in *Blade Runner* (1982) features a newspaper that announces 'Farming the Oceans, The Moon and Antarctica'.

57   When we see clips, it is clear that this fictional show's aesthetic parodies Snyder's balletic, speed-ramping action, further distinguishing the 2019 series from the 2009 movie.

58   Lindelof has also played previously with word puzzles hidden on shop signs: in *Lost*, the Hoffs-Drawlar Funeral Parlor, an anagram of 'Flash Forward', explained the series' enigmatic time shift.

59   Alan Moore, 'Introduction', Miller, Janson and Varley, *Batman: The Dark Knight Returns* Book Two, n.p.

60   Steve J. Ray, 'DKN Exclusive Interview: Jorge Fornés – Artist on *Batman*', *DarkKnightNews* (1 August 2019, accessed 13 July 2022), https://darkknightnews .com/2019/08/01/dkn-exclusive-interview-jorge-fornes-artist-on-batman/.

61   Miller, Janson and Varley, *Batman: The Dark Knight Returns* Book Two, 8. A crucial 'BLAM' sound effect, late in *Rorschach*'s penultimate chapter, is rendered in *Watchmen*'s yellow capitals.

62   Graeme McMillan, '*Rorschach* Writer Pulls Back Curtain on "Very Angry" *Watchmen* Follow-Up', *HollywoodReporter.com* (10 September 2020, accessed 21 July

NOTES

243

2022), https://www.hollywoodreporter.com/movies/movie-news/rorschach-writer-pulls-back-curtain-on-very-angry-watchmen-followup-4056798/.

63 Morrison, Quitely and Fairbairn, *Pax Americana*, n.p.

64 There is a possible reference, also, to Grant Morrison and Cameron Stewart's 2006 comic *Seaguy*.

65 Len Wein moves the boundaries of the *Watchmen* universe in the opposite direction with the introduction of three cartoonish lawyers, Dewey, Cheatem and Howe; the existence of implausibly punning names in Moore and Gibbons's previously 'realistic' storyworld shifts the rules again. See Len Wein and Steve Rude, *Before Watchmen: Dollar Bill* 1: 'I Want to Be in Pictures', in *Before Watchmen Omnibus*, 854.

66 See Brian Azzarello and Lee Bermejo, *Before Watchmen: Rorschach* 4: 'Damntown Chapter 4', in *Before Watchmen Omnibus*, 675. There is even a possible gesture towards including the author in the comic: one panel shows a character posing in front of the Victory Arch in Baghdad, an image very similar to Tom King's photograph of himself during his CIA career. See Rich Johnson, 'Did *Batman*'s Tom King Work For the CIA? Yes, He Did', *Bleeding Cool* (2 January 2019, accessed 13 July 2022), https://bleedingcool.com/comics/batman-tom-king-cia/.

67 Note that Fornés also names Darwyn Cooke as an influence, alongside 1980s artists like Miller and Mazzucchelli and 1960s giant Ditko. See Ray, 'DKN Exclusive Interview: Jorge Fornés'.

68 Moore, Gibbons and Higgins, *Absolute Watchmen*, n.p.

69 The final page of the first issue seems to show Dr Manhattan on a mortuary slab, in keeping with his death at the end of HBO's *Watchmen*, and a 'Come Back to NYC' billboard is also in keeping with details of the TV show, where New York tourism plummeted after the squid attack. (See Episode 5, 'Little Fear of Lightning'.) Tom King confirmed that his story took place 'in the same timeline' as the Lindelof series: see Tom King, *Twitter.com* (1 November, 2020, accessed 13 July 2022), https://twitter.com/TomKingTK/status/1322957293034606592.

70 See Catherine Padmore, 'A Coquel Set "Far Away, Where The Fighting Was"', in Parey (ed.), *Prequels, Coquels and Sequels*, 65.

71 This detail is suggested in the role-playing game, which Winninger says inspired aspects of *Before Watchmen*. 'A cab driver stopped and offered me a ride . . . told me I was his hero.' See Winninger, *Watchmen Companion*, 170.

72 https://bleedingcool.com/comics/alan-moore-talked-dc-comics-watchmen-sequels-back-2010/.

73 Moore and Gibbons, *Watchmen*, chapter 9, 20. 'Just don't ask where I was when I heard about JFK', Blake chuckles.

74 There are comic-book precedents for this reveal: Cooke's *Minutemen* has two costumed heroes unmasked as Japanese allies to the American cause. Grant

Morrison's *Multiversity* similarly reveals that Dr Fate is Black under his mask, in a retro 1940s story of pulp heroes like the Minutemen: see Grant Morrison and Chris Sprouse, *Multiversity: Society of Superheroes* 1: 'Conquerors from the Counter-World' (Burbank: DC Comics, November 2014).

75   He was 'found brutally beaten to death'. See Johns and Frank, *Doomsday Clock*, chapter 1, 34.

76   'He exploited the small fame he gained from making this lucky find to launch a career as a scholar of post-modern culture and his work often overlaps with mine. I've met the man at many conferences, and let me tell you, he's an embarrassment to our oft-maligned field of study.' 'Vigilantes in Pop Culture', *Peteypedia* (3 September 2019, accessed 13 July 2022), https://www.hbo.com/content/dam/hbodata/series/watchmen/peteypedia/02/masked-vigilantes-in-pop-culture-memo.pdf.

77   Cooke, *Before Watchmen: Minutemen* 6: 'The Last Minute', in *Before Watchmen Omnibus*, 814. Moore simply mentions, through Hollis Mason's autobiography, that she was 'murdered . . . by one of her former enemies'. See Moore and Gibbons, *Watchmen*, chapter 2, 31.

78   *Before Watchmen: Comedian* offers an explanation by introducing J. Gordon Liddy, one of Gibbons's inspirations for the character, as a lookalike. See Brian Azzarello and J. G. Jones, *Before Watchmen: Comedian*, in *Before Watchmen Omnibus*, 984.

79   See Cronin, 'Before *Watchmen*: The Plotting For Ozymandias' Famous Plan Ends With A Whimper'.

80   See Moore and Gibbons, *Watchmen*, chapter 2, 5–7.

81   Meghan O'Keefe, 'Damon Lindelof Reveals the One Line in *Watchmen* That Almost Ruined their Hooded Justice Backstory', *Decider.com* (24 November 2019, accessed 13 July 2022), https://decider.com/2019/11/24/watchmen-episode-6-damon-lindelof-talks-hooded-justice-retcon/.

82   Klock, *How To Read Superhero Comics*, 30.

83   Ibid., 30–1.

84   Mireia Aragay and Gemma López, 'Inf(l)ecting *Pride and Prejudice*: Dialogism, Intertextuality, and Adaptation', in Mireia Aragay (ed.), *Books in Motion: Adaptation, Intertextuality, Authorship* (Amsterdam: Rodopi, 2005), 217.

85   See 'The Origin of Sister Night', *Peteypedia* (22 September 2019, accessed 21 July 2022), https://www.hbo.com/content/dam/hbodata/series/watchmen/peteypedia/07/memo-sister-night.pdf.

86   *Rorschach* seems to depict the encounter with Captain Carnage, but a Millennium poster on the wall indicates that this must have happened after Kovacs was killed, and so both combatants must be copycats.

87   Commentators struggle to reconcile this inconsistency, like the others: 'perhaps it was reopened at a different location or Burgers'n'Borscht was closed because of the returned tension between the US and Russia.' See Frida Keränen, 'Keeping a Watch

on *Doomsday* Clock', *Multiversity Comics* (13 December 2017, accessed 13 July 2022), http://www.multiversitycomics.com/annotations/doomsday-clock-01/.

88   See Brian Cronin, '. . . And the Superhuman Review – *Before Watchmen: Rorschach 1*', *CBR.com* (20 August 2020, accessed 13 July 2022), https://www.cbr.com/before -watchmen-ozymandias-plot-ends-with-whimper/; https://www.cbr.com/and-the -superhuman-review-before-watchmen-rorschach-1/.

89   Grant Morrison and Chaz Truog, *Animal Man* 23, 'Crisis' (New York: DC Comics, May 1990), 7.

90   Adam DiLeo, 'Batman Exists in the HBO *Watchmen* Series Universe . . . Kind Of . . ', *Ign.com* (3 December 2019, accessed 21 July 2022), https://www.ign.com/articles /2019/12/03/batman-watchmen-hbo.

91   Brandon Schreur, 'Batman Collides With *Doomsday Clock*'s *Watchmen* Universe in First Flashpoint Beyond Preview', https://www.cbr.com/dcs-flashpoint-beyond -batman-doomsday-clock-watchmen-universe/.

92   Mike Cecchini, '*Watchmen* Timeline Explained', *Den of Geek* (16 December 2019, accessed 21 July 2022), https://www.denofgeek.com/comics/watchmen-timeline -explained/.

93   John Orquiola, 'HBO's *Watchmen* World & Timeline Changes Explained', *ScreenRant .com* (20 October 2019, accessed 21 July 2022), https://screenrant.com/watchmen -hbo-show-world-timeline-explained/.

94   MattTheNerd42, 'Tom King's *Rorschach* Series is in Canon With HBO's *Watchmen*', *DCFandom.com* (1 April 2021, accessed 21 July 2022), https://dc.fandom.com/f/p /4400000000003188211.

95   Ashkera, 'Academic Research About Watchmen', *Reddit: r/watchmen* (July 2019), https://www.reddit.com/r/Watchmen/comments/e4jd3r/academic_research_about _watchmen_some_discussion/.

96   Arachnophilia, ibid.

97   Isz82, ibid.

98   Dekeita, ibid.

99   ChinatownKicks, ibid.

100 Arachnophilia, ibid.

101 See for instance Tony Bennett and Janet Woollacott, *Bond And Beyond: The Political Career of a Popular Hero* (London: Routledge, 1987), Stephen Knight, *Robin Hood: A Complete Study of the English Outlaw* (London: Blackwell, 1994), Ken Gelder, *Reading the Vampire* (London: Routledge, 1994).

102 Anon, 'Bibliography of Jane Austen Sequels', *Pemberley.com* (no date, accessed 21 July 2022), https://pemberley.com/janeinfo/austseql.html.

103 See R. J. Carter, *Alice's Journey Beyond the Moon* (Kent: Telos Publishing, 2004), and Gilbert Adair, *Alice Through the Needle's Eye* (London: Macmillan, 1984).

104 See Andrew Scahill, 'Serialized Killers: Prebooting Horror in *Bates Motel* and *Hannibal*', in Amanda Ann Klein and R. Barton Palmer, *Cycles, Sequels, Spin-offs, Remakes and Reboots: Multiplicities in Film and Television* (Austin: University of Texas Press, 2016).

105 See for instance Anon, 'Jeter Continuity', *Blade Runner Off-World* (no date, accessed 21 July 2022), https://bladerunner.fandom.com/wiki/Off-world:Jeter_continuity.

106 Michael Kennedy, '*Hannibal*: How The TV Show Fits into the Movie Timeline', *ScreenRant.com* (27 May 2020, accessed 21 July 2022), https://screenrant.com/hannibal-tv-show-connections-movie-franchise-timeline/.

107 See Haleigh Foutch, 'Mike Flanagan Says *Doctor Sleep* is in the "Same Cinematic Universe" as *The Shining*', *Collider.com* (13 June 2019, accessed 21 July 2022), https://collider.com/doctor-sleep-the-shining-cinematic-universe/.

108 See William Proctor, 'The Fault in Our *Star Trek*: (Dis)Continuity Mapping, Textual Conservationism, and the Perils of Prequelization', in Mark J. P. Wolf (ed.), *Exploring Imaginary Worlds* (London: Routledge, 2020), 208.

109 Similarly, the time-travel nature of the *Terminator* series allows fans to perform a similar get-out: 'Fortunately the saving grace of *Terminator* is if you like, you can say all of it is canon and all of it has happened in different timelines.' KingSkaar, 'Is *Terminator: Sarah Connor Chronicles* Canon?' *Reddit: r/terminator* (July 2016, accessed 21 July 2022), https://www.reddit.com/r/Terminator/comments/4rgv34/is_terminator_sarah_connor_chronicles_canon/.

110 An interpretation of the Schrödinger's Cat thought experiment, which originated in 1935. We might regard Oz, Wonderland and the fanciful lands of *Gulliver's Travels* as literary precedents.

111 See William Proctor, 'United States: Trans-Worldbuilding and the Stephen King Multiverse', in Matthew Freeman and William Proctor (eds), *Global Convergence Cultures* (New York: Routledge, 2018), 103.

112 See Stephen Follows, 'Hollywood Sequels By The Numbers', *StephenFollows.com* (15 June 2015, accessed 21 July 2022), https://stephenfollows.com/hollywood-sequels-by-the-numbers/.

113 This was also the reason for *Hannibal*'s incompatibility with the existing texts: writer/producer Bryan Fuller did not have the rights to any characters from *Silence of the Lambs*.

114 Similarly, Lady Gaga is slated to play Harley Quinn in *The Batman*'s sequel, while the character was previously associated with Margot Robbie in *Suicide Squad* (2016), *The Suicide Squad* (2021) and *Birds of Prey* (2020).

115 In August 2022, DC announced that it had no plans to release the *Batgirl* movie. *The Flash*, at the time of writing, is still scheduled for Summer 2023.

116 See PillarOfDeception, 'If We're Able To Get *Star Wars: Visions*, Then I Don't See Why Separate Timelines Aren't Possible', *Reddit: re/saltierthancrait* (April 2022, accessed 21 July 2022), https://www.reddit.com/r/saltierthancrait/comments/tyczln/if_were_able_to_get_star_wars_visions_then_i_dont/.

NOTES

247

117 Eileen Meehan observed that in 1989, Batman merchandise was split between promoting the characters and branding of the comics and those of the new Burton movie. How much easier and more profitable to unite the two and sell both strands together! See Eileen R. Meehan, '"Holy Commodity Fetish, Batman!" The Political Economy of a Commercial Intertext', in Pearson, Uricchio and Brooker (eds), *Many More Lives of the Batman*.

118 Anon, 'Word of the Year 2016 Is . . .' *Oxford Dictionaries*, https://en .oxforddictionaries.com/word-of-the-year/word-of-the-year-2016 (accessed 19 July 2022).

119 *Oxford Dictionaries*, ibid.

120 Dorian Lynskey, *The Ministry of Truth: A Biography of George Orwell's 1984* (London: Picador, 2019), 263.

121 Ibid.

122 Ibid., 265.

123 Ibid., 264.

124 Reuters Fact Check, 'Chris Rock Did Not Wear a Cheek Pad During Academy Awards Slap' (29 March 2022, accessed 21 July 2022), https://www.reuters.com/ article/factcheck-chris-pad-idUSL2N2VW25M.

125 Luke Zaleski, *Twitter.com* (17 March 2022, accessed 22 July 2022), https://twitter .com/ZaleskiLuke/status/1504485683779411983.

126 Kimberley Hilier and Christopher J. Greig, 'The Art of the Con: *Inventing Anna, The Tinder Swindler,* and Gender', *The Conversation* (10 March 2022, accessed 21 July 2022), https://theconversation.com/the-art-of-the-con-inventing-anna-the-tinder -swindler-and-gender-177121.

127 Kim Willsher, '"Lots Of Great Actors Are Not Exactly Oil Paintings"', *Guardian* (23 March 2022, accessed 21 July 2022), https://www.theguardian.com/music/2022/ mar/23/lots-of-great-actors-are-not-exactly-oil-paintings-valerie-lemercier-on-her -horrifying-celine-dion-biopic.

128 Adam, 'The Darkest Timeline', *KnowYourMeme.com* (July 2017, accessed 21 July 2022), https://knowyourmeme.com/memes/the-darkest-timeline.

129 *Good Housekeeping* Editors, '50 Mandela Effect Examples That Will Make You Question Everything', *Good Housekeeping* (25 May 2022, accessed 21 July 2022), https://www.goodhousekeeping.com/life/entertainment/g28438966/mandela-effect -examples/?slide=1.

130 See Lynskey, *The Ministry of Truth,* 265.

131 Jameson, 'Postmodernism and Consumer Society', in Brooker (ed.), *Modernism/ Postmodernism*, 167.

132 Jean Baudrillard, trans. Sheila Faria Glaser, *Simulacra and Simulation* (Michigan: University of Michigan 1984), 6. 'When the real is no longer what it was, nostalgia

assumes its full meaning', he writes. Nostalgia was Veidt's canny name for a cologne in *Watchmen*: in the HBO series, it has acquired new (full) meaning as a time-travel drug that motivates major plot twists.

133 Jean-Francois Lyotard, 'Answering the Question: What is Postmodernism?' in Brooker (ed.), *Modernism/Postmodernism*, 140–1.

134 Jesse Singal, 'Here Are My Contemporaneous Articles About The Kyle Rittenhouse Shootings, Now Unlocked', *JesseSingal.Substack.com* (10 November 2021, accessed 21 July 2022), https://jessesingal.substack.com/p/here-are-my-contemporaneous -articles.

135 Jesse Singal, *Twitter.com* (10 March 2022, accessed 22 July 2022), https://twitter.com /jessesingal/status/1501927893995298822.

136 See for instance Mike Merritt, 'J.K. Rowling Attacks "Orwellian" Transgender Rape Policy', *The Times* (13 December 2021, accessed 20 July 2022), https://www.thetimes .co.uk/article/jk-rowling-attacks-orwellian-transgender-rape-policy-hxs7mw76h.

137 Kathleen Stock, 'Entering the Parallel Universe of Transactivism', *KathleenStock .Substack.com* (21 March 2022, accessed 21 July 2022), https://kathleenstock .substack.com/p/entering-the-parallel-universe-of.

138 Jesse Singal, *Twitter.com* (12 July 2022, accessed 22 July 2022), https://twitter.com/ jessesingal/status/1546914843508330499.

139 Christoph, *Twitter.com* (13 July 222, accessed 22 July 2022), https://twitter.com/ Halalcoholism/status/1547022530124435456.

140 Longjumping_Ad8515, 'Law Professor Humiliates Josh Hawley during Senate Committee Hearing', *Reddit: r/politics* (12 July 2022, accessed 20 July 2022), https:// www.reddit.com/r/politics/comments/vxi4m5/law_professor_humiliates_josh _hawley_during/.

141 Jesse Singal, *Twitter.com* (12 July 2022, accessed 22 July 2022), https://twitter.com/ jessesingal/status/1546941345067110402.

142 Helen Joyce, *Twitter.com* (13 July 2022, accessed 22 July 2022), https://twitter.com/ HJoyceGender/status/1547147309372391424.

Conclusion

1 Emily Holden and Julian Borger, 'Doomsday Clock Lurches to 100 Seconds to Midnight – Closest to Catastrophe Yet', *The Guardian* (23 January 2020, accessed 22 July 2022), https://www.theguardian.com/world/2020/jan/23/doomsday-clock-100 -seconds-to-midnight-nuclear-climate.

2 Anon, 'Coronavirus: Face Masks and Coverings to Be Compulsory in England's Shops', *BBC.co.uk* (14 July 2020, accessed 23 July 2022), https://www.bbc.co.uk/news/ uk-politics-53397617.

NOTES

3 Joe Biden, 'Remarks By President Biden on Russia's Unprovoked and Unjustified Attack on Ukraine', *WhiteHouse.gov* (24 February 2022, accessed 23 July 2022), https://www.whitehouse.gov/briefing-room/speeches-remarks/2022/02/24/remarks -by-president-biden-on-russias-unprovoked-and-unjustified-attack-on-ukraine/.

4 This was true at the time of writing but, as I predicted, is already out of date. In October 2022, Geoff Johns introduced new characters 'Nostalgia' and 'The Watchman' into the DC comic book universe, hinting at the possibility of a sequel to, or continuation of, *Doomsday Clock*.

5 Scott Campbell, 'A Tortured Superhero Movie that Peaked Early Reconnects with Streaming Fans', *WeGotThisCovered*.com (17 July 2022, accessed 25 July 2022), https://wegotthiscovered.com/movies/a-tortured-superhero-movie-that-peaked-early -reconnects-with-streaming-fans/.

6 Eric Vespe, '*Peacemaker* Is The Biggest TV Series in the World Right Now', *SlashFilm .com* (27 January 2022, accessed 23 July 2022), https://www.slashfilm.com/748757/ peacemaker-is-the-biggest-tv-series-in-the-world-right-now/.

7 Brendan Tobin, 'Reign of the Rorschachs', *BrendanTobin.com* (15 February 2012, accessed 23 July 2022), http://brendantobin.blogspot.com/2012/02/reign-of -rorschachs.html.

8 Nico Parungo, 'This *Venom* Cover Pays Tribute to *Watchmen* and That's Awesome', *Epicstream.com* (7 November 2018, accessed 23 July 2022), https://epicstream.com/ article/this-venom-cover-pays-tribute-to-watchmen-and-thats-awesome.

9 John Saavedra, '*The Flash:* Batman Set Photo Teases Michael Keaton's New Batsuit', *Den of Geek* (4 June 2021, accessed 23 July 2022), https://www.denofgeek.com/movies /the-flash-batman-michael-keaton-batsuit-symbol-watchmen-set-photo/.

10 Jamie Burton, 'YouTuber's Videos Dragging Amber Heard May Make Him Up To $64000 A Month', *Newsweek.com* (22 June 2022, accessed 23 July 2022), https://www .newsweek.com/youtuber-umbrella-guy-negative-amber-heard-videos-earn-64000 -month-1718017.

11 Kofi Outlaw, 'Wendy's Fans Are Concerned After Bizarre *Watchmen* Tweet', *Comicbook* (24 June 2021, accessed 23 July 2022), https://comicbook.com/irl/news/ wendys-watchmen-doctor-manhattan-meme-tweet-joke-reactions/#3.

12 Wendy's, *Twitter.com* (23 June 2021, accessed 22 July 2022), https://twitter.com/ Wendys/status/1407749585049686017.

13 Matt, 'I Am Tired of Earth. These People', *KnowYourMeme.com* (July 2020, accessed 22 July 2022), https://knowyourmeme.com/memes/i-am-tired-of-earth-these-people.

14 Moore and Gibbons, *Watchmen*, chapter 4, 25.

15 Matt, 'I Am Tired of Earth. These People.'

16 Will Brooker, *Batman Unmasked* (London: Continuum, 2000), 333.

17 Brandon, 'Dr Manhattan Kills Rorschach', *KnowYourMeme.com* (November 2021, accessed 22 July 2022), https://knowyourmeme.com/memes/dr-manhattan-kills -rorshach.

SELECTED BIBLIOGRAPHY

Alan Moore and *Watchmen*

Ayres, Jackson. *Alan Moore: A Critical Guide*. London: Bloomsbury, 2021.

Bensam, Richard (ed.). *Minutes to Midnight: Twelve Essays on Watchmen*. Edwardsville: Sequart, 2012.

Berlatsky, Eric L. (ed.). *Alan Moore: Conversations*. Jackson: University Press of Mississippi, 2012.

di Liddo, Annalisa. *Alan Moore: Comics as Performance, Fiction as Scalpel*. Jackson: University Press of Mississippi, 2009.

Green, Matthew J. A. (ed.). *Alan Moore and the Gothic Tradition*. Manchester: Manchester University Press, 2013.

Hoberek, Andrew. *Considering Watchmen: Poetics, Property, Politics*. New Brunswick: Rutgers, 2014.

Khoury, George, Dave McKean, Todd Klein, Jose Villarubia, John Morrow, Marc McKenzie, Steven Tice and Eric Nolen-Weathington. *The Extraordinary Works of Alan Moore*. Raleigh: TwoMorrows Publishing, 2003.

Klock, Geoff. *How To Read Superhero Comics And Why*. London: Continuum, 2002.

Larance, Jeremy. 'Alan Moore's *Miracleman*: Harbinger of the Modern Age of Comics', *Works and Days* 32, no. 1–2 (2015): 117–38.

Link, Alex. 'Psychogeography's Legacy in *From Hell* and *Watchmen*', *European Comic Art* 9, no. 2 (Autumn 2016): 77–99.

McCue, Greg S. with Clive Bloom, *Dark Knights: The New Comics in Context*. London: Pluto Press 1993.

McLean, Duncan. 'HBO's *Watchmen* and Generic Revision in a Genre of Adaptation', *Journal of Popular Film and Television* 49, no. 4 (Winter 2021): 196–209.

Millidge, Gary Spencer. *Alan Moore Storyteller*. New York: Universe Publishing, 2011.

Moore, Alan. *Alan Moore's Guide to Writing Comics*. Rantoul: Avatar, 2010.

Morton, Drew. '"Watched Any Good Books Lately?" The Formal Failure of the *Watchmen* Motion Comic', *Cinema Journal* 56, no. 2 (Winter 2017): 132–7.

Parkin, Lance. *Magic Words: The Extraordinary Life of Alan Moore*. London: Arum Press, 2013.

Taylor, Aaron. 'The Continuing Adventures of the "Inherently Unfilmable" Book: Zack Snyder's *Watchmen*', *Cinema Journal* 56, no. 2 (Winter 2017): 125–31.

Van Ness, Sara J. *Watchmen As Literature*. Jefferson: McFarland & Co, 2010.

White, Mark D. (ed.). *Watchmen and Philosophy*. Hoboken: John Wiley & Sons, 2009.

Wolf-Meyer, Matthew. 'The World Ozymandias Made: Utopias in the Superhero Comic, Subculture, and the Conservation of Difference', *Journal of Popular Culture* 36, no. 3 (March 2003): 497–517.

Related comics studies

Brooker, Will. *Batman Unmasked: Analysing A Cultural Icon*. London: Continuum, 2000.

Brooker, Will. *Hunting the Dark Knight: Twenty-First Century Batman*. London: I B Tauris, 2012.

Carpenter, Greg. *The British Invasion! Alan Moore, Neil Gaiman, Grant Morrison, and the Invention of the Modern Comic Book Writer*. Edwardsville: Sequart, 2016.

Domsch, Sebastian, Dan Hassler-Forest and Dirk Vanderbeke (eds). *Handbook of Comics and Graphic Narratives*. Berlin: De Gruyter, 2021.

Gravett, Paul. *Graphic Novels: Stories to Change Your Life*. London: Aurum, 2005.

Jones, Gerard and Will Jacobs. *The Comic Book Heroes*. Roseville: Prima Publishing, 1987.

McLaughlin, Jeff (ed.). *Comics as Philosophy*. Jackson: University of Mississippi Press, 2005.

Morrison, Grant. *Supergods: Our World in the Age of the Superhero*. London: Jonathan Cape, 2011.

Pearson, Roberta, William Uricchio and Will Brooker (eds). *Many More Lives of the Batman*. London: BFI Palgrave, 2015.

Round, Julia. *Gothic in Comics and Graphic Novels*. Jefferson: McFarland & Company, 2014.

Related film and literature studies

Aragay, Mireia (ed.). *Books in Motion: Adaptation, Intertextuality, Authorship*. Amsterdam: Rodopi, 2005.

Bazin, André. *What is Cinema? Volume 1*. Berkeley: University of California Press, 1967.

Cartmell, Deborah and Imelda Whelehan (eds). *Screen Adaptation: Impure Cinema*. London: Palgrave Macmillan, 2010.

Doležel, Lubomír. *Heterocosmica: Fiction and Possible Worlds*. Baltimore: Johns Hopkins University Press, 1998.

Freeman, Matthew and William Proctor (eds). *Global Convergence Cultures*. New York: Routledge, 2018.

Horton, Andrew and Stuart T. McDougal (eds). *Play It Again, Sam: Retakes on Remakes*. Berkeley: University of California Press, 1998.

Kendrick, James (ed.). *A Companion to the Action Film*. Hoboken: Wiley & Sons, 2019.

Klein, Amanda Ann and R. Barton Palmer (eds). *Cycles, Sequels, Spin-offs, Remakes and Reboots: Multiplicities in Film and Television*. Austin: University of Texas Press, 2016.

Michelson, Annette (ed.) and Kevin O'Brien (trans.). *Kino-Eye: The Writings of Dziga Vertov*. Berkeley: University of California Press, 1984.

Parey, Armelle (ed.). *Prequels, Coquels and Sequels in Contemporary Anglophone Fiction*. London: Routledge, 2019.

Stam, Robert and Alessandra Raengo. *Literature and Film: A Guide to the Theory and Practice of Film Adaptation*. Oxford: Blackwell, 2005.

Wolf, Mark J. P. (ed.). *Exploring Imaginary Worlds*. London: Routledge, 2020.

Theories of intertextuality

Allen, Graham. *Intertextuality*. London: Taylor & Francis, 2000.

Bakhtin, Mikhail. 'Discourse in the Novel', in *The Dialogic Imagination: Four Essays by M. M. Bakhtin*, edited by Michael Holquist. Austin: University of Texas Press, 1981.

Bakhtin, Mikhail. 'From Notes Made in 1970–1', in *Speech Genres & Other Late Essays*, edited by Caryl Emerson and Michael Holquist. Austin: University of Texas Press, 1986.

Barthes, Roland (trans. Steven Heath). *Image Music Text*. London: Fontana, 1977.

Deleuze, Gilles and Felix Guattari. *A Thousand Plateaus*. London: Continuum, 2011.

Moi, Toril (ed.). *The Kristeva Reader*. Oxford: Blackwell, 1986.

Related critical theory

Barthes, Roland. *Camera Lucida*. London: Vintage, 2000.

Baudrillard, Jean (trans. Sheila Faria Glaser). *Simulacra and Simulation*. Ann Arbor: University of Michigan, 1984.

Bloom, Harold. *The Anxiety of Influence: A Theory of Poetry*. Oxford: Oxford University Press, 1997.

Bolter, Jay David and Richard Grusin. *Remediation: Understanding New Media*. Cambridge, MA: MIT Press, 2000.

Derrida, Jacques (trans. Alan Bass). *Margins of Philosophy*. Sussex: Harvester Press, 1982.

Jameson, Fredric. *Postmodernism: Or, The Cultural Logic of Late Capitalism*. London: Verso, 1991.

Jameson, Fredric. 'Postmodernism and Consumer Society', in *Modernism/Postmodernism*, edited by Peter Brooker. Essex: Longman, 1992.

Kaplan, E. Ann (ed.). *Postmodernism and its Discontents*. London and New York: Verso, 1988.

Williams, Raymond. *The Long Revolution*. Middlesex: Pelican Books, 1965.

INDEX

9/11 (terrorist attack)   137, 146
300 (movie)   92, 99, 101–2, 115
1963 (comic book)   50, 122
2000AD (comic)   16, 29, 32, 38–9, 88–90, 120, 157, *see also Future Shocks; individual story titles*

Abar, Angela (character)   168, 171, 180
adaptation   2, 91–116, 159, 187, 189
Alcott, Louisa May, *see Little Women*
Alec (comic book)   145, 147, 149
Alice in Wonderland   160, 176, 186
Alternate Earth, *see* multiverse
Animal Man (character and comic book)   90, 117, 120–3, 131, 136, 182
Archie Comics   18
Arkham Asylum, see Batman: Arkham Asylum
Austen, Jane   100, 160–2, 181, 186

Baikie, Jim   88
Bakhtin, Mikhail   4, 100, 116
Barthes, Roland   3, 7–8, 22–4, 44, 126, 140, 197–9
Batman   14, 16, 24, 27, 42, 57, 62–4, 66, 69, 74, 76, 78–80, 111, 127, 139, 180–1, 186, 188–9
Batman: Arkham Asylum (graphic novel)   90, 119, 127
Batman Begins (movie)   92
Batman: The Dark Knight Returns (comic book and graphic novel)   56, 59, 61–2, 64–5, 69, 74, 76–7, 79, 85, 94, 127, 173–4, 180
Batman: The Killing Joke (comic book)   31, 43, 57, 76, 170, 175
Baudrillard, Jean   193

Before Watchmen (comic book series)   3, 158, 161, 164–7, 173–9, 181–5, 188
Berger, Karen   87
Bible John (comic book)   122
Bickle, Travis (character)   174–6, 179
Big Numbers (comic book)   50
Black Canary (character)   14, 82, 85
Blackhawk (comic book)   81
Blade (movie)   92
Blade Runner (movie series)   105, 186
Blake, Eddie, *see* Comedian
Bloom, Harold   60, 132–4, 138, 141, 168
Blue Beetle   15–16, 39, 52, 65–74, 78, 82, 123, 125, 128–9, 131, 147–8, 154
Bolland, Brian   43, 170, 175
Bond, James (character)   50, 184, 186
Bowie, David   24
Bridget Jones (novel series and movie adaptations)   100, 181
Brontë, Charlotte, *see Jane Eyre*
Bronze Age of comics   59, 64–5
Burroughs, William   19, 23
Burton, Tim   91
Byrne, John   63, 79, 86

Campbell, Eddie   50, 145–50
Cannon, Peter, *see* Peter Cannon, Thunderbolt
Captain Atom (character and comic book)   50, 65–9, 72, 74, 77–8, 123–5, 136–9, 158
Captain Britain (character and comic book)   30–1, 47, 62, 64, 74, 120
Captain Metropolis (character)   12, 20, 42, 163
Carroll, Lewis, *see Alice in Wonderland*
Catwoman (character, comic book series and movie)   62, 81, 93, 119

INDEX

254

Charlton Comics and characters   14–17, 28, 62, 65, 67, 72–8, 90, 123–51
Chaykin, Howard   79, 81, 85–6, 90, 154
Chronocops (comic book story)   38–9, 51
Collins, Suzanne, *see Hunger Games, The*
Comedian (character) origins and influences   14–18, 39, 60, 67–8, 77, 88, 148–9, 156, 197
    fan interpretations   21
    in role-playing game   163
    in *Watchmen* (2009)   108–9, 111–12
    in *Watchmen* (2019); in *The End is Nigh*   177
    in *Before Watchmen*   178–9
Conner, Amanda   164
Constantine, John, *see Hellblazer*
Cooke, Darwyn   164–5, 168, 178
Coquel   160–1
Courtyard, The (comic book)   50, 52, 119
Crisis (comic book event and series)   58, 63, 74, 76, 79–80, 86, 89, 120, 143, 182, 188–90
Crisis (Fleetway comic book)   88
Crisis on Infinite Earths, *see Crisis*
The Crow (movie)   92
Cthulu, *see* Lovecraft, H.P.

Daredevil (character and movie)   16, 62, 64, 93, 154
Dark Age of comics   59, 146, *see also* Grim and gritty
The Dark Knight Returns (comic book), *see Batman: The Dark Knight Returns*
Davis, Alan, *see Captain Britain*; *D.R. and Quinch*
Dawn of the Dead (movie)   114–15
Death of the Author, *see* Barthes, Roland
Defoe, Daniel, *see Robinson Crusoe*
Delano, Jamie   87
Deleuze, Gilles and Guattari, Félix   4, 14, 100
DeMatteis, J.M.   57, 81–2, 90
Derrida, Jacques   3, 100, 150
DIE (comic book)   144
Ditko, Steve   16, 48, 73, 75, 77, 87, 125, 131, 173, 174, 179

Doom Patrol (comic book)   57, 87, 90, 122, 127
Doomsday Clock (comic book)   3–4, 158, 165–9, 173, 176–8, 181–3, 185, 188
Dracula (character and movie adaptation)   101, 200
D.R. and Quinch (comic book story)   39, 47, 120
Dreiberg, Dan, *see* Nite Owl
Dr Manhattan (character) origins and influences   15–16, 121, 124, 131, 147–9, 158
    in *Doomsday Clock*   168
    fan interpretations   20–1, 119–200
    in *Rorschach*   175
    in *Watchmen* (2009)   103, 111–12
    in *Watchmen* (2019)   170–2, 180
    in *Before Watchmen*   161
Dylan, Bob   9, 12, 112, 115, 167

Ellis, Warren   127, 145–6
Emma (novel and adaptations)   100, 160, 176, *see also* Austen, Jane
End is Nigh, The, *see Watchmen: The End is Nigh*
Equel, *see* Coquel
Everything Everywhere All At Once (movie)   189

Fabry, Glenn   157–8
Fairbairn, Nathan   130, 174
Fake news   191–2
Fantastic Beasts, *see Harry Potter*
Fantastic Four (characters, comic book and movies)   65, 73, 93
fidelity, *see* adaptation
Fifty Shades of Grey franchise   176
Final Crisis (comic book)   123, 137, 140
Flash, The (character, comic book, movie and TV adaptations)   14, 27, 59, 63, 80–1, 89, 155, 168, 190, 198
Fornés, Jorge   173, 175
For The Man Who Has Everything (Superman comic book story)   32, 42–3, 50, 53
Frank, Gary   166

INDEX

255

From Hell (comic book) 19, 50, 122
Future Shocks (comic series) 36, 38, 53, 120

Gaiman, Neil 61, 87–8
Gibbons, Dave
  art style 97, 106–10, 121, 157–8, 162, 164, 166
  involvement with *Watchmen* role-playing game supplement 163
  relationship with Alan Moore 144, 168
  response to *Saturday Morning Watchmen* 99
  response to *Watchmen* (2009) 101
  response to *Watchmen* (2019) 168
Gillen, Kieran 142–51, 158, 201
Gimmick, Jimmy The (character) 36, 176–9, 181
Golden Age of comics 10, 18, 59, 87, 89, 92, 111
Green Arrow (character and comic book) 47, 57, 64, 82–5, 89
Green Lantern (character and comic book) 33, 47, 50, 64, 119, 141–2, 168
Green Lantern Corps, The, *see* Green Lantern
Grell, Mike 82, 85–6, 90
Grim and gritty (comic book trend) 29, 31, 56–69, 92, 146, 155

Halo Jones (character and comic book) 29, 31, 37, 47, 51
Hamlet, see Shakespeare, William
Harry Potter franchise 157, 160, 186
Hellblazer (comic book) 87–8
Heroes (TV series) 93
Higgins, John 1, 11, 95, 104, 106, 157, 164, 166, 201
His Dark Materials (novel series, movie adaptations) 161, 188–9
Hooded Justice (character) 10, 18, 20, 163, 177–9, 181
Hughes, Adam 164, 181
Hunger Games, The franchise 176

Incredibles, The (movie) 93, 99
In Pictopia 26, 147
intertextuality 4, 7–55, 75, 100, 146, 149, 174
Invisibles, The (comic book) 117, 119, 122

Jacobi, Edward, *see* Moloch
James, E.L., *see Fifty Shades of Grey*
James, P.D. 162
Jameson, Fredric 26, 129, 153–5, 193
Jane Eyre 160
Jean Rhys, *see Wide Sargasso Sea, The*
JFK, *see* Kennedy, President John F.
Johns, Geoff 166–7, 178–9, 201
Judge Dredd (character and comic book) 24
Jupiter, Sally, *see* Silk Spectre
Juspeczyk, Laurie, *see* Silk Spectre
Justice League (superhero team, comic books and movies) 27, 57, 82, 154, 189

Kennedy, President John F. (JFK) 9, 12, 16, 111–13, 139, 179
Kent, Clark, *see* Superman
Kid Eternity (comic book) 90, 119
Killing Joke, see Batman: The Killing Joke
King, Stephen 187–8
King, Tom 173, 179, 183
Kirby, Jack 20, 65, 122
Klock, Geoff 26, 40–1, 60, 66, 132–3, 180
Kovacs, Walter, *see* Rorschach
Kristeva, Julia 4, 100

League of Extraordinary Gentlemen 12, 26, 31, 50–3, 122
Lee, Jae 165, 174
Lee, Stan 65, 73, 122
Legend of the Guardians: The Owls of Ga'Hoole 116
Lindelof, Damon 2–4, 12, 168–73, 175, 178–81, 183
Little Women (novel) 161
Long, Reggie, *see* Rorschach

256 INDEX

The Longbow Hunters, see Green Arrow
Lovecraft, H.P. 5, 50–3, 118, 144
Lubomír Doležel 160
Lyotard, Jean-Francois 194

McCarthy, Brendan 119–20
McKean, Dave 82
McKelvie, Jamie 142–5
MAD magazine 18, 23, 38, 51, 155–8
Martian Manhunter (character and comic
book) 57, 78, 81–2, 119, 154
Marvel Cinematic Universe (MCU) 5,
92, 112, 137, 146, 189–90, 192
Marvelman, *see* Miracleman
Marvel Studios, *see* Marvel Cinematic
Universe
Mason, Hollis, *see* Nite Owl
Maus 61
Mazzuchelli, David 173
MCU, *see* Marvel Cinematic Universe
Meyer, Stephenie, *see Twilight*
Millar, Mark 145–7
Miller, Frank (comic book creator and
character) 59, 62–6, 69, 76–81,
85, 92, 101–2, 106, 127, 154–5,
173–5, 179–80, 188
Milligan, Peter 87, 119
Miracleman (character and comic
book) 26, 28–33, 47, 49, 62, 64,
69, 74, 78, 90, 117–18, 120–3, 153
Moloch (character) 36, 104–5, 107, 115,
164, 176, 179, 181
Moorcock, Michael 188
Moore, Alan, *see also individual story titles*
authorial style 24–54
involvement with *Watchmen* role-
playing game supplement 162
relationship with Dave Gibbons 144,
168
relationship with Grant Morrison 90,
123–42
relationship with Kieron Gillen 144
reputation 23, 139
response to *Before Watchmen* 164,
177
response to *Watchmen* (2009) 99, 164

response to *Watchmen* (2019) 169
Morrison, Grant 87, 90, 117–46, 150,
154–5, 158, 173–4, 182, 188, 194,
201
Motion comic, *see Watchmen: The Motion
Comic*
Mr A (character and comic book) 16–
17, 77, 125
multiverse 123, 187–91, 194–5

Neonomicon (comic book) 31, 50–3,
119
New Statesmen (comic book) 88–90,
134
Nightshade (character) 15, 123, 125,
128–9, 147
Nineteen Eighty-Four, see Orwell, George
Nite Owl (character) origins and
influences 14–16, 18, 39, 74–5,
77, 88, 128, 144
in *The End is Nigh* 163–4
fan interpretations 20–1
in role-playing game 163
in *Watchmen* (2009) 111–13, 181
in *Before Watchmen* 178–9
Nixon, President Richard 9, 113, 162,
171, 176–7
Nolan, Christopher 92, 114

Obama, President Barack 192
Oliver Queen, *see* Green Arrow
O'Neil, Denny 64, 74–8, 86, 90, 154
Orwell, George 24, 51, 191–4
Osterman, Jon, *see* Dr Manhattan
Owls of Ga'Hoole, The, see Legend of the
Guardians
Ozymandias (character) origins and
influences 14–16, 125, 131, 133,
147–8, 156
in *Doomsday Clock* 176, 178
in *Rorschach* 175
in *Watchmen* (2009) 109, 112–15,
170
in *Watchmen* (2019) 171–2
in *Before Watchmen* 175, 179, 181
Ozymandias (poem) 138, 167

INDEX

Parallel universe, *see* multiverse

parody 11, 18, 38, 122, 129–30, 134, 142, 153–60

pastiche 11, 26, 35, 50–1, 122, 129, 143, 146, 151–4, 158, 164, 197

Pax Americana (comic book) 90, 123–41, 143, 146, 155, 158, 174, 198

Peacemaker (character, comic book and TV show) 65–9, 72, 78, 125, 127, 129, 136, 197

Pérez, George 79

Peter Cannon, Thunderbolt (character and comic book) 9, 50, 143–51, 158, 169, 198

Phillip Pullman, *see His Dark Materials*

postmodernism 3, 9, 11, 26, 37, 56, 153–4, 178, 193–4

post-truth 191

prequels 2–3, 5, 54, 117, 158–64, 183, 186

Pride and Prejudice (novel and movie adaptations) 100, 161–2, 181, *see also* Austen, Jane

Prismatic Age of comics 146

Promethea (comic book) 26, 50–1, 122, 130

Providence (comic book) 50–2, 119

Queenan, Joe 58, 62

The Question (character and comic book) 15–17, 39, 50, 66–7, 74–8, 123–9, 174

Quitely, Frank 123–4, 127, 130, 132, 139, 141

reboots 62–4, 74, 76, 92, 174, 188

Redford, Robert (character, fictional president) 16, 171, 174

remixes 2, 25, 118, 153–95, 168

retcons 62, 74, 134, 175, 180, 185–6, 194

retroactive continuity, *see* retcons

Rhys, Jean, *see Wide Sargasso Sea, The*

Robin Hood (character) 17, 24, 83, 200

Robinson Crusoe (character and novel) 160

Rogue Trooper (character and comic book story) 16

role-playing game (RPG) 144, 159, 161–3

Romeo and Juliet, see Shakespeare, William

Rorschach (character) origins and influences 14–17, 38–9, 50, 72, 75–7, 79, 83, 125–8, 131–4, 143–4, 148–9, 155–8, *see also* Rorschach (comic book)

in *Doomsday Clock* 3, 166–7, 178, 181

in *The End is Nigh* 163–4

fan interpretations 20–1, 198–200

mask-killer theory 36

in role-playing game 163

in *Rorschach* 4, 159, 173–5, 177–8, 181, 183

in *Watchmen* (2009) 92, 94–6, 104–10, 113, 115

in *Watchmen* (2019) 172, 178

in *Before Watchmen* 176, 182

Rorschach (comic book) 4, 159, 173–8, 181, 183

Rowling, J.K., *see Harry Potter*

RPG, *see* role-playing game

Sandifer, Elizabeth 43, 57, 59, 117, 134

Sandman, The (comic book) 88

satire 129, 184–8, 200, *see also* parody

Saturday Morning Watchmen 97–8, 164

Schumacher, Joel 113

sequels 2–5, 25, 85, 93, 100, 158–89, 197, 200

Shade, the Changing Man (character and comic book) 87

Shadow, The (character and comic book) 18, 24, 57, 79

Shakespeare, William 51, 101, 132, 160, 176

Shelley, Mary 101, 200

Shelley, Percy Bysshe 9, 132, 138, 167

Sherlock Holmes (character) 184, 186, 200

Sienkiewicz, Bill 82

Silk Spectre (character) origins and
influences   14, 17–18, 93, 125, 129,
144, 147, 156–8
fan interpretations   21
in *Watchmen* (2019)   170, 176
in *Before Watchmen*   176, 182
Silver Age of comics   10, 27, 59, 63–4,
148
Sin City (comic book, movie
adaptation)   101–2
Sister Night, *see* Abar, Angela
Skizz   29, 32, 37, 88
Smith, John, *see New Statesmen*
Snyder, Zack   91–116, 158–9, 164, 169–
73, 177–8, 181–3, 189, 197, 199
Spider-Man (character, comic book and
movie adaptations)   65–6, 70–3,
77–8, 92, 189–90
Spiegelman, Art, *see Maus*
Star Wars franchise   186–7, 190, 192
Stechschulte, Tom   93
Stoppard, Tom   161, 176
Superman (character and comic
book)   27, 29, 32, 42, 50, 53, 63,
78–9, 86, 90, 123–4, 127, 131, 137,
168–9, 176, 181, 198
Superman Returns (movie)   92, *see also*
Superman
Superman: The Movie   93, *see also*
Superman
Supreme (comic book)   25, 50, 122–3
Swamp Thing (character and comic
book)   14, 19, 28–34, 37, 42,
46–50, 62, 64, 73–4, 80–2, 87–8

Taxi Driver (movie)   113, *see also* Bickle,
Travis
Terminator film series   186
Thunderbolt, *see* Peter Cannon,
Thunderbolt
Time Twisters, see Future Shocks
Tom Strong (comic book)   50
Top Ten (comic book)   50
Totleben, John   30, 120

Trump, President Donald J.   191–4
Twilight franchise   176
Twilight Lady (character)   179

Updike, John   160, 176

Varley, Lynn   92
Veidt, Adrian, *see* Ozymandias
Vertigo (DC Comics imprint)   60, 87–8
V for Vendetta (comic book)   24, 26, 31,
37, 41, 45, 47, 156
video games   2, 114, 159, 161, 163–4,
166, 177, *see also Watchmen: The
End is Nigh*

Warrior (comic book)   18, 117
Watchmen movie (2009)   2, 12, 91–116,
158–9, 164, 169–70, 172–3, 177–8,
181–3, 197, 199
Watchmen: The End is Nigh (video
game)   2, 159, 161, 163, 166, 177,
179, 181
Watchmen: The Motion Comic   2, 93–7,
164, 204–5
Watchmen TV series (HBO, 2019)   2–4,
158–9, 168–75, 178
Watergate (political scandal)   164, 177
Wayne, Bruce, *see* Batman
We3 (comic book)   124, 127
Wein, Len   71–3, 75, 154, 164
Wicked (novel)   160
Wicked and the Divine, The (comic book
series)   143–4, 148
Wide Sargasso Sea, The   160
Wolfman, Marv   79
Wonder Woman (character and comic
book)   27, 53, 79–80

X-Men (characters and movie
franchise)   12, 92, 189

Zapruder film footage   112–13, 137, 139
Zenith (character and comic book)   90,
118–20